ORANGEVILLE

ORANGEVILLE

The Heart of Dufferin County

Wayne Townsend

Nov. 21/06
Wayne Townsend

NATURAL HERITAGE BOOKS
TORONTO

Copyright © 2006 by Wayne Townsend

All rights reserved. No portion of this book, with the exception of brief extracts for the purpose of literary or scholarly review, may be reproduced in any form without the permission of the publisher.

Published by Natural Heritage / Natural History Inc.
PO Box 95, Station O, Toronto, Ontario M4A 2M8
www.naturalheritagebooks.com

All visuals courtesy of the Dufferin County Museum & Archives, unless otherwise credited. *Front cover*, Blanket box lid, painted by Orange Jull. Photograph by Peter Herlihy. *Courtesy of Peter Stewart.* Back cover visuals *courtesy of the Town of Orangeville and John Woolner, Orangeville.*

Cover design by Neil Thorne
Book design by Norton Hamill Design
Edited by Jane Gibson

Printed and bound in Canada by Hignell Book Printing

Library and Archives Canada Cataloguing in Publication
Townsend, Wayne, 1952-
  Orangeville : the heart of Dufferin County / Wayne Townsend.

Includes bibliographical references and index.
ISBN 1-897045-18-2

1. Orangeville (Ont.)—History. 2. Orangeville (Ont.)—Biography. I. Title.

FC3099.O73T69 2006   971.3'41   C2006-906117-3

Natural Heritage / Natural History Inc. acknowledges the financial support of the Canada Council for the Arts and the Ontario Arts Council for our publishing program. We acknowledge the support of the Government of Ontario through the Ontario Media Development Corporation's Ontario Book Initiative. We also acknowledge the financial support of the Government of Canada through the Book Publishing Industry Development Program (BPIDP) and the Association for the Export of Canadian Books.

To my partner, John, who loves Orangeville as much as I.
And to my parents, who encouraged me to move
to "town" and make a life for myself here.

CONTENTS

Acknowledgements		ix
Introduction		x
Maps		xiii

1	IN THE BEGINNING	3
2	EARLY STORIES OF THE SOURCE OF THE CREDIT	9
3	THEM DAMN YANKEES	27
4	ROADS AND RAILWAYS: GETTING TO TOWN	38
5	EARLY INDUSTRY: ENTERPRISE AND ENTREPRENEURS	52
6	SUDDEN GROWTH, SUDDEN DECLINE	66
7	TOWN OF CHANGE, 1900 TO 1914	83
8	ORANGEVILLE BETWEEN THE WORLD WARS	92
9	LOOK AT US NOW	104
10	MUNICIPAL HISTORY: GETTING THINGS DONE	119
11	BROADWAY: STREET OF DREAMS	137
12	LANDMARKS IN TOWN	154
13	JUST FOR FUN	169
14	AND BAD TIMES TOO	186
15	VILLAINS AND HEROES	198
16	OFF TO WAR: CITIZENS WHO SERVED	219
17	ORANGEVILLE MOMENTS: SIGNIFICANCE IN CANADA	233

EPILOGUE   241

APPENDIX A *Ketchum Family Tree*   244
APPENDIX B *Lawrence Family Tree*   246
Notes   247
Bibliography   260
Index   262
About the Author   281

ACKNOWLEDGEMENTS

I wish to acknowledge my friend George Pylypiuk for his continuing support. Thanks to the staff of the Town of Orangeville, past and present, for putting up with me all these years as an advocate for my little town. I want to acknowledge the wonderful friends that I have in, and from around, Orangeville. You are part of my story.

A very special thank you to Steve Brown, Archivist at the Dufferin County Museum & Archives (DCMA), for his assistance and support; and to Kim Peters-Millman, Darlene Moorse, Rosanne Rutledge, Marilyn Wright and the volunteers at the DCMA for research, proofreading, word processing and more.

While every effort has been made to ensure accuracy of the historical detail, the responsibility remains mine. Any errors or major omissions brought to the attention of the publisher and myself will be dealt with in subsequent editions.

INTRODUCTION

This is the story of my town, Orangeville. It is not a chronological or historical thesis, but more like a scrapbook of researched memories and mementos put together in an attempt to give the reader a sense of a place and time. This is about how Orangeville began and where it is going in the future, with a whole lot of stories about the town in-between. This is a unique piece of history, told in the words of the people who have lived here, including me. These words will, perhaps, allow the reader to feel the soul of Orangeville, to understand what has given life to the town, and what it is that will move the town forward, making the community one of the best places to live in Canada.

When I started to read the mountains of research that had been gathered in preparation for writing the story of Orangeville, I realized that the actual recorded words as said by the residents, were also the story. The style they used to present their stories provided character and soul. The subtleties of the English language when crafted by a skilled writer of a period, especially a good Victorian newspaper editor, in my mind, should be allowed to stand on their own. The result is that this book is not just the writer interpreting stories and research, but it is often also the words of the people who originally wrote or spoke them. It is as close to being there that one can be, reading the original words as though they were pictures taken at the time, rather than "seeing" them after someone has interfered with their colour and shape.

Over the years much has changed in Orangeville, but it is that change that has shaped the town's progress and formed its history. Not all that has happened was planned, it just happened. The motto adopted by the town in 2003 says it all—"Historic Past-Dynamic Future." Orangeville is a town whose history lives on in its streets and its architecture and its stories that remain. But Orangeville is also a town that looks forward to its future, to the generations who, it is hoped, will live here and leave their stories for posterity as well.

Orangeville and area is for me, and was for my ancestors, a wonderful place to live. I believe it will also be so in the future for whoever may choose to live here. It is hoped that through the stories of Orangeville's places and people, the reader will understand why.

This book is a tribute to those people who have recorded the stories of this town, and kept them intact. These stories have not only interested me but also influenced me as well, ones such as the writings of John Foley and A.D. McKitrick in their newspapers, *The Sun* and *The Orangeville Banner*; the stories of Sidney Dickens and Alan Rayburn, also published in *The Orangeville Banner*, stories these authors so painstakingly researched and gathered; the stories of historians that I have known, Bess Marshall, Helen Matheson and Jean Turnbull; and the stories of the Orangeville historian and the person who has kept Orangeville's history alive, Steve Brown, presently the archivist at the Dufferin County Museum & Archives. He has hundreds more stories tucked safely in his head still left to tell. These were the stories that kept me interested and wanting to learn more.

A sign welcomes visitors to the Town of Orangeville. The town boundaries will continue to expand until the population reaches a maximum of 40,000. This is a figure that both the local and provincial governments hope to reach but not exceed. *Courtesy of John Woolner, Orangeville.*

As part of this introduction I will use the words of an earlier Orangeville historian, Sidney Dickens, who wrote this in 1965 as his introduction to an unpublished history of Orangeville:

Orangeville is a wonderful town and has an honourable history that far surpasses any other town in Ontario, and has produced some of the province's leaders and Canada's greatest citizens. Today they may be found in almost every part of the country and in every profession. Few towns have undergone such an uphill fight for its existence and have come through the struggle as Orangeville has, and become the prettiest spot in all of Ontario. It is worthy of the honour of being the county town for Dufferin County. In its history it has made a contribution to Canada's life.[1]

I couldn't have said it better.

MAPS

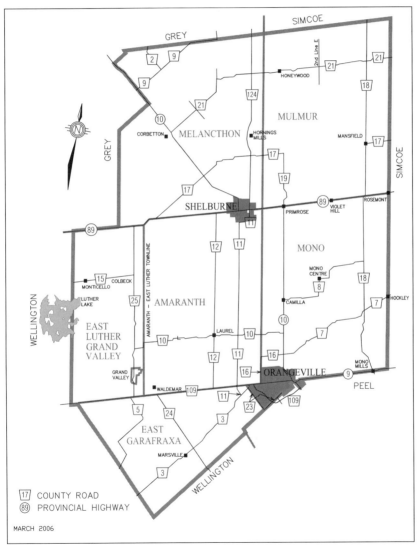

Map of Dufferin County. *Courtesy of the County of Dufferin.*

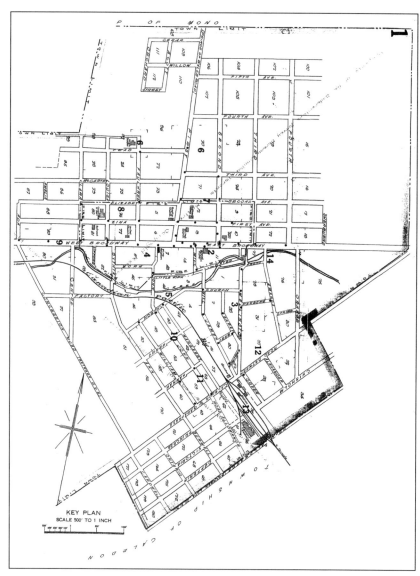

Map of Orangeville, Ontario, dated 1907, revised 1938. Taken from the Goad Insurance Map. *Courtesy of the Dufferin County Museum & Archives.*

ORANGEVILLE

I

IN THE BEGINNING

IT IS DIFFICULT TO IMAGINE what it was like at the source of the Credit River before settlement arrived. There are paintings that exist of areas similar to the Credit Flats, so we can conjure an image of the wetlands and dense bush where Orangeville now stands: "How savagely, how solemnly wild it was! So thick was the overhanging foliage that it not only shut out the sunshine, but also the daylight."[1]

We can close our eyes and imagine the look of the past or walk along sections of the Bruce Trail and catch traces of what the landscape might have looked like. However, you and I will never be able to recreate the smell of hundreds of years of humus, or feel the cool of the air on the forest bottom where sunshine seldom reached, even in the middle of the summer. We will never see the sight of the sun or moon filtering through a towering canopy of branches or hear the sound of hundreds of thousands of passenger pigeons[2] on their flight overhead. This is the past of the Orangeville that we will never know—the history before the arrival of humans; the longest period of our history covered hundreds of thousands of years.

It is the diversity of geological features around Orangeville that gives the town its uniqueness. Geologically, the land on which the town stands was the bottom of a shallow lake close to the equator millions of years ago. It drifted with the rest of the North American tectonic plates to the latitude where we are now. Locally, the geology has been determined by both the formation of the Niagara Escarpment and the work of the glaciers.

Dr. Walter M. Tovell,[3] former director of the Royal Ontario Museum (ROM) and a past Orangeville resident, described the formation of the Niagara Escarpment:

The escarpment records changes that began in the Paleozoic era about 450 million years ago, when an immense delta was being formed by many rivers whose headwaters rose out of a range of mountains, now long gone, that occupied part of the area of today's Appalachian Mountains. A modern version might be the delta at the mouth of the Ganges River in India, whose headwaters flow out of the Himalayas."[4]

In talking about the terrain closer to Orangeville, Dr. Tovell describes the Hockley Valley to the northeast of Orangeville as one of the "over 30 valleys or re-entrants of the Niagara Escarpment, which are the features that give the escarpment its jagged outline. These valleys vary in size and shape, but have broadly similar trends. The valley floors are generally covered with gravel, sand and silts. Most of the valleys have rivers that carry far too little water even in flood to have eroded such large valleys. Such rivers are called misfits."[5] Dr. Tovell explains that the Nottawasaga (Hockley) Valley, which cuts through to the escarpment just east and north of Orangeville, is one of these misfit rivers. The Credit River, which gathers its water from springs in the Orangeville area, falls over the escarpment, and over the years has eroded its path through the soft limestone. The escarpment itself is still continually eroding and undergoing change.

The glacial activity in southern Ontario had two major effects on the Orangeville area. Firstly, it wore down the sharp faces of the escarpment and secondly, left glacial deposits of silt and gravel in the form of moraines. Orangeville is situated where the Oak Ridges Moraine[6] and the Orangeville Moraine meet, and where both intersect the Niagara Escarpment.

Northwest of Orangeville the landmass attains altitudes of more than 1,600 feet above sea level. From there, both the Credit and Humber rivers find their way to Lake Ontario. As well, the area is the source of the Grand River, which rises in the Townships of Amaranth, East Luther and Melancthon and flows southward into Lake Erie. Less than one mile north on the Niagara Escarpment, the Nottawasaga River, swollen with water from its tributary, the Boyne River, flows northward into Georgian Bay. Small tributaries of the Saugeen River system flow more northwesterly from the top of Melancthon Township and on into Lake Huron. Natural springs surround the site of the town and the limestone of the Niagara Escarpment surfaces to the east, south and north. But it is the tributaries of the Credit River

In the Beginning 5

that gave the town its beginnings. These creeks were constant. The water was clear and it flowed with a consistently strong force, dropping 150 feet in two miles.

It is possible that mastodons may have visited the area. In the 1880s, mastodon bones were discovered in nearby Amaranth and East Luther townships. The Amaranth find is the most northerly discovery to date:

> The mastodon was a magnificent and imposing animal, closely related to the modern elephant, but slightly larger. The evidence from the mastodon sites indicates that they inhabited spruce forests between 10,000 to 12,000 years ago, just after the glacial ice had melted away from southern Ontario.[7]

The forest cover of the Orangeville area depended on geology and climate. Just north and west of town there are numerous swamps that were populated with cedars, tamarack, poplar and birch. To the east, on the hills of the moraine surrounding the Niagara Escarpment, were forests of mixed deciduous hardwoods of sugar maple, beech, red oak, black cherry, bass, elm, white ash and others. These woods are evident in the pioneer furniture that was made locally, samples of which can be examined at the Dufferin County Museum. The types of woods were quite varied and the tree rings indicate the large sizes of the trees and their great age. To the north was found the versatile white pine that grew on plains created by the glaciers, and there would have been oak plains in the district as well. Occasionally, there probably would have been thickets of scrub growth, the remnants of the ravages of fire or the force of winds:

> There are fundamental relationships between trees and sites. It is quite clear that spruce and cedar would usually inhabit damp sites, whereas pine was found on sandy, well-drained land. The hardwoods did not have such clear relationships, except that they seemed to grow on soils generally usable for agriculture.[8]

The trees were responsible for bringing the first industry into Orangeville, namely the sawmill. And these trees challenged the pioneer farmers who laboriously carved out a piece of land to create their settlement. Some of the cut logs were squared off or notched to make their first shelter, but that did not use up much of the forest. Many acres of forest were simply cut down and burned, the stumps removed and the roots grubbed. When the wood was burned, the residue of ash often provided the first source of cash for families, as the ash was often sold for potash and lye. Excess lumber could sometimes be sold off to the numerous sawmills that were springing up across the central part of Upper Canada (later named Canada West) in the 1830–50s. Sawn lumber was easier to transport to the markets in larger cities that were growing at an incredible rate, the result of increasing immigration from the old country. "Timber was also an integral part of the agricultural economy, based on sawmills located as close as possible to where settlers were cutting trees on their bush farms and wanting lumber. The opportunity to continue to augment income through the sale of saw logs, fuel wood and potash from the clearing of a farm, likely made the difference for many pioneer between staying on the farm or retreating to the town."[9]

Of all the aspects of history that once were part of today's Orangeville, our First Nations population has left the least trace. Portions of our virgin forests can be found and the remnants of the once powerful streams are evident. All around town the limestone outcroppings of the Niagara Escarpment are clearly visible, but of the Indigenous People we know little. Arrowheads used to be found on Purple Hill, immediately to the east of town, and I remember seeing some when I was a young lad. An early painting of Orangeville completed in 1850 by Orange Jull, grandson of Orange Lawrence (the founder) shows a Native encampment. In a 1975 newspaper article, the Orangeville Historical Society claimed that there was "a long established summer Indian village located on Purple Hill. These Indians belonged to the Mississauga tribe and spent their summers hunting and fishing to provide their food supply for the winter months in their villages further south along the Credit River. The historical society has in its possession several arrowheads from the old Purple Hill camp."[10] How the society acquired this information is not clear, but it has become part of the town's folklore and no one knows what has become of the arrowheads. In truth, little remains.

Modern research indicates that for the Native Peoples, rivers were important spiritually and that the sources of these rivers were viewed as very sacred. Hence, it is likely they would have visited the area for spiritual reasons if not for trading. Game animals were plentiful in the forest as were fish in the waters and so the area may well have been used as a source of food. An outcropping just to the south of Orangeville, towards the old quarry, has always been referred to locally as "the chief's chair." A legend exists that Native elders in the past

In the Beginning

Examples of Native arrowheads and points found around the Orangeville area. *Courtesy of John Woolner, Orangeville.*

would sit on the rock and view the source of the Credit from this picturesque outlook. But there is no evidence to support this the tale.

Judging from what evidence that does still exist, I believe that the Natives probably were more predominant in the areas surrounding the site of the present town than they were in what would now be the town limits. Many of the early settlers recorded their encounters with the local Natives and their families, so we do know that they had several spots in the nearby vicinity where they would come to hunt each season. It is also known that there were areas of First Nations' activity in the area of Mud Lake in East Garafraxa. Original Aboriginal trails, used for hundreds of years by moccasined feet, were located in the Hockley Valley area as well as at Mono Mills and along the Grand River. Before 1649, the Huron First Nation traded with Petuns and Neutrals along the Nottawasaga portage to the Grand. This portage was used later by the Mississauga and the Ojibwa First Nations.

It is believed that Aboriginal people made their appearance in Ontario approximately 12,000 years ago, coming into the fertile areas left by the retreat of the ice age, "Their arrival was contemporary with that of the first tree species—spruce and willow. For many millennia, the human impact was minimal to non-existent."[11]

It is generally known that the Petun First Nation, first inhabited this region of Ontario, "the Ontario Island [Dundalk uplands] were notably unpopulated compared to areas closer to Lakes Huron, Ontario, and Erie"[12] The Petun people were mainly farming people and had such agricultural practices as burning off the forest growth to allow open meadows, savannah and prairie to develop for game and to grow crops such as tobacco. These tribes were often referred to as the "Tobacco Indians." However, when Champlain explored the Huronia area, he wrote, "Most of the land is cleared of trees. The soil is good...The whole district is thickly settled and so, I was told, are the neighbouring districts."[13] It is probably safe to state that the number of Natives that the early settlers in this area would have come into contact with would have been minimal as almost 200 years had passed between first contact and the organized surveying of the townships around Orangeville. By then "European contact is estimated to have resulted in the death of up to 90% of the Aboriginal People through disease, displacement and warfare"[14] Historically we know that the Mohawks of the Six Nations lived along the Grand River and that the Iroquois raided the Tobacco tribes. Therefore, we can assume that the Orangeville area was, at the very least, visited by members of the Mississauga, Petun, Mohawk and Iroquois nations.

Also part of local folklore is the coming into the area of Samuel de Champlain. It is known that on at least one of his explorations of southern Ontario, he came up the Credit River to reach Georgian Bay by way of the Nottawasaga River. Could he have been the first person to see the area where the sources of these two rivers meet, within a half of a mile of each other?

What views met the first settlers who had purchased or were granted land at the present site of Orangeville? The area would have been a location that may have been travelled through by explorers, traders, surveyors and other settlers on their way to their property, and thus would have been only slightly disturbed. As with other sections of Upper Canada of the time, there may have been a few squatters in rudimentary log cabins or trappers who earned their livelihood in the forest. The forests were virgin woods, the rivers high and wildlife abundant. But there was also the winters and the winds, the relentless insects and types of fauna and flora that would challenge the hardiest of pioneers. There was frost, which the natural environment had adapted to, but which made farming almost impossible. Crops with a shorter growing period and from more hardy varieties were developed later for these extremes of the Canadian climate and growing conditions. What the pioneers found had to be conquered and altered in order to be of any use to an agricultural way of life.

Interestingly today, it is the rivers, the forests, the fauna and the flora that attract the new wave of urban escapee settlers who are moving to Orangeville. The difference with these new settlers, however, is that instead of trying to tame the natural environment, they are working to protect what is left and to encourage natural regrowth.

2

EARLY STORIES OF THE SOURCE OF THE CREDIT

ALEXANDER McLACHLAN, AN EARLY CANADIAN poet closely connected to the history of Orangeville, wrote of the pioneer experience:

> This generation ne'er can know,
> The toils we had to undergo,
> While laying the great forest low."[1]

The areas to the east, west and north of today's Orangeville were some of the last to be settled in central Ontario. The area is some distance from any large bodies of water or navigable river systems. As well, the terrain is rough. The hills are many and the swamps even more plentiful, and the Niagara Escarpment wraps itself around the town.

For those early pioneer settlers who did come into the area, there were two rivers available to the northeast of York (Toronto) that could be used to used for travelling to interior Crown lands in this part of Upper Canada, the Credit and the Humber. The Humber was more accessible with much less gradient to the banks. Mono Mills (Market Hill as it was then known), is located at the source of the Humber River. A community developed there well before Orangeville, which is at the source of the Credit River. The Credit, however, did provide excellent sites for potential grist and sawmills to support the growth of any pioneer community. Orangeville is situated about 1,460 feet above sea level. From there, the Credit takes a quick drop as it rushes along the Niagara Escarpment to present-day Port Credit.

From their sources to the west of town, no less than five strong streams ran through the present site of Orangeville, although, today some of them have disappeared, victims of the lowered water table. Only three of them remain: the branch through the centre of town visible at KayCee Gardens, the branch that today flows from Island Lake to become the Credit River and the one that flows to the north of the Fairgrounds Mall and into Island Lake. The one that goes through the centre of town is the one that attracted the interest of pioneers. For its size it had a great drop of 140 feet from west to east, providing enough force to power any water-driven wheel. As well, the abundance of flat workable limestone, which was readily available along the river, made it easy to add ponds and small dams at the various mill sites. The water also tended to flow readily throughout the summer since it was primarily spring-fed. This changed quickly, however, as the settlers cleared away the forest, leading to erosion and the rapid run off of water, which, in turn, lowered the water table. There also were smaller springs in the area that could supply water for domestic purposes, particularly when a well had to be dug. Several community wells developed early, the most important being the one at the corner of First Avenue and Second Street on the property of Jesse Ketchum the Younger.

The fast-flowing water of the streams was often used to carry away the industrial waste, such as the noxious discharge from Campbell's Tannery. This worked well for the businessman, but played havoc on the fish and plant life of the delicate Credit Flats between Orangeville and Melville and the lush cedar swamps in the same vicinity. The practice would not be condoned in our more environmentally conscious times. Today, a little stream winds its way through town and is not noticeable except in areas such as the KayCee Gardens Park and behind the light industries located along Armstrong Street and lower Broadway.

It is fairly evident, from what little traces and legends that have survived from the earliest settlement period, that the present Town of Orangeville had its beginnings on Purple Hill, about a mile east of downtown. Taverns had developed there as earlier settlers made their way en route to the regions of the Queen's Bush[2] and Georgian Bay. At the beginning of the 19th century, the Credit River was jammed with dead falls and only cleared out in the spring run-off or in floods. The Credit Flats flooded every spring and generally was a treacherous mire for most of the rest of the year. In the spring it was necessary to barge across the river. Services and hotels were established and pioneer families would wait on the Purple Hill side for Abraham Hughson (who had

Early Stories of the Source of the Credit   11

settled in Amaranth about 1819) to "locate" them on their property that
had been purchased from the Crown, or given as payment for military
service. In the case of the latter, the land lay to the east of the Credit.

Purple Hill and Orangeville, when initially established, were competitive settlements, Purple Hill being older. In the late 1840s, they
were linked together by the Seneca Ketchum project,[3] a primitive log
causeway that ran through the swamps of the Credit Flats. Even well
into the 1850s, each settlement maintained a distinct identity, each
even having its own Orange Lodge.

But it was on the other side of the Credit that the quick streams
flowed and it was there that industry developed. The 1837 *Directory of
the Home District*[4] includes Caledon and Mono, but Orangeville is not
listed as it did not yet exist. Most of the area was still unoccupied. It
was created as the Nassau District in 1788 and renamed Home District in 1792, remaining under that name until 1849. In 1837, the site
on the west of the Credit River was patented to Robert Dodds who
farmed in Mono Township. He, in turn, sold it to James Griggs who
build a mill there about 1838. The property title was Lot 1 Conces-
sions E and F in Garafraxa Township. It is reported that when Griggs
sent to Trafalgar for his wife to join him, she refused to leave as she
was "afraid of the Indians."[5] Griggs only held the property a short
time before selling to his son George Griggs in 1841, who, in turn,
sold to Orange Lawrence of Trafalgar Township in 1844. Lawrence
had established a second mill, store and tavern by 1847, ten years after
the *Directory* was published. The second mill built by Mr. Lawrence
burned down in 1856. Lawrence's mill ran seven days a week. He
thought that, if the water ran seven days a week, so should the mill.
Ironically, the mill burned on a Sunday.

There is little remaining to permit much tracking of the settlement's
history from the 1830s until the establishment of the newspaper in
1861. What we do know is that game and fish provided much of the
food for the few hardy residents. Many of the earlier buildings had bark
roofs, or were covered in pea straw for insulation in the cold winters.
Much of the cloth required for clothing was woven on simple looms in
the small cabins. Furniture was crude, usually made by the settler himself. Although the land records show activity, it is evident from the
archives that many people owned land that was sold and resold, but
few of these people ever lived in Orangeville.

The exception to the lack of archival evidence pertaining to settlement is an interview with Abiathar Wilcox, published by *The*

Orangeville Advertiser in 1895. Mr. Wilcox had settled on his property in 1840. The interviewer stated that Mr. Wilcox, "being a modest man, was not disposed to talk much for publication." The reporter was able, however, to extract sufficient data for a column of interesting reminiscences. The column reads:

Mr. Wilcox was born in 1811. His father was a Yankee, while his mother was of Pennsylvania Dutch extraction. When but a lad, Mr. Wilcox struck in to the wilderness and for 10 or 11 years lived in Caledon. Here he married and learned the stern realities of pioneer farming. Through the U.E.L. Crown grants, his mother had acquired the ownership of 100 acres in Mono [Township]. Mr. Wilcox traded this property for what was then known as Lot 2, Concession 2, Mono W.H.S. [west of Hurontario Street]. [His farm was located on what is now Bredin Parkway and the Goldgate subdivision.]

In the spring of 1840, with his wife and three children, he entered into possession of the land that was destined at no distant future to form a valuable portion of the prosperous Town of Orangeville. There was only one man here before Mr. Wilcox. His name was James Griggs and he owned a saw and gristmill. Griggs had a wife and one or two children. Orange Lawrence, who is generally supposed to have been the founder of the town, did not arrive until several years after Mr. Wilcox came to keep James Griggs company in the howling wilderness. After Mr. Wilcox came Isaac Newton. He was also a miller.

Mr. Wilcox lost no time in idle speculation. He constructed a log house and lived in it without the luxury of a floor. The cracks between the logs were filled with moss. Bears, wolves and deer were plentiful. Oxen were the only available beasts of burden. There were very few Indians in the neighbourhood. The early settler did not live extravagantly. Scorched flour or corn took the place of coffee and peppermint or sage made tea. Cow cabbage and potato tops were good enough for vegetable purposes. Mr. Wilcox wintered four head of cattle on the tops of trees one year. A saucer of grease with a piece of twisted rag for a wick was the best thing to a candle for illumination purposes. When the man of the house wanted an extra stylish pair of pants he bought some factory cotton and dyed them with hemlock bark. Vest and coats were worn only on Sundays and visiting days.

Mr. Wilcox was personally acquainted with Wm. Lyon Mackenzie and sympathized with that patriot in his struggles for responsible

Jull's gristmill was built on the banks of Mill Creek in 1857, by Orange Lawrence's two sons-in-law, Thomas Jull and John Walker Reid.

government. The first vote Mr. Wilcox recorded was for Mackenzie himself and he travelled all the way to Streetsville to exercise his franchise on this occasion.[6]

Isaac Newton is acknowledged as the first child born in Orangeville. He was the son of Mary Ann and William Newton who had a log cabin on the site of today's Town Hall. Newton was Orange Lawrence's Mill foreman. Isaac Newton was born in 1846 and lived his entire life in Orangeville. He worked on the construction of the old stone post office building and the Dufferin County building on Zina Street. He died in 1929.[7]

It was during the early development of the village that water rights[8] were established along the creeks. The mills that were beginning to locate south of what is today's Broadway, relied on water power to drive them. Orange Lawrence, owner of some of these early mills, very busily bought up water rights wherever he could, to divert the flows into the mill races to power his mills. On June 30, 1856, he bought the rights from Jesse Ketchum the Younger to divert water from a stream through the Ketchum property. Ketchum had arrived in Orangeville in the early 1850s, settling on land he obtained from his Uncle Seneca Ketchum's estate. Just because there was a hill between the Ketchum stream and

14   ORANGEVILLE

the Lawrence mill races didn't deter Lawrence. He put an hydraulic ram (a type of pump) in the stream and forced the water through a pipe up the hill across from what would become Zina Street and Broadway and into the open races, the man-made "creeks" by Mill Creek.

Interestingly, these water rights were not relinquished by their subsequent owners until 1909. The mills had converted to steam power in the 1870–80s, and the races had been abandoned for many years. The sale of the lands reserved for water rights marked the official end of the water-power era in Orangeville.

It was the availability of this water power that created the tiny settlement in the first place. However, the mill races and the ponds powering the mills, caused new problems, those of the human kind. While the mills brought prosperity to the town, they also brought tragedy:

> It is with deep regret that we have to chronicle the death by drowning of the eldest child of W. Rutledge, merchant, of this village—a fine little boy of about three years of age. The deplorable accident occurred yesterday afternoon, as follows: In the rear of Mr. Rutledge's store is a pond connected with the sawmill. The family missed their eldest child, and immediately commenced to look for him, but without avail, and it was not until the elapse of an hour that the idea of the child being drowned in the millpond occurred to the agonized parents. On searching the pond with grappling irons, the body of the unfortunate child was immediately found. Life appeared to have been long extinct, as the body was quite cold. We in common with the church and the whole community deeply sympathize with the family in the irreparable loss he has sustained.[9]

The industries that began to develop in the small settlement depended on two local economies—agriculture and lumbering. In fact, all settlers were dependent ultimately on agriculture or timber for their livelihood. The sawmills and gristmills that were being built along Mill Creek were also dependent on both. Foundries and furniture factories followed. Records show that some of Orangeville's early industries included a foundry, a furniture maker, a tannery and a woollen mill. Stores supplied the basic needs of the families, if they had the cash or produce to trade. Because of the difficulties of travelling any distance to acquire goods, smaller industries such as potteries, tin shops and shoemakers quickly developed.

Early Stories of the Source of the Credit   15

Although no information exists on the exact population, in the 1851 Census, after extracting names from Garafraxa and Mono entries, a population of approximately 280 persons are recorded as living in the Orangeville area. The laws of Canada West (Ontario) indicated that a centre with a population of 500 could incorporate as a village. By the time of the 1861 Census, Orangeville had achieved that number, but it took until 1863 to get all the required government formalities in place. The actual day of incorporation is January 1, 1864. The new Village of Orangeville became part of Wellington County.[10]

During the early history of Orangeville the land in the adjoining townships was still rough and largely unsettled, well into the 1850s. Large populations of wild animals roamed nearby. Wolves often visited the homes of settlers for what might seem to them an easy meal. In 1869 in nearby Luther Township, the following account was noted:

Wolves are very numerous this season. They sally forth in large packs from the swamps and attack sheep, cattle and horses in the clearings and are sometimes daring enough to chase the farmers from their fields. A large bounty is set on wolves but the animals are wary and captures are seldom made.[11]

Bears were also quite plentiful when the settlers arrived and did not disappear until the 1880s. In the fall of 1863 one farmer alone, Mr. John Large of Amaranth, shot three bears including one weighing over 500 pounds, "When discovered, his bearship was sitting on his haunches munching a fat hog, which he had carried off for breakfast and which he would have devoured alive had not the leaden messenger of death abruptly interrupted his festive enjoyment."[12] Bears were of some commercial value and, in 1869, a good hide would fetch $12 in the Canadian dollars of the time and the carcass an additional $12. Lynx also were plentiful and known to bother livestock, causing local farmers to try and destroy the animal without bothering about the meat or fur. By about 1890, the lynx had disappeared.

The land was rich and fertile. The first crop yields were plentiful provided that the crop could survive the late frosts of spring and the early frosts of fall. Due to the high altitude the growing season was quite short. Long winters were good news, however, if one were involved in the lumbering and logging business. Logs were easier to move over the snow and without heavy foliage to impede the way.

Within town many smaller acreage farms appeared, the larger holdings being cut into smaller holdings. A family could grow enough food to eat on these small parcels of land. Some lots were large enough for such uses as orchards, gardens or even small fields for hay or grains. The site of the present Town Hall was once a wheat field owned by Granny Newton, mother of Isaac. Originally an immigrant from Darlington, County of Durham, England, she died at age 84 on October 14, 1875, the very year the new Town Hall was built on her former farm.

More people moved in, most of them seeking prosperity in a new country. Orangeville had become a jumping off point for settlers heading to the outlying townships. Mono and Mulmur townships were settled in the 1820–30s and Garafraxa saw its major settlement during the 1850s. Amaranth was settled primarily from 1850 to 1870, while Melancthon and Luther were not fully settled until the 1860–80s. A number of people stayed because they liked the area. Many of their descendants still remain generations later, despite the many changes and overall growth. Orangeville was there to stay.

Schooling was very important to the early settlers. People of the era saw education as the way of bettering oneself and getting ahead in this new country. It is known that the early settlers or their wives held informal learning sessions and Sunday Schools in their homes. Orange Lawrence started a small school in one of his buildings in 1848 and his son Ferris was the teacher. In Orangeville, a real schoolhouse was finally built in 1850, long before many of the early factories and businesses:

The little log schoolhouse, with its thatched roof of pea straw, was erected in the year 1850 or thereabouts on the corner of John Street and Broadway, where stands the present fire hall. John James Nichol was the first teacher in this section to wield the birch in this, the first school. About the years 1859 or 1860 the log schoolhouse was burned down. It is said that two of the pupils were sent to extinguish the fire, which had started in the thatched roof, but these embryo firemen by some means started another blaze on the other side of the roof and so ended the little log schoolhouse. In the year 1859 the following persons or residents of the district donated cash for prizes in school for the amount of $7.25: Jesse Ketchum, C.J. Wheelock, Thomas Hunter and Abiathar Wilcox. In the interval, while the timber and brick were being teamed, and the foundations were being laid for the second school on the corner, which is now Bythia and York streets, school was conducted by Miss Polly Bennett in the cooper shop at the corner of First and Zina streets. The brick school was erected in 1862. About the year 1872 this latter school was abandoned for lack of accommodation and our present public school was erected.[13]

About the same time as the schoolhouse burned, F.E. McBain opened a private school at a nominal charge of 25¢ a month on First Avenue. The existence of this private school is confirmed by a notation in the diary of Jesse Ketchum, "Went to McBain's school—afternoon—says he has 101 scholars."[14]

Religion and religious freedom were also important to the early residents of Orangeville. Methodists were among the first settlers in the Orangeville district. Abraham Hughson settled on Lot 3, Concession 1, (now County Road 16 on the west side of Orangeville) Amaranth. He was deeded the property in 1823 but could have been living there as early as 1819. He was instrumental in holding early religious services and providing a school of sorts in his log barn. Abiathar Wilcox arrived in 1840, determined to organize the local Methodists into a regular church, instead of relying on the occasional visits of itinerant missionaries, the famous "saddle bag preachers." Children were baptized and

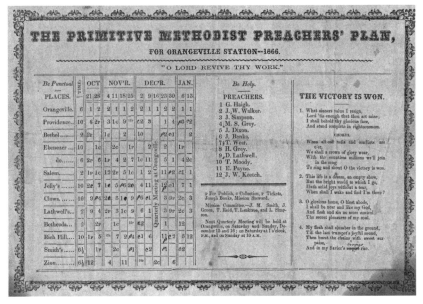

An 1859 broadsheet listing the various branches of the Amaranth Mission of the Methodist Circuit. Various branches of Methodism were active early in the Orangeville area. The Amaranth Mission had its headquarters in Orangeville.

weddings performed by these travelling ministers, and burials were handled by the local church members. Wilcox, Hughson, James Johnston, John Tweedy and Miles Bacon organized "the Amaranth Mission station" based at Orangeville in 1849. The mission had a resident clergyman, Rev. J.W. Byam, to assist the lay preachers serving congregations at other nearby settlements—The Maples, Cataract, Melville and Glen Cross, as well as Orangeville. In 1850, the name was changed to the Orangeville Mission:

> The new congregation decided a chapel was necessary for their work and in 1850, Abiathar Wilcox gave them a lot on his farm on the current First Street and Bredin Parkway. The congregation thought it was too far out of town, so Wilcox purchased an acre from Orange Lawrence at the corner of Church and Wellington Street. It was used for a church and burying ground. The building committee acquired two more acres for a site for a parsonage, too.[15]

The chapel was constructed during 1850, and had the distinction of being the first brick building, and for a few years, the only brick building in Orangeville. It is from this building that the name Church Street was given. While the congregation was ambitious, as can be seen by its construction of a brick building at a time when every other congregation in the district had one built of logs, it does not necessarily mean they were prosperous. Things started off well, but the interior of the church was not completed until 1856. It took a further five years to pay off the $1,850 it cost to build the 26 × 36-foot chapel.

From 1853 to 1863, seven preachers served this mission, their salaries consisting of forty pounds from the station and an equal amount of missionary grant. Often more practical contributions were made, such as wheat, oats and wood. The credit system flourished. In 1858, the currency of the country changed from pounds to dollars.

> In October, 1856, Brother Jones informed the "Canada Christian Advocate" that The Lord is reviving his work in Orangeville. Several have professed to find peace in believing and others are earnestly seeking salvation, while old professors are being revived and quickened in spirit. And the following year, he claims that Satan has a great popular agent who does much harm to the progress of beloved Methodism. Love of strong drink or the inebriating bowl is the prevailing evil.[16]

Early Stories of the Source of the Credit   19

Complaints of hard times were not uncommon. A story is told of the congregation's desperation. They had mortgaged the parson's cow for $10.70. Abiathar Wilcox paid off the loan so the minister could take his cow when he left town for a new post. A special collection was later taken by the congregation to repay Mr. Wilcox.

Early congregations rarely provided grandiose homes for their preachers, and the Orangeville congregation was no exception. Their stone parsonage was about the same size as a log house of the time would have been and probably followed a similar plan: two or three rooms downstairs and a loft upstairs. Dividing walls would likely have been added later in the upper floor.

Life in early Orangeville was not all work. There was some fun and mischief. About 80% of the settlers prior to 1850 were from Ireland or the children of Irish immigrants. Many were from the north of Ireland, primarily from the Counties of Tyrone and Armagh. The rest were from the west of Ireland from County Sligo. They were predominantly Protestants, and brought their distinctive Ulster accent and culture with them. The Irish had the temperament for a good laugh and a good trick, and perhaps a dry sense of humour got many a person through the hardships of pioneer life. And for the Irish, perhaps the only thing that was dry was the humour. Stories of mischief kept creeping its way into my research notes:

> The person who removed a large wash tub from the cellar of Elgie's Hotel, on the evening of the Fair Day, is well known, and is requested to leave it at the cellar door, and save any unpleasantness that might otherwise arise from its retention.[17]

Another notation was found:

> On Wednesday night a number of disorderly persons assembled in front of Mrs. Norris's residence to charivari a young couple lately married, and whom they expected to be in the house. They made night hideous with the discordant music of kettles, bells, tin horns, etc and proved a source of nuisance to the whole neighbourhood. Nuisances of this character are getting too common and ought to be suppressed by the strong arm of the law.[18]

Almost every early home in Orangeville prior to 1870 had three things that few homes in town have today, an outhouse, a garden and a

This early photograph shows the north side of Broadway as it appeared in 1866. The store in the middle belonged to the reeve, Falkner Stewart. Later, he was elected first warden of Dufferin County and became an MPP.

barn. Outhouses have long been replaced and it has been many years since I have known of one in the town area. A good garden went a long way to feed the larger families of the period when families of six to nine children were not uncommon. Good seed was readily available in many of the stores on Broadway as well as from peddlers who travelled up and down the roads, making a living by selling their wares from a wagon. Mail-order catalogues were not to come along for another thirty years.

There were plenty of jobs in a garden for a growing brood of children. The stealing of pea pods and apples was a popular pastime along the lanes of town, and the early newspapers are filled with stories of the town youth getting into gardens and helping themselves. Throughout the summer season, locals could supplement the family dinner with fish from the Credit, and plenty of wild fruit. In the summer of 1870, the huckleberry marshes of Amaranth, west of the town limits, yielded over one thousand bushels of berries. Chokecherries gathered along fence lines could be used for either jam or something a little more medicinal in nature, depending on the religion of the family or their feelings on temperance.

The barn was suited for a variety of uses. It would house the family horse, needed to get about, as well as a carriage or buggy and provide storage space for food. Sometimes a cow or two would be included and chickens were not uncommon within the town limits. Chickens provided eggs for the pan and meat for the pot. Early mornings were filled with the sound of the town roosters calling the townsfolk to work. Pigs were kept to eat swill (the peelings, leftovers and edible

Early Stories of the Source of the Credit 21

refuse) as well as providing cured and salted pork that would keep all winter without refrigeration. Manure from the barn would either be used in the gardens or in orchards. but would never be hauled out of town. Manure piles created a real problem in town, clogging the back lanes and reeking in hot weather.

By the 1890s, only limited farming existed in the town. Gone too were the farms that once edged the small cluster of buildings that made up the growing village. The one small agricultural business that did exist, was a small one-half-acre celery farm operated by Orange Lawrence Jr. The fields were along what is now Amanda Street.

By the end of the pioneer era in Orangeville, human habitation was already having a detrimental effect on the growing town. Trees had been lumbered off in and around the town or simply burned to make way for farmland. The waters of the Credit were polluted from the dumping of refuse from the streets and the local factories, the worst offender being the tannery. Sawdust from Thomas Jull's mill was dumped into the stream as well. Potable water, essential for the residents, was becoming difficult to find. As early as 1863, with the town having been in existence for less than 20 years, the negative effects of rapid growth were evident:

> Nothing, we imagine, contributes more to the prosperity of Orangeville than its water power. As the forests recede it has been observed that the volume of water in Mill Creek decreases, and fears are entertained that in a few years more it will so far diminish that it will be inadequate to turn its present complement of machinery. We confess we are not without our fears in this respect, but we are not of those who think that the difficulty cannot be surmounted. There are several small steams fed by durable and continuous springs in the immediate neighbourhood of Orangeville whose course might be diverted into Mill Creek, thus securing an inexhaustible supply of water. The expense and labour attending the enterprise would of course be considerable but not such as to prevent the project from being speedily carried out. Of the streams that might be conveniently turned into Mill Creek, an imperfect inquiry has shown us that a branch of the Nottawasaga, which crosses the Prince of Wales Road is the chief.[19]

The scheme never happened. Orange Jull, who worked in his father's gristmill, developed an improved turbine wheel that increased the power that could be extracted from the existing flow. Steam engines of ever-increasing sizes were also being introduced to provide reliable power for the mills.

In 1850, Orangeville was only one of many small hamlets in the headwaters region. As farms were taken up and cleared by settlers, roads improved, allowing the pioneers to diversify the crops they had been growing. From the earliest days wheat had been the mainstay of early central Ontario agriculture. But better roads allowed farmers to transport their goods to town to sell to agents, who would travel to the towns and buy commodities. Peas, oats and turnips began to replace wheat in local fields. However, travelling to a larger centre such as Guelph or Toronto was expensive, time-consuming and often dangerous.

In November 1848, the people of Orangeville organized monthly "fairs" for the purpose of trading livestock, and a more formal market was initiated in 1859. It was perhaps the market that made the settlement grow at a faster rate than the other surrounding hamlets. It brought the farmers as well as the agents into town. Agents, acting as middle men, would buy local products and ship them south in wagons to the urban centres, always having to turn a profit.

With the farmers coming into the village, manufacturing businesses such as foundries began to develop and exhibit their wares at the agricultural market. On July 9, 1868, *The Sun* reported that the local display of agricultural implements and artisan work was larger than last year and reflected great credit on the part of the manufacturers. Roads, indeed, did bring money to town, but the railway coming in 1871 brought profits in by the carload. Now traders could reach Orangeville and return daily, and goods could be transported quickly to the growing urban centres clustered along Lake Ontario. Livestock as well as agricultural produce travelled well on rail cars and soon the local farmers began to ship animals for sale to the beef markets located in the vicinity of the rail yards in Toronto, the area that became known as the Junction.

Lumbering was another industry that profited from the arrival of the "iron horse." Prior to the railway, it was very difficult to transport larger logs on the poor road system. Some logs were floated down the Grand River through Grand Valley, Waldemar and Belwood, but neither the Credit or Nottawasaga rivers were suitable for the transportation of logs. Lumber began to be produced not just for local use but for export as well. Throughout the 1870s, *The Sun* contained numerous references to large quantities of cordwood, telegraph poles and lumber being shipped from town by rail.

This load of cross ties demonstrates a time when Orangeville was a lumbering town. For a while sawmills and lumberyards flourished along Mill Creek. The coming of the railway led to a second lumbering boom with its demand for wooden ties and wood to fuel the steam engines that travelled the tracks.

All was not quiet in early Orangeville, as it grew in population. By 1863, *The Sun* reported a population of 700 persons with another 300 scattered around the village on farms and smaller hamlets. Within the village there now were all types of new commercial building and residences more permanent than the earlier log or stone cabins. With that growth came the problems credited by a busy centre. Horse traffic on Broadway caused many collisions involving both pedestrians and other drivers. Newspapers of the era reported many accidents on the main street in almost every issue. Horses were often easily startled and owners were sometimes irresponsible.

Newspapers also began to report criminal activity, particularly along the main thoroughfare. Drunkenness in the streets was common in Orangeville, and the eleven hotels and three liquor stores did a riproaring good business:

> An affray which might have been attended with fatal consequences, took place at the "Marksman's Home," on Broadway, on Saturday evening. It appears that a young desperado named Andrew Hamilton entered into the bar room of the Marksman's Home about nine o'clock and addressing the proprietor, Mr. A. Lennox, offered to wager $5 that he could bind four acres of wheat in a day, Mr. Lennox

From as early as 1848, Orangeville inns, taverns and hotels provided hospitality. Bar rooms were always crowded on market days, as shown in this photograph inside the bar of the Queen's Hotel.

replied, by observing that he could certainly loose the wager, as the task was enough for two men. At this Hamilton rushed at Mr. Lennox; a struggle ensued in which Mr. Lennox, overcoming his assailant, ordered him out of the house. Hamilton, however, refused to leave, and Mr. Lennox, to avoid any difficulty with him, went out. After the lapse of some time he returned, and taking a seat in the bar room, was again set upon by Hamilton, when another struggle ensued, in which Mr. Lennox ejected his adversary from the room. In this encounter Hamilton must have used his knife with fearful effect for at the close, the bystanders noticed blood flowing copiously from Mr. Lennox's side; and, on examination, it was found that his shirt and pants had been pierced in fourteen places, and that four thrusts had taken effect, inflicting dangerous wounds in the left breast, back, groin and thigh The news of the outrage committed on Mr. Lennox, who is highly esteemed and respected, created intense excitement in the neighbourhood, and Hamilton, the perpetrator of the deed, was pursued, and arrested at the residence of a friend, on West Broadway, and brought before Messrs. G. Leslie and S.H. McKitrick, both Justices of the Peace, who committed him to jail to await his trial at the Assizes to be held in Guelph in October. The knife, which is supposed he used in the murderous assault, was found upon his person, stained with blood. Hamilton bears the reputation of a dangerous character, who first provokes a quarrel and then employs a knife against his unwilling antagonist.[20]

The end of the pioneer period was marked by the removal of an old log cabin, with its front addition, from Broadway. It was dismantled to make room for the erection of the new Orangeville Town Hall, built in 1875:

Early Stories of the Source of the Credit

The old log cabin, erected more than a quarter of a century ago in the midst of the forest on the very identical spot destined to be chosen as the market site for the populous and prosperous Town of Orangeville, has at last succumbed to the encroachments of modern improvements. Last Saturday it was taken down, as it had been put up, log by log, and removed to make room for a town hall and a market building. It was the oldest monument left of the patient labours of the founders of the town, and though overshadowed by the magnificent structures of stone, brick and mortar, which had risen around it, was itself doubtless considered by its builders, a piece of matchless architecture, and even in its old age it showed that much care had been taken in its erection.

Granny Irvine's original log cabin became the back kitchen of her frame house on First Street, now the site of the Lord Dufferin Centre.

We are sorry that this old monument of the early settlement of Orangeville had to be pulled down. It awakened thoughts, and gave rise to reflections which must now slumber in the brain, because there is nothing else left to revive them and call them into action. Who could pass along East Broadway, or 2nd East Street, and see the old "log biggin" on the corner, with Mrs. [Mary Ann] Newton, the old lady who had occupied it for over twenty-five years, and who herself now close upon 90, yet still strong and vigorous, standing before the door, and not recall the struggles, the failures, triumphs and final victory of the early settlers? Who could look upon the humble old hut, as the lonely starting point of the populous town around it, without a feeling of awe at the magnitude of the changes which have taken place within the last thirty or forty years? Where dwelt the lonely axeman in the wilderness, patiently toiling as the pioneer of civilization, satisfied with the simplest fare, and enduring the severest hardship, has become the mart of trade and commerce, a hive of human beings, living in the utmost security, and enjoying all the luxuries which can be supplied by their own and other countries.

Even the very features of the country have undergone great changes, and so rapid is the transmutation now, that it may almost be said without exaggeration that should the visitor yesterday come again tomorrow, he could scarcely recognize a single spot. We are verily moving at a pace whose speed we do not pause to calculate, because if we should stop to look behind us we should lose our place in the march of progress.

Whither, it may be asked, are we drifting? Where is the final goal? No one can tell. Our duty is to march on without flagging, leaving behind us monuments which our descendants, if they travel faster than we, may find encumbrances in their way, and pull down as ruthlessly as we do the works of our ancestors, and with as little concern as paid labourers did the Old Log Cabin.[21]

Indeed, by the time of the arrival of the railway, traces of the early settlement period were largely gone, as were many of the first generation of settlers. Their sons and daughters had taken over while new people continued to stream into the town, which by now was showing all the signs of prosperity and growth. Orangeville had been incorporated as a town as of January 1, 1875. The new Town Hall, a symbol of not only Victorian architecture but also of Victorian prosperity, was designed by the Orangeville architect and lawyer, Francis Grant Dunbar. It was to be erected in combination with a market house and council chamber. Orangeville's pioneer period was over and the town was entering into a new era.

3

THEM DAMN YANKEES

IT WAS NOT THE FIRST settlers into the tiny settlement at the source of the Credit River that had the greatest impact, nor was it the many Irish Protestants who began to move in. The "fathers" of the present Town of Orangeville, if there be such a thing, were, in fact, latecomers and American by birth. And that's not all the peculiarities. Orange Lawrence, after whom the town is named, did not arrive until 1843 and Seneca Ketchum, its earliest developer, actually lived on nearby Purple Hill.

In 1914, Mrs. Nathaniel Sproule (née Tweedy) was interviewed by *The Sun*. She recalled Orangeville of 1850:

When I was about a year and a half old, my father Samuel Tweedy moved from the Humber to the Town Line. [lots 4 & 5, Concession East Garafraxa—across from Greenwood Cemetery] That was about 1850. Orangeville at that time hadn't a name at all. It was simply spoken of as "the Mill." My father would take a bag of grain to the mill on his back, wait for it to be ground and bring it home the same day. The bread would be as black as black as there was then no way of separating the smut. The mill was run by a man by the name of [James] Griggs and was a small log building. The roads were so swampy and bad that no one could thresh until the first frost came. It was the wildest place you ever saw. I can remember when there were only three houses in Orangeville. After a while Mr. [Orange] Lawrence came to town. He had a fine lot of nice looking girls. The day they named the village after him I saw him carried up the street in a chair. Some did not want it called Orangeville and some did. Mr. Lawrence wanted it, was pleased and it was right as he built places and made things lively.

Many's a wedding I went to in Mr. Seneca Ketchum's church in Mono. That was where all the weddings were held. In those days we went on horseback. There were no roads fit for buggies even if we had the buggies. I remember Seneca Ketchum well. He rode a big bay mare, wore a dark blue cloak and went about teaching the young people their catechism. After he died, Jesse Ketchum [Seneca's nephew] came. He had the most money of anyone that ever came to the village and spent it in improving and laying out the roads and making a fine place of it.[1]

Seneca Ketchum, a volunteer missionary with Church of England, was licensed by Bishop John Strachan[2] to come to the wilds of Mono Township in the early 1830s. He had farmed successfully at York Mills, married Sarah Ann Mercer and was active in business, community and social work in the area. Seneca had arrived in Canada as an United Empire Loyalist and had gone first to Kingston, then on to York Mills. He acquired his first land in the Orangeville area in 1822, one hundred acres in Mono Township the year that it was surveyed, and a year after the first settler to the area, Abraham Hughson, another United Empire Loyalist, had moved to Lot 3, Concession 1, Amaranth. Ketchum was a protegé of Strachan's old friend, Reverend Dr. Okill Stuart, who had arrived in Kingston during the American War of Independence. Stuart was a very prominent Anglican clergyman of the 1820s. Ketchum was known to be a very religious man, but his ideas sometimes were a little "off-beat" for the conservative Anglican Church of the time.

The Orangeville area was little more than a series of primitive trails with a few families scattered in the bush. Perhaps it was thought that Seneca could do little harm in such a remote area. He worked endlessly for God, establishing Sunday Schools and teaching catechism. By 1837 he had built a log church on Lot 1, Concession 2, E.H.S. (east of Hurontario Street) Mono Township. This church became the foundation of the present-day congregation of St. Mark's Anglican Church. Ketchum was loved by the settlers, and soon became a leader in the community with everyone coming to him for help and advice, both religious and business. His generosity in helping with municipal matters, such as road building, was well known. As well, he ran a children's library for the education of the young residents of Mono and The Gore of Garafraxa (the point of a surveyed triangle between townships). His brother, Jesse, a tanner, had stayed in York (Toronto) and had founded the Upper Canada Religious Tract and Book Society,

Them Damn Yankees

which would eventually be merged with the Canadian Bible Society. Like his brother, Jesse held a particular interest in education and founded York's first Common School in 1819.

At a meeting of the Church Society of the Diocese of Toronto on November 5, 1845, the committee sent thanks to Seneca Ketchum for the donation of 100 acres of land on what is now Purple Hill. It was to be held in trust for the maintenance of divinity students. Seneca was known in the church circles in Toronto as both a fervent believer and a supporter of the church. He also offered to donate three hundred acres of the approximately 700 acres he had acquired, to the Diocese to promote a scheme that he had of having a township settled entirely by men of the Church of England and their families. And he had picked the Township of Mono and the future site of Orangeville as that place.

Although a stanch supporter of the early Anglican Church, he was sometimes radical in proposing particular schemes and was fearless in expressing his personal opinions. In a letter to the Diocese of Toronto, dated April 26, 1850, he states his views on the minister sent out to the Mono Mission, "They send me a brandy tippler to entertain and preach to my people. I had him for five months last year. He had [the use of] my two servants, all my bedding, house, bread, meat, candles, salt, butter, honey, fat geese, and feed for his horse. I thought him a gentleman and said so, but his conduct has proved the reverse. All it cost him and the Bishop was a lock for the door. How careful is the Bishop of hurting the devil."[3]

Seneca Ketchum died in 1850 at the age of 78, while on a trip to visit Bishop Strachan. He was buried at his former churchyard in York Mills. Before he died he left Orangeville a rich municipal heritage. He had spent considerable amounts of money to improve the area, including $54 to clear off the market square, fence it and have it sown for mowing. It was he who cut through the swamp (the Credit Flats on East Broadway) at his own expense, and built 156 rods (about 785 metres) of causeway, complete with seven bridges, to create an easier access into Orangeville. He also opened two roads—one from McLaughlin's (Mono Mills) and one down to Bracken's place near Charlestown (later Caledon).

When he died, and having no children, his several hundred acres of land holdings went to his nephew Jesse Ketchum (who became known as "Jesse the Younger"), including the land north of Broadway. It was he who planned the subdivision of North Ward in the present Town of Orangeville and began to develop it. Rural life was unfamiliar to

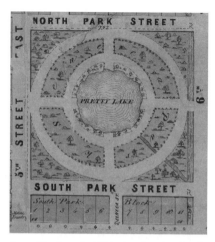

Jesse Ketchum's 1856 plan for the development of Orangeville north of Broadway included a landscaped lake and park to be laid out on the swamp in the Credit Flats.

Jesse, as he had been raised in Toronto. His diary tells of many personal and financial difficulties he experienced after inheriting his uncle's land. With the co-operation of local businesses and residents, and with the aid of some planning, the town began to grow quickly. Jesse became a member of the committee formed to create a new county for the area in 1862.

Jesse was about 34 years of age when he took up his new holdings. He saw the potential of the little settlement and wanted to become as successful as some of his relatives. Having visited New York, he thought this fledgling town could be something "big." He changed the name of the dirt track Orange Lawrence had called Main Street to Broadway, and had Charles Wheelock resurvey one of Seneca's farms (today's Historic District) into streets and city-sized lots, all north of present-day Broadway. Alan Rayburn suggests that "it was Wheelock who came up with the idea of increasing the width of Broadway from 66 to 100 feet, making it one of the most handsome main streets in Ontario."[4] The streets and avenues were given numerical names like those in New York. A park built around a man-made pond was planned for the Credit Flats, the site today of Idlewyld Park. It was laid out very formally, as were the streets, orderly and even, unlike the streets south of Broadway that were being developed about the same time on Orange Lawrence's property. When Jesse was developing his end of town, he named one street Sherburne in honour of his sister-in-law's grandmother, Elizabeth Sherburne, wife of Baron de Fleur.

Jesse the Younger's life in the little town was not always easy, as he was not used to the bush life and he did not have his uncle to go to for advice In his diary of 1859, he wrote, "this has ended a most unfortunate year for me of trouble and loss—I trust such another may never occur. I trust also the trials here gone through may be a warning and lesson to me and that Providence may smile on me in my pecuniary matters and if such should be the case, may wisdom give me from above to be a Good Stewart while suffering under the rod of afflicting penury. I consider that a very great portion of my difficulties have been deserved—not being content when I had abundance nor using that abundance in a sufficiently praiseworthy manner."[5] And it would seem that things may not have improved the next year, "Mr. Reverend Gray will give me my note for $200 after he sells lots for enough to pay himself and give me balance—whether I am the victim of misplaced confidence in this instance as in most others remains to be seen.[6]

Jesse Ketchum owned the community water well, located at the corner of First Avenue and Second Street (across from Alexandra Park), that was used by residents located on his lot. Ownership of the well meant holding considerable power since the water from the rivers was becoming unsafe for use, the result of ever-increasing pollution from the factories built along the waterway. But despite his position of strength in the town, he never was able to secure a government position or gain prominence in the church as his uncle had done before him. Nor did he not have the influence that Orange Lawrence held in the town, but he was an astute businessman, nonetheless. Not only was he surveying his lands into lots to increase his revenue, but, by 1869, was in the business of selling brick to the very people to whom he had sold land. At one time he was making up to ten thousand red bricks available to builders.

After Jesse the Younger's early death from consumption in 1874, the influence of the Ketchum family was still felt in Orangeville. His widow, Mary Colvin, had the Ketchum Block of commercial buildings erected at the corner of Broadway and First Street, on the land she inherited from Jesse. Most of these brick buildings still stand and the original interior woodwork, unmatched in town for detail and quantity, is intact in the apartments above. The architecture is

Mary Colvin, widow of Seneca Ketchum, inherited land from her nephew Jesse Ketchum following his death. She had the Ketchum Block built on the corner of Broadway and First Street after the fire of 1873. Today it still anchors this commercial section of the Historic District of Orangeville. *Courtesy of John Woolner, Orangeville*

very similar to the Town Hall as it was constructed by the same builders, with Hugh Haley as carpenter and Robert Hewitt as bricklayer.

The Ketchum family[7] was very inventive. One of Jesse's sons, Oliver, operated the Orangeville Pottery for a period of time, but when it failed he moved to Baltimore, Maryland, where he pursued a career as an inventor. His patent stoneware was warranted to hold coal oil or liquors without any soaking through the porous material. Another descendant, Mrs. Percival of Ottawa held a number of patents, one of which was for metal ear tags for cattle. Yet another descendant, Mary Gladys Ketchum, worked as an actress in both Canada and the United States, under the name of Miss Ainsworth. Son Zebulon started a sporting goods store in Ottawa in 1895, and, in 1915, founded the Ketchum Manufacturing Company, a producer of heavy farm equipment.

Another pioneer family that seems to be connected to the Ketchum family, either by blood or propinquity, is the Hannahson family. They arrived in the area about the same time as Seneca Ketchum and settled on land they had purchased from him in the late 1840s. George Hannahson was married to Mary (maiden name unknown) who was born in 1827 in Switzerland. Her obituary states, "thence through an almost pathless country to the Township of Mono, to be her late home, which was then unbroken wilderness.[8] Where the mystery arises is in the census records of Mono Township that list George and all his children as African. The census of the township dictated that the nationality of the father be given to the children being listed.

Locally, it has always been told that Hannah Ketchum, sister of Seneca and Jesse Sr., was born in 1786 in the USA, and that she had given birth to a child at York in the early 1800s. It is believed her son, George, came to live with her brother Seneca in Toronto before the two of them took up land at Orangeville in 1829. The surname, chosen, it is said, was Hannahson, for Hannah's son. There are other references to the Hannahsons being African in local and church records. In Jesse Ketchum's diary it says, "met Hannahson who says he has a claim from Uncle Seneca's will for 100 pounds—[he] looks upon the sugar bush as his own."[9]

George and Mary Hannahson built a stone house for themselves and had at least ten children. One son, Rev. John J. Hannahson, became a well-known Presbyterian minister who served several churches across Ontario. A daughter, Miss Elizabeth, was one of Ontario's first female telegraph operators, working in Mono Mills. The family lived on the next farm to Seneca Ketchum and remained there until the early 1900s.

In 2004, human remains were disturbed by a construction company preparing a subdivision on the former Hannahson farm. It is believed that this discovery was the Hannahson family plot, as identified by older residents and through local "folklore." The Hannahson story will be of interest to researchers for many years, but whatever truth lies therein, the family contributed much to the early life of Orangeville and will be part of the Ketchum contribution to our history.

When Orange Lawrence, another American-born entrepreneur, bought 200 acres of land from George Griggs in The Gore of Garafraxa in 1844, little did he know that only a few years later a thriving little town would be named after him. His wife, Sarah, already owned land, a 200-acre UEL grant, in nearby Garafraxa Township. He had been born in Canaan, Connecticut, in 1796, the son of William and Esther (Dutton) Lawrence. They moved to Halton County when he was four years old. In the 1820s, he married Sarah House of Beamsville and purchased a farm in Trafalgar, west of York (Toronto). They lived there until 1847 when the family made their way into the small settlement near Grigg's mill where Orange had purchased his land.

Reverend Alfred E. Hannahson was also a son of Mary and George Hannahson. He was a popular minister in the Sarnia area until his death in 1939. His son Arthur returned to Orangeville and was an organist at St. Andrew's Church for many years.

Lawrence built a sawmill, a gristmill, the community's first hotel and first store where he opened the first post office in 1851. By that time he had proved himself as a relentless promoter of the town, interested in his fellow citizens and politically active. Orangeville as the name of the settlement dates from the time that Lawrence opened his mills in 1847. The name of the town was formalized when the post office was opened and named in his honour. There was an attempt in the 1880s to change the name of the town to Lawrence but that idea was "met with strong opposition from the seven Orange Lodges[10] in and around the community. They were happy with the name just the way it was."[11] Interestingly, Orange Lawrence never belonged to the Orange Lodge.

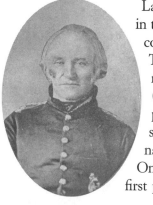

Orange Lawrence (1786–1861) was the entrepreneur who "made things lively" in the little bush settlement that soon would carry his name.

Lawrence and his family became very involved in the emerging community, In 1861, Lawrence commissioned Chisholm Miller of Garafraxa Township to survey the area between what is now Wellington Street and today's Town Line (then known as Garafraxa Street) so he could provide access to the town lots he had up for sale. Sarah Street in the new survey was named after Lawrence's wife, Sarah House. One of Sarah's relatives, J.B. House, opened the first photographic studios on Broadway in 1862. Photography was just in its infancy and was considered both a novelty and an art form.

One of Lawrence's sons, Ferris[12] became Orangeville's first schoolteacher in 1848 (they could collect the education grant). A daughter, Mary, married Thomas Jull, who had emigrated from Kent, England, to Trafalgar, Canada, then moved to Orangeville. In 1857, in partnership with John Walker Reid, he set up a gristmill on Mill Street in 1857, on the site where his father-in-law's wooden gristmill had burned the previous year. Reid was married to Rhoda, another of Lawrence's daughters. (The mill operated until the 1970s under various owners, the last being Fred Stagg, and has since been demolished.) Son Orange Lawrence Jr. (so named to confuse historians and writers for years) was a captain in the local militia and was interested in local matters, especially in acquiring water for the town and diverting the Mill Creek bed to better serve the industries along the creek.

Dated 1848, this overshot coverlet was presented to Mary Lawrence and Thomas Jull by her father, Orange Lawrence. That was the year that the Julls moved from Trafalgar to Orangeville. *Courtesy of the DCMA Artifact Collection.*

Orangeville's town father was very interested in politics, although never truly successful in this endeavour. Allan Rayburn summarized his interest as, "Orange Lawrence had a strong interest in political matters, running in 1861 as an Independent in Wellington North. In his campaign, he railed against magistrates who wrenched away the hard earnings of new settlers. He wrote to *The Sun* of helpless families losing their cow, their seed, their furniture, which were sold off by the magistrates, 'minions, who, to my certain knowledge, owe their offices in this vicinity to the number of cases they pick up.' Lawrence also promised to secure legislation to prevent tippling on the Sabbath."[13]

As the first postmaster, Orange Lawrence must have been at the very heart of the little town. Early postmasters of the period were political appointees and had a lot of influence as they had contact with the government and its many departments, not only involving mail services but also immigration and excise matters as well. In addition, he had some militia experience, and while still living at Trafalgar had organized a voluntary militia during the Rebellion of 1837, earning the rank of captain. Later he was instrumental in establishing the militia in Orangeville.

Orange Lawrence's tombstone in Greenwood Cemetery stands near the original front gate of the cemetery. His body was moved here sometime after Greenwood opened in 1876. *Courtesy of John Woolner, Orangeville.*

The Lawrence family was not without its own troubles, however. In 1864, one of Orange Lawrence's grandsons, William, was charged with stealing a carpet bag and $13. The young man escaped from the custody of Magistrate Samuel Wallace. When captured several days later, he was sentenced to four months of imprisonment at hard labour.[14]

Fortunately, Orange Lawrence did not live to see his grandson's incarceration, as the founder of Orangeville died in December of 1861 at age 65. His obituary reads, "LAWRENCE, Orange, an old resident of Orangeville, was found dead at the end of his own house last Sunday afternoon. It appears there was a clothesline extending between 2 poles and that Mr. Lawrence made a noose in the slack of the rope, which he placed around his neck, and so strangled himself. He left considerable property, and leaves a widow and grown family."[15] It was generally believed that he was depressed after having just lost an election.

After Lawrence's death, the duties of postmaster passed to Dr. William Hewat. In an unusual combination of diverse businesses, a resident could get a cure for summer complaint and a stamp all in one stop.

Several of Mr. Lawrence's family were to play an important role in the history of Orangeville. His son-in-law, Thomas Jull, as well as operating the grist and flour mill with his brother-in-law, also operated a foundry and a sawmill. The latter burned to the ground. According to rumour, the mill was torched, likely by a supporter of the town's liquor trade, as Jull, a local magistrate, was a fervent temperance man. A busy man was Thomas Jull since he was also a town reeve and councillor and held a position on the first Orangeville Board of Health. A grandson, Orange Jull, would go on to become a well-known inventor.

Descendants of Orange Lawrence live in town to this day and many have spread across North America. A number still visit the town named after their ancestor, especially during the Founders Fair[16] held in town each in July to honour Orange Lawrence and other early entrepreneurs.

The home of Mary Lawrence and Thomas Jull on Little York Street. Mr. Jull always referred to the house and its once-extensive grounds as "the homestead."

Them Damn Yankees 37

We will probably never know the relationship between these two town fathers, Jesse Ketchum and Orange Lawrence. Orange Lawrence arrived in town in 1847, and Jesse Ketchum the Younger arrived in 1856. Orange Lawrence died in 1861. They certainly would have known each other, living in such proximity. Jesse Ketchum would have had many occasions to do business with Orange Lawrence as they both were concerned with the water rights along Mill Creek. The 1859 *Tremaine Map of the County of Peel* shows part of the community of Orangeville in Caledon Township, Peel County. There were five subscribers from Orangeville who advertised in the book, with both Orange Lawrence and Jesse Ketchum listing themselves as "a dealer in real estate." Whatever their relationships, the names of Ketchum and Lawrence became synonymous with the founding of the Town of Orangeville.

It was Jesse Ketchum and Orange Lawrence who were the relentless promoters and early developers of the early settlement. Their heirs carried on the family tradition and became an important part of Orangeville's history as well. No doubt there were countless others who contributed in their own way, but it was these two men with American roots, who settled in a community of predominantly Irish immigrants, that have always been considered the town fathers. The Irish population, although they experienced tough times, had the drive to succeed. It was that drive that was needed in a small pioneer town to get the work done and the town firmly rooted and on its way to prosperity.

4

ROADS AND RAILWAYS:
GETTING TO TOWN

MANY TIMES IT HAS BEEN said that all roads lead to town. As with all fledgling communities, access roads were critical for future development. It would be the settlement or colonization roads that finally brought stability to Orangeville.

The first settlers came on foot, following trails through the bush. The early roads of Upper Canada, the Governor's Road (Dundas Street) and Yonge Street that ran from York to Georgian Bay, were both some distance from the Dufferin area. In 1820, the Huron Colonization Road was surveyed to connect York on Lake Ontario with Goderich on Lake Huron, as part of the settlement scheme of the Canada Company.[1] This rudimentary road travelled through Guelph, but again at no point was it near Dufferin. The very earliest of the pioneers had no choice but to strike out for their land by foot. A few were United Empire Loyalists, some were Pennsylvania Dutch, but most were Irish immigrants from Ulster and Sligo counties. Getting to the area was not an easy task. The bush trails were rough and incredibly difficult to traverse in anything but perfect weather. And even under the best of conditions, the insects along the way made the trip quite uncomfortable, not to mention the frequent hazards created by tree branches, fallen logs and other formidable obstacles. For women the fashion of the day did not help travelling much, their heavy skirts at a length only a fraction of an inch above the dirt as they walked.

After settlers travelled as far as they could on a colonization road, the only route into the region became a primitive path through the bush, sometimes barely wide enough for an ox cart. Some followed old aboriginal trails, some followed old military roads, others simply followed

Roads and Railways: Getting to Town 39

the crude trail cut out by the surveyors who were marking off the townships and somehow working out straight lines through a very rough terrain. Over time the roads improved somewhat through constant use, but not because of any government support. When ultimately the pioneers reached their land allotments, they were required by statute labour to improve the roadway in front of their property.[2] But building a road was not the first priority for someone needing both a shelter for the winter and a clearing in the bush for the planting of a first crop.

Ironically, it was the first road built into the Orangeville area that took the longest to have any influence on the development of the village. It was the first road in, but certainly the last to be developed. Hurontario Street, also known as Centre Road, was the first surveyed route to the area. By the mid-1830s, this road brought settlers to the taverns of Purple Hill, a stop on the way to their farms in Mono Township and points north. Originally surveyed as one of Lieutenant-Governor Simcoe's "Roads of Communication,"[3] it had been crudely built, and remained in abysmal condition for many years. To many it seemed that the road had been laid out on the worst possible route, through swamps, over steep hills, and down treacherous inclines. Moreover, there was no completed route connecting this road to Orangeville. It seemed to take forever to complete the last stretch across the Credit Flats. The existing deplorable portion was left to be maintained by statute labour, and was not completed until the 1850s.

Sometime in the mid-1850s, a "coach" line was set up between Brampton and Orangeville along the Hurontario route. Corduroy logs were used to somewhat improve the swampy portions. The "coach" was "a two-wheeled affair" used when the road was all but impassable. The powerfully built wheels were six feet in diameter, and the body was a twelve-foot box, balanced on the axle and capable of accommodating anywhere from ten to fifteen passengers as necessity demanded. With four horses, encouraged by a blacksnake whip, the driver generally got through even the roughest stretches. Bill Phillips and the Giffin Bros. managed this transportation line for years and "in imagination the sound of the old tin horn used to announce the departure still echoes around Orangeville at 5 a.m."[4] Transportation into the small village from this Centre Road had been improved by Seneca Ketchum before his death in 1850. As noted, it was Seneca, with his "Causeway Project," who had built the seven bridges out of town across the swamps and streams of the Credit Flats and in so doing connected Orangeville to the outside world.

The second colonization road that led into the site of Orangeville was the Garafraxa Road, designed to connect Oakville with Owen Sound on Georgian Bay. Completed in 1837, it reached nearby Garafraxa Township at Reading, a few short miles to the southwest of Orangeville. The road followed the 7th line of Trafalgar Township, through Esquising and Erin, then to the 14th line of Garafraxa and westward on 5 Sideroad, then north to the village of Fergus. From that point it continued north on the survey line of what is now Highway 6. It was along this road that Orange Lawrence would bring his family, all of them walking the final distance from Reading.

By 1842 the Amaranth Settlement Road (5 Sideroad) connected Reading to Orangeville. Many of the early of families were to use this route. The site of Orangeville was in The Gore of Garafraxa, that triangular shape where the township survey lines met up and formed a triangle. Those last few miles from the end of the road to The Gore were tough going. Large sections of swampy land, thick bush on the gravel hills and even a few areas of dangerous quicksand greeted the intrepid pioneers.

In time the roads improved and were used for travel back down to Lake Ontario for reasons of commerce or to connect with other people. Many grown sons used these same roads to leave the area to seek work on the Welland Canal,[5] work needed in order to supplement the meager income of a settler. In Jesse Ketchum's diary of 1859, he writes about a day trip taken by him on September 5 of that year. His description suggests a more acceptable road system, allowing the use of a buggy instead of riding a horse, "Fine day rather cool—got Smith's mare and Leslie's buggy—went to Elora got there at one o'clock—saw Frank paid him thirty off interest—started from there at five—got in before ten—a fog about the village."[6]

It was not until 1875, however, that the road from Orangeville to the Trafalgar Road and Fergus was much improved, allowing for safer transportation of goods and permitting a longer season of travel. A local road development scheme was set up to improve the existing road:

We are glad to be able to announce that work was commenced on the Orangeville and Reading Road, just beyond Springbrook, on Tuesday. The contractor, Mr. Al Dryden, intends putting on large gangs with teams at different points, and pushing the work to completion as rapidly as possible. He expects to have the whole road graded and gravelled by the end of August, or, at the furthest, by the middle of

Roads and Railways: Getting to Town

The Prince of Wales Road in Orangeville. In 1860, a gravel road was laid out from Broadway to the village of Camilla. It was named in honour of the visit by the Prince of Wales that year. The name stuck until 1963 when the post office introduced home mail delivery and insisted on using the registered name, which is First Street.

September. When completed, this road will form a most important line of communication between Orangeville and the Garafraxies.[7]

As a result, the route to the Garafraxa Road was considerably better.

But it was not the route over to Fergus and Guelph that took priority in the minds of the local promoters of the town. As early as the 1850s, it was felt that Orangeville needed to be connected by better roads to the expanding population to the south in Toronto and Port Credit. As well, improved connections to the growing communities in the back townships to the north of Orangeville were needed.

The Toronto Sydenham Colonization Road,[8] opened with haste in 1848 to accommodate the land-hungry settlers flooding into Upper Canada, was the third route built into the Orangeville area. It not only opened up military access, but also allowed entry to the unclaimed lands in central Ontario, the area then known as the Queen's Bush. The route was surveyed Charles Rankin, a surveyor experienced with the bushland of Canada. The road began in Toronto and followed the route of the Albion Road and Mono Road to Mono Mills. It then crossed Mono Township and on into Melancthon Township. It was this road that opened the floodgate of Irish settlers into Melancthon and Proton townships.

The difficult terrain of Mono Township made it impossible to maintain the road, and so that portion of the route was abandoned in 1858. Traffic was diverted west to Orangeville and from there, north on the

Prince of Wales Road to Primrose. The route continued west to Shelburne then north to connect to the existing Toronto Sydenham Road at "cemetery corner," the site of Shelburne Cemetery where today's Highway 10 curves around the cemetery

The solution to connecting with the townships in the north became the upgrading and completion of the Prince of Wales Road, so named in honour of Queen Victoria's son, Edward, the heir to the throne who toured Canada in 1860. This rural northerly extension of First Street in Orangeville, was the first line west of Hurontario Street in Mono. In 1860, the Prince of Wales Road travelled north from Orangeville through Mono Township to connect with Camilla and the Victoria Road from Camilla via Whittington, Rich Hill, Coleridge and on to Shelburne. A bridge was built across the Nottawasaga River and, except for a hill around Lot 26, the route was relatively flat, making the transportation of heavy wagons from the farms relatively easy. Orangeville businessmen hoped that all settlers would go through town on their way to the newly available land in Grey County, even those en route to Lake Huron. They also hoped that settlers would return for medical and legal services as well as to buy and trade goods, the services in Orangeville being closer to their land than those in Toronto, which were another full day's travel south.

Originally, the Road only reached as far north as Camilla but later was extended to Primrose. Before that extension, persons travelling north would turn left at Camilla, then travel through the small communities and ultimately reach Shelburne. From Primrose, the route was extended further north into Mulmur Township. Several taverns popped up along this new road and began to compete for the traveller's business with those inns already located along the Toronto Sydenham Road.

In a letter to the editor of *The Sun*, a writer states,

Having recently made a trip to the northwest part of Mulmur, I am much impressed with the defective nature of the roads and desirability of easier communications between this place and the fine country in the rear. Surely, while seeking readier means of access to the outer world which the projected railway will give, it is worthwhile to open up—inlandward—facilities for travel and commerce. Were there a good road leading from this place to the rear of Mulmur and Melancthon, a large share of the business of those localities would doubtless come this way instead of going north to Collingwood.[9]

This log bridge carried the Prince of Wales Road over the Boyne River in Mulmur Township, photo 1905.

The Prince of Wales Road soon proved to be successful at bringing in the commerce.

With the improvement of Hurontario Street to the south and the building of the Prince of Wales Road north into Mono and Mulmur, there was a passable road connecting with the Toronto Sydenham Road. Now a clear route from Toronto to Owen Sound was in operation, and Orangeville was located right in the middle. In 1865, the northerly route through Primrose was abandoned and redirected through Shelburne, the route of today's Highway 10.

By 1871, for the first time, two stage lines were running daily between Orangeville and Brampton. Since the 1860s the line had been operated by William Lewis, who not only provided passenger and freight service but also was responsible for the mail. Lewis sold his business to the Griffin Bros. of Edmonton (now Snelgrove) and stayed on as the manager of the company. A new stage line opened that same year, operated by a group of Brampton businessmen. Although there was not enough business for the two lines, for a short while passengers enjoyed the spirited competition around fares, which dropped as low as $.50 one way. Also that same year, 1871, a new stage heading north was opened by a Mr. Trimble of Orangeville. It left the Witter's Hotel on Broadway on a daily run to Owen Sound, the partway coach fare to Shelburne being $1.00.

Probably one of the most important roads to bolster commerce in Orangeville was the Hockley Road. The original bush trail, which followed an old Aboriginal trail, was widened in 1876–77. "The road is 66 feet wide, the land being acquired from the farms along the river [the Nottawasaga]. The entire scheme was funded by local businessmen buying in, hoping to regain their investment in increased revenue. Messrs. Green, Parsons, Campbell and Stewart were appointed [to] a Committee on Leading Roads, and a petition presented from Mr. J. Paisley and others, praying the Council to adopt such measures as would secure the construction of a road from Orangeville to Hockley, along the valley of the Nottawa, was referred to said Committee.[10]

Although everyone understood the importance of roads, those that surrounded Orangeville remained in poor to inconsistent condition well into the 1870s. "A petition was presented from Mr. Hugh Haley of Orangeville, asking for compensation from Mono council for loss alleged to have been sustained by him in consequence of the bad state of the roads, which, he states, prevented him from hauling bricks so fast as he otherwise would have done, costing a loss to him of 300 dollars."[11]

A road gang in East Garafraxa circa 1887. This is a typical crew, many of whom were performing statute labour in front of their properties. Orangeville is located in the Gore of Garafraxa Township. Town Line marked the line between Garafraxa and Caledon townships while the point of The Gore marked the juncture of Simcoe, Wellington and Peel counties.

Roads and Railways: Getting to Town   45

Soon a decision had to be made by the town fathers of the growing village. Would they lobby to improve Centre Road to Brampton or lobby for the railway?

In 1869, a decision to build a gravel toll road between Orangeville and Brampton was abandoned, making the arrival of the railway almost a certainty. Costs for the toll road were considered too high, the public seemed indifferent to the plan and it was generally felt that the traffic would not support the wages of the tollkeepers. The local paper promoted the railway, and stated, "The advantages of railway communication to any section of country cannot be too highly prized. Lands within easy access of railway stations rise rapidly in value; agricultural, commercial and manufacturing interests are all benefited. In this enlightened age the superior advantages of the iron horse are so well understood and so generally appreciated as to render any reference to them entirely unnecessary."[12]

As early as the 1860s there had been much discussion of building a tramway from Brampton to Orangeville where it would connect with the Grand Trunk Railway.[13] The tramway, with horse-drawn cars on a rail line had local support. The route was surveyed by C.J. Wheelock of Orangeville, and a couple of miles of track were built south of town. However, the enterprise came to a halt, in 1868, when the Toronto, Grey & Bruce Railway (TG&B) scheme was floated.[14] If the proper people were persuaded, it would be built right into town. This idea quickly gained the support of the residents of Orangeville and nearby Amaranth and Mono townships. Public meetings were organized by supporters at several hotels in Orangeville and similar ones scheduled to be held at Trueman's Inn at Coleridge, Bowsfield's Inn at Whittington and Wallace's Inn at Farmington, all hamlets located in Amaranth.

After much discussion and much persuasion, Orangeville was included on the rail route. When the TG&B Railway reached Orangeville on April 20, 1871, everyone in the area had an opinion as to the potential benefits. The line left Weston and travelled through Bolton, Mono Road, Caledon, Alton and Melville before arriving at Orangeville. The workmen who were laying down the tracks reached town limits about four p.m., and shortly thereafter the locomotives, "Kincardine" and "A.R. McMaster," richly decorated with evergreens, flags and bunting, slowly made their appearance. The roadbed for the tracks was yet to be ballasted and with no gravel yet in between the ties, the engines could only move at "crawling" speed.

The new Orangeville station was located in the undeveloped south edge of town where just a month before a lynx over 5 1/2 feet long had been shot. When the first official train with TG&B officials and dignitaries on board arrived, the town was decorated in "triumphant arches and streamers bearing [such] inscriptions as 'Goodbye To The Old Stagecoach,' 'Look Out For The Train' And 'Welcome, The Iron Steed.' Evergreens gaily decorated the town hall together with flags and drapery and the walls [were] studded with mottos and with the names of the chief promoters of the railroad."[15]

The first freight to be shipped out of Orangeville left on August 10, 1871. Four hundred tubs of good butter, packed in wooden butter boxes and ice, were shipped to Toronto bound for Liverpool, England. The first rail excursion from Orangeville was held on a special civic holiday, August 24, 1871. The train left Orangeville at five a.m., heading to Toronto then returning home at nine p.m. Regular train service began operating on September 18 of that year. Two trains, hauling both passenger cars and freight cars, departed Orangeville at 7 a.m. and 3:45 p.m., and left Toronto to return to Orangeville at 7:45 a.m. and 3:45 p.m. The Toronto newspapers, which did not reach Orangeville till 11 p.m. when brought by stagecoach, were now being received by 11 a.m.

The TG&B Railway really altered life in the town. From the time the line was first proposed in 1863 until the end of its first full year of operation, the village had doubled in population, reaching a total of almost 2,000 people. Some of this expansion was due to the railway.

In August of 1872, to encourage travel to and from the railway station, a wooden sidewalk was laid all the way from Broadway down Mill Street, right to the station entrance. The Railway Hotel was established on Mill Street and much of the cottage housing found in the area today was built for the use of railway workers and their families living in Orangeville while the rail line was under construction. A tunnel from the rail yard leading to one of the homes on Mill Street is still in existence. No one knows its actual use, but rumour has it that the tunnel provided a secret route for lifting whisky from the cars to a worker's home.

Several new businesses came into existence almost immediately after the opening of the railway. Mrs. James Moote operated a boarding house on Town Line and advertised rooms available for ten people to sleep. The square red brick house still stands on Town Line near Green Street. And amazingly, yet another new form of transportation came into being:

Roads and Railways: Getting to Town

Part hotel and part boarding house, Mrs. James Moote's large home on the lower Town Line provided room and board to railway workers and travelling salesmen in the heyday of the CPR.

As an evidence of the enterprise and progressive spirit of Orangeville, we have to record the appearance of a passenger wagon on Broadway on Thursday. It was built by Messrs. Buyers & Meredith, of this place, for Mr. J. Paisley, of the Paisley House, [on the south side of Broadway] and will run regularly between the Paisley House and the railway station. It is substantially built, handsomely painted, and well-finished, and shows that the ability of our carriage factories to turn out good work is equal to any town in the Province. Mr. Paisley's enterprise in furnishing so fine a conveyance to and from the station will no doubt be duly appreciated by the public.[16]

Orangeville was a divisional point for the railway where the rail crews changed, and a water and coal stop as well as the point of origin for local trains. When the engines were run by wood, Orangeville was the second "wood up" station after Bolton between Toronto and Owen Sound. Steam locomotives took on water from the wooden tower and filled their tenders with coal funnelled in through long chutes. If a locomotive had to be turned around, it was accomplished on a huge circular hand-operated turntable. It was said the railway restaurant, which opened in 1871 next to the passenger terminal, served the best apple pie in the area. But a passenger would have to find that out quickly as there was only a ten-minute stop in Orangeville.

The Toronto, Grey and Bruce Railway reached Orangeville in 1871 and things were never the same again. With its future as a market town assured, Orangeville boomed during the 1880s and 1890s, years that were marked by a depression in other parts of Canada. In the background is the first TG&B railway station.

In use from 1871 to 1881, the woodburning engine was called "The Caledon." It was known as a "double header" as it had two enormous stacks from which great bellows of smoke would mark the location and arrival of the train from countless vantage points both north and south of town. The views from the train as a passenger travelled through Caledon were spectacular, with lots of curves, rocky outcroppings and beautiful scenery. After the great horseshoe switchback curve built to climb Caledon Mountain (the escarpment), the train headed through prosperous farming country to Orangeville. At the height of railway usage, eight passenger trains a day stopped at Orangeville, plus numerous freight trains. Trains also arrived from the Elora and Teeswater branch lines coming through the villages of Orton and Grand Valley. The Credit Valley Railway, following the Credit River north from Streetsville, reached Orangeville in 1879. Five years later both railways were merged into the Canadian Pacific Railway network. The last passenger train to Orangeville was on October 30, 1970.

The Orangeville CPR passenger terminal was built circa 1906 in a style recognizable throughout Ontario. The design was unique with its round waiting room and unusual conical roof structure. The building still stands in town but not on its original site. It was relocated to Armstrong Street in 1990 and is currently being used as the "Train Station Restaurant." The entire building was moved from its location on Town Line down to the junction of Highways 9 and 10, then up the hill on Broadway. Hundreds of Orangeville's residents lined the streets to watch the building "crawl up" the street, taking almost a day to move the distance of one mile to its new location. Unfortunately, the interior of the building burned in 2004, but the exterior was saved by local volunteer firefighters. The outside was painstakingly restored, however, it was not possible to save any of the original tongue and groove boards on the inside walls and ceiling nor the benches that once had lined the walls.

This building replaced an earlier station that had burned in a fire in 1906. "At 12:30 o'clock this morning the CPR station caught fire and two hours later it was a complete wreck. Night operator Ben Tansley Jr. discovered the roof of the building to be in flames and he first carried out the books and then gave the alarm. A spark from a passing train is thought to have been the cause. For a number of years the CPR authorities had been discussing building a new station here, but it always was shoved over until another year. The fire, however, has solved the problem. It was admitted by the CPR people that Orangeville should have a fine station. This is the most important and best paying point on the two lines."[17]

Orangeville was a significant division point on the CPR after 1884. A number of important facilities, including the turntable were part of the station grounds.

Although a boon to the town, the railway was not without controversy. Most of the concern focused on the number of tracks and the commotion created on Town Line as the trains moved through and cars were shunted about, hooked up or rearranged. When the building of the new station was underway, some town residents objected to the many changes that would increase usage of the railway. In an interview the former editor of *The Orangeville Banner*, A.D. McKitrick, stated, "a group of citizens took it upon themselves to picket the railway at the crossing at Town Line and went to considerable trouble in an endeavor to prevent the railway installing extra trackage."[18]

A second railway, the Credit Valley line, came into town in 1879, but it only operated for four years. The line travelled from Streetsville, through Brampton, Inglewood, Alton, Melville and ultimately to the Orangeville terminal located at the intersection of Broadway and Fourth Street. The company, formed by Toronto financiers including George Laidlaw, planned to run lines into Orangeville and to St. Thomas in southwestern Ontario. "The Credit Valley Railway, while becoming a competing line to the TG&B perhaps hastened the upgrading and standard gauging of the latter railway. It became quickly apparent that the Orangeville line was not pulling its weight financially, however."[19] In 1883, the line was purchased by the Ontario and Quebec Railway Co., a shell for the Canadian Pacific Railway, and added it to the CPR in 1884.

After the CPR took over from the TG&B Railway, a spur line following the old bed of the Credit Valley Railway was built from the railway station to Broadway, then on to the Owen Sound Quarry, located at Hockley Road and Hurontario Street. Stone was hauled out for several years before the quarry closed around 1900 and the rail line was no longer needed. A very small section of the old rail bed of this spur can be glimpsed from the Hockley Road at Sideroad 5.

The sound of the train whistle is missed by longtime residents. Engineers were required to signal each time the train intersected a street, which meant lots of noise, but no one ever seemed to mind. Large transport trucks replaced the trains, making Broadway crowded and noisy but not in the more romantic fashion of the railway. Orangeville finally ridded itself of the truck traffic on Broadway in 2005 when the County of Dufferin completed a bypass to the west and south of town, making it the alternative route for both trucks and through traffic. The road cost an estimated 12 million dollars, more than the original cost to build the rail line between Orangeville and Georgetown.

Roads and Railways: Getting to Town   51

Today's Orangeville is readily accessed by road. Highway 9 comes in from Newmarket to Orangeville, then continues as County Road 109 to Arthur and Walkerton. The town sits midway between Port Credit and Collingwood on Highway 10 as well as on County Road 124 between Guelph and Owen Sound. A well-maintained county road system, including the Hockley Road and the Orangeville-Fergus Road, brings rural inhabitants into town to schools and churches, for shopping, the theatre and all the range of services the town has to offer.

5

EARLY INDUSTRY:
ENTERPRISE AND ENTREPRENEURS

THE GRIST AND SAWMILLS LOCATED along Mill Creek, which ran through the centre of town, were the first industries in Orangeville. James Griggs operated the first mill, later purchased by Orange Lawrence. In 1856, Lawrence's sons-in-law, Thomas Jull and John Walker Reid, built a gristmill that stood until the late 1980s. This mill was constructed of cut stone that would have been quarried near the site of the mill itself.

The multiple inns and taverns that quickly sprang up along the roadsides began to shape what would become Orangeville. These hotels provided a variety of purposes in a new community, offering food and lodging for the traveller and a place for businessmen to conduct business or trade. Salesmen would take a room, use it as an office, then move on in a few days to the next town. The inns also provided a place of rest and a place to quench the thirst of settlers coming into town to bring produce to the new mills along the river. Orangeville historian Alan Rayburn once noted that in the last quarter of the 1800s, no less than eleven hotels operated in Orangeville with at least another three on the outskirts.

The first hotel in the area may have been established at Purple Hill on the other side of the Credit River, before any inn was built in town. In 2005, a Best Western Hotel was established roughly on that same site, but today that hotel is within the town's limits. It is believed that the first tavern was built by Orange Lawrence in 1845. It sat on the corner of Broadway and Wellington and had a small general store attached to the side. The Marksman's House, operated by Ed Bloomer, was constructed to the west. James Graham may have owned

Early Industry: Enterprise and Entrepreneurs

The Gordon House was built after the great fire of 1875 had destroyed Bell's Hotel. In turn, it burned in 1903. This hotel is typical of the imposing buildings constructed during the railway boom.

a tavern on Purple Hill before he came into town to operate the new stone tavern in 1854. It still functions today as the Greystones Restaurant, more than a century and a half later. James Curry opened the Paisley House, followed by the West Simcoe Hotel, built about 1860 on the site of the present-day CIBC building. Curry was the one to move the hotel business into a whole new section of town.

Bell's Hotel, run by George Bell, was chosen as the regular site for town council meetings after the village was incorporated in 1863. The hotel burned, and was rebuilt in 1875 and renamed the Gordon House. Three storeys high, it had 75 rooms for guests. After it burned again, in 1903, the site was used for a bank and the present Carnegie Library building. The building erected as the American Hotel in 1883 still stands and is the office of *The Orangeville Citizen* on First Street. For a short time at the turn of the century, a hotel known locally as the Red Onion was owned and operated on Broadway by Jim Booth. Other hotels included: the Queen's Hotel, the Royal Hotel, the Commercial House, the Dufferin House, the Forest Lawn Hotel, the Royal Temperance Hotel and the Globe Hotel. The Railway Hotel was located near the railway yards and the Perfect House was at Springbrook at the corner of C Line and Broadway. The Coffin House, so named for the shape of the building, sat at the junction of the Fergus Road and County Road 109.

Records indicate that women were sometimes operators of the hotels in Orangeville. Mary Beater was granted a liquor license as an innkeeper in 1870, but the name of her establishment remains elusive.

The Railway House Hotel was built on Mill Street by William Ryan in 1870 before the railway arrived, but everyone knew that the "iron horse" was on its way.

The availability of liquor in the town centre did cause problems, but the inns and hotels kept business coming into town, and served many uses in Orangeville—meeting rooms for public issues, polling booths, concert hall, banquet hall...somewhat like the community centres of today.

In 1861, at least one resident of Orangeville thought that either a brewery or a distillery would not only boost the hotel business, but the whole area as well, "I don't look upon the subject with a view to teetotalism, or as an encouragement to intemperance as my suggestion has in reality has nothing to do with either, but simply a matter of commercial advantage. Doubtless, were both a distillery and brewery in Orangeville to-day neither would add to nor diminish from the actual consumption of beer and whisky, but instead of sending annually a large sum abroad for liquors, we once create a home market for barley, rye and inferior grains."[1]

The variety of liquor available in town was astounding. In 1870, an ad for the Monaghan House bragged, "We have on hand wines and liquors which for cheapness, quality and freshness, eclipses anything of the kind this side of Montreal."[2] The ad also contains a listing of some of the stock, including wines, liquors, a cellar filled with choicest brandy, fine old rye distilled on the south bank of the Detroit River, malt mountain dew, Old Crow, Diamond Whiskey, Dunville's V.R. Whiskey from old Belfast snuggly packed in the heather from Ireland's bogs, port wines, old Madeira in wood or bottle, Premartin, Thistle

Whisky and Cramp Sutter. And just in case that was not enough temptation for the shopper, one could also purchase Black Swan, Minnie Warren, Prince of Wales, Pride of Canada, Seldom Equalled Never Excelled, Sailor's Solace, Princess Alexandra, Fine Bird's Eye and Little Joker tobacco products.

The old-time log, stone and rough-cast taverns gave way to the modern palatial brick hotels about the time the railway went through, with only the present Greystones Restaurant left to remind us of Orangeville's pioneer taverns. The present owner has managed to retain the original architecture and integrity of the building despite the necessities of modernizing a restaurant that is 150 years old.

According to an 1857 Ontario Directory, the population of Orangeville had reached a population of 500 persons. The town is described as "a village on the Credit River in the Gore of Garafraxa at the junction of the three counties of Wellington, Grey and Simcoe." An analysis of the businesses listed indicates that Orangeville showed all the characteristics of a healthy and rapidly growing pioneer village. While artisan life was strongly represented, professional life was much less so, except for the clergy, which represented five per cent of those listed. The cause of Christian Methodists religion was well looked after by three Methodist ministers, while there was one clergy each for the Church of England and the Church of Scotland. There was no Catholic priest at the time. Other professional persons and officials formed ten per cent of the list, with storekeepers and tailors accounting for another ten per cent. Ten

Greystones Restaurant is arguably Orangeville's oldest hotel building. Erected about 1860 by James Graham, it replaced an older wooden structure. *Courtesy of John Woolner, Orangeville.*

per cent of the professions were represented by shoemakers, saddlers and tanners, innkeepers seven per cent and miscellaneous occupations eight per cent. Of the remainder, twenty-five per cent was made up of carpenters, building masons, plasterers and brick makers with the other twenty-five per cent represented by millmen, blacksmiths, wagon makers and cabinet makers.[3]

The first tannery is believed to have been built by Walter Bowsfield, sometime in the late 1840s, but little information could be found. In 1850, William Campbell, owner of a tannery in Mono Mills, came to town and opened up his second tannery, which he operated for over 30 years. His product had a reputation of being of excellent quality. The three-storey tannery of frame construction, was located just west of Jull's Mill on Little York Street, known as Sunnybrook Street before the turn of the century.

Foundries followed shortly after the mills appeared, supplying the needs of the local farmers with an assortment of ploughshares and machinery parts. In Orangeville the first foundry to open, in 1858, was operated by the partnership of McKitrick, Penfold and Huskinson. The building was a large cement structure built on the site now used by the franchises of A&W and Tim Horton's. A few years later Huskinson moved to Texas and Penfold also left the company. Samuel and Robert McKitrick opened up a new foundry on Mill Street that operated until the turn of the 20th century. The McKitrick Foundry could handle large jobs as well as the needs of local farmers. A pit wheel made for Mr. Newell's gristmill in Mono weighed over two tons. A cog wheel produced for Thomas Jull's gristmill weighed over thirty-four hundred pounds; it was cast in 12 sections. The only other foundries able to produce such huge items were located in the larger centres of Toronto and Hamilton. The early days of the company, however, were not easy. *The Sun* reported:

> the company started into existence in the fall of 1858, the business had, of course like all new undertakings of the kind, great difficulties

William M. Campbell, along with his brothers, built both the Mono Mills Tannery and the Orangeville Tannery during the 1850s and 1860s. A very popular businessman, he was selected as a justice of the peace for the area. The photo dates from the late 1870s.

to encounter and which perhaps cannot be truly said to be all finally overcome yet. Still, from the well-known skill, energy and perseverance of the practical and obliging men who conduct it will make a first rate substantial job.[4]

In 1853, the first tinsmith opened in town. Sepha Donner, born in Germany, opened Orangeville Tin Ware, but in 1857 he switched to running a general store. That same year, William Parsons opened a tinsmith shop, reportedly when he was only 18 years old. Parsons was very active in the local militia and ultimately became Major Parsons. A street is named in his honour.

A woollen mill came into being somewhere around 1855, when William Waite of Brampton moved to Orangeville. The building stood at the bottom of Bythia Street, beside the creek providing the power. It was taken over by Messrs. Ingram and John Stephenson around the mid-1860s. Part of the stone foundation of the mill still can be seen to this day in KayCee Gardens, where it is now used as a perennial flowerbed. The Stephenson home, located beside the mill, still stands. From the sidewalk of Bythia Street it looks odd as the front of the home faces the creek and the mill site.

The first drugstore opened in 1860 under the ownership of Thomas Buckham. His shop sold a full range of drugs and medicines as well as groceries and shoes. Although he only remained in the community for

Sepha Donner was one of Orangeville's first businessmen, operating a tinsmithing business on the south side of Broadway.

five years, he was very active in the town affairs. "He also dickered in real estate, general insurance and the issuing of marriage licenses. In 1861, he was appointed deputy postmaster, to aid the ailing Orange Lawrence. In 1863, Buckham was appointed one of the two auditors of Garafraxa Township. [He] became the captain of the Orangeville militia and organized a company of volunteers to prepare for the incursions of the Fenians across the border from the United States. In 1864, the Debating and Mutual Improvement Society was organized in the village and Buckham was elected its first president. He sold his Medical Hall in 1864 to Thomas Stevenson and a year later he went to Philadelphia to study medicine. He decided to specialize in the new science of psychiatry and wrote an authoritative book on insanity."[5]

The establishment of the town's first newspaper, *The Sun*, in 1861, brought the outside world into the growing community, and kept the community informed of local news and issues. Much of the research material for this book has come from early volumes of *The Sun*, as it is well written with excellent use of the subtleties common to the language of the day. The editor and co-owner was John Foley, and the first edition[6] was printed in January of 1861. The masthead of *The Sun* stated that it served the areas of Garafraxa, Erin, Caledon, Albion, Adjala, Mono and Amaranth. Mr. Foley claimed to be neutral in politics, and the title on the front page also included the slogan, "All Extremes are Error and Truth lies Between." John Foley was candid in his editorials and kept citizens aware of the issues that would affect them, by covering local, national and international news. Each issue contained a continuing short story and over half of the issue was advertising. No one of the period had more influence on the thinking of Orangeville citizens, still predominantly Irish Protestants, yet John Foley was a Catholic from the Oshawa area. However, the Orange Lodge news was always included and he proved to many an "Orange" settler that there were indeed "good" Catholics.

After his death in 1882, his son John Jr., at the tender age of 16, took over the paper with assistance from his uncle, the printer Patrick Meany. He later (1890s) left town to forge a career in the gold fields of the Klondike. Margaret, Foley's sister, contributed from time to time. Imagine, editorials from female Catholics. Possibly the reputed intolerance from our past may not be true. But the paper was not without competition. Strong Liberal promoters founded *The Orangeville Advertiser* in 1867. The owner, Fisher Munro, was a justice of the peace and a strong temperance man. In the 1880s, his buildings were

Early Industry: Enterprise and Entrepreneurs   59

attacked by arsonists, but the paper managed to survive as a weekly until 1907. Another weekly, *The Gazette* was started in the late 1870s. The *Dufferin Post* may have operated as early as 1873. It was published by Dennis Mungovan, another Catholic, who had studied for the priesthood and law before moving to Orangeville.

Blaney McGuire Jr. founded *The Orangeville Banner* in 1893 after a brief period of owning *The Gazette* in partnership with Seneca G. Ketchum. Mr. McGuire had grown up in town; his father, Blaney McGuire, had operated a shoe store on Broadway. As well as being a popular job printer, McGuire was a member of Orangeville lacrosse teams, served as president of the Ontario Lacrosse Association, and, in 1911, was president of the Canadian Lacrosse Association. He also served as a town councillor, but was defeated in his bid for deputy reeve in 1913, probably because he supported the platform allowing the local sale of liquor. In 1895, Alexander Dunlop McKitrick from East Garafraxa joined the firm and two years later bought a partnership in the paper. He had intended to study law, but after working as a student in the newspaper business, decided to make journalism his career.

Mr. McKitrick took over full ownership in 1931 when Blaney McGuire died. He then purchased *The Sun* in 1933 when John Foley Jr. died and it was amalgamated with *The Orangeville Banner*. After McKitrick's death in 1949, his daughter Helen B. Matheson (married to a county agricultural representative, Bruce Matheson), often wrote the editorials, following in the footsteps of Margaret Foley by being a woman writing in Orangeville newspapers. She also ran the paper with her brother Victor. A.D. McKitrick's eulogy was given by his neighbour, Judge Walter T. Robb, who stated, "his pen was mighty and his style inimitable. His hometown, Orangeville, was to him the capital of Canada. And to his hometown he was whole heartedly and loyally devoted."[7]

These were the influential men and women of the community whose stories have been recorded. Several businesses just disappeared without a trace, along with an array of smaller enterprises or cottage industries that may never be known. There were weavers, soap makers, spinning-wheel makers and countless other artisans. It seems that at one time a gunsmith may have existed in town, although he is not listed in any of the directories. "In the morning down to foundry to enquire about a man who talks of starting a gunsmith business."[8]

Another example of a former business comes from, "Mr. E. McLean has opened an Auction Room and General Commission Agency on East Broadway. His Thursday evening sales are very popular and

60   ORANGEVILLE

attract a large attendance."⁹ A complete list of business in the early
history of Orangeville would be quite extensive and the goods available quite surprising. For some of them with curious names or goods
all that remains are listings in old directories:

1857	Mrs. Mary Newton	midwife
1857	C. Clark	reedmaker
1862	Youman's Store	oysters, sardines, oranges and lemons
1862	Mrs. Merryweather's	apples, peaches, pears and plums, sweets of all kinds
1868	Husband & Galbraith	dentists, the first Tues. of every month
1868	Longeway & Bros.	Advertised a new stock of Waubuno Bull Frogs
1871	The East Indiaman	whisky, tea, wines, Hurst's Sausages, cash only
1871	The Bun House	iced creams, soda water, temperance drinks, sardines

The working men of the town, as well, are hard to trace and their
names may never be known. "WANTED, A GOOD ACTIVE BOY.
About fourteen years of age, to learn the tinsmithing business. None
need not apply unless well recommended. Sepha Donner."¹⁰ Who was
the successful applicant? What became of him? Was he successful? Or
did he move on or did he become a name on a tombstone in Greenwood Cemetery? Orangeville has hundreds of such stories.

A poem published in *The Sun*, on November 12, 1864, advertised
what might have been the town's first barber. After this poetic render-
ing was published, the newspaper editor noted that the shaving off of
beards had become the craze in town. Wives did not even recognize
their spouses when they arrived home, never having seen the face
beneath the typical full beard of the pioneer period. One wonders if
they were happy with what they found!

> Behind his razor sharp that never hath drawn tears
> Wishing to be understood this difference he traces
> Between himself and "shaves" who touch not faces.
> It is this: the honey-tongued and well-paid shavers
> Use their wits, and he his soap and razors.

Early Industry: Enterprise and Entrepreneurs 61

Farm implements and vehicles were a necessity in early rural Ontario. Brothers Samuel and Robert McKitrick, who operated a successful foundry on Mill Street, manufactured and sold farm equipment.

Things in the world of personal cleanliness became in vogue. "Mr. G.S. Nelson has opened a splendid bath room, in connection with his hair dressing establishment on Broadway. Hot, cold or tepid baths may be had at any hour during the day at 15 cents each, a charge so light that all may enjoy this health inspiring luxury."[11]

Not to be outdone by the poetic flair of the barber, when a new shop opened in 1868, the owners extolled the recent invention, known as a photograph,[12] by writing the following poem:

> Here Art triumphant our attention claims,
> Here life seems spread from a hundred frames
> Belles, merchants, statesmen fill the pictured walls,
> Each face, each form, its living type recalls!
> Features, complexion, attitude, attire, beauty's soft smile
>   and manhood's glance of fire,
> Truly reflected from the burnished plate
> Astonished life with its own duplicate.[13]

At the time poetry had been popularized by numerous English writers whose work frequently appeared in the newspapers. Poetry was also being published in book form and made available in the local general stores.

Another of the early industries associated with the pioneer era was an ashery run by Mr. Tindley on the site of the present Fairgrounds Shopping Mall. Trees being cleared from local farmland were burned and the ashes sold. These ashes were leached with water, producing lye that would be later mixed with fat derived from rendered down meat to make a soft soap, the only type of soap available at the time.

Sometime in the early 1860s Orange Lawrence Jr. and Jack Lawrence started a celery farm on land along today's Amanda Street to Parsons Street, which at the time was very swampy. The celery was transported to Toronto by wagon and sold to the wholesale market there.

Broadway, the main street of a busy growing town, also attracted many businessmen who wished to start a new life in Canada. In 1867, an ad announced C. Cullen (late of London, England) Watchmaker, "Having had twelve years experience in first class establishments in England, feels confident of giving satisfaction to those who may entrust him with orders."[14]

Many early merchants would extend credit to their customers, often at such outrageous interest as 25% annually. The town courts were always jammed with cases of businesses suing for their bills and the newspapers full of warnings from the shop owners that they would be taking such action. But providing credit did not always work. Local butcher J.W. Jarvis added this poem to his ad in *The Sun* on July 22, 1869:

> FRESH & DRIED MEAT—FOR CASH ONLY
> For customers came and I did trust them,
> By doing so, I lost both meat and customs,
> To loose them both did grieve me sore,
> I am resolved to trust no more.

Others dealt with cash in different ways, such as offering a percentage off for the use of cash. The Mammoth Store, which sold clothing, shoes and yard goods, ran an ad that stated, "Notwithstanding the scarcity of money, our stock is twice as large as it was in the corresponding period of last year, which enables us to sell at smaller profits."[15]

Orangeville's post office is built on the site of an early cemetery. The first post office, in Orange Lawrence's store, opened in 1861. The location was moved several times before 1886, but was never convenient to the downtown area. A the time (1876), the town had three cemeteries, each responding to the needs of different religious denominations and all in the downtown area. All were full. A controversy raged over where to put a new cemetery, and, as a result of people not being able to agree on a location, the town ended up with two: a publicly owned cemetery, Greenwood, and a privately owned one, Forest Lawn.

Early Industry: Enterprise and Entrepreneurs 63

This Orangeville Post Office building served the community from 1886 to 1962. It was built on the site of the former Bethel Presbyterian Cemetery. Some people were surprised when bones were discovered when the present building was constructed on the site in 1963.

Over the next few years, the interred bodies were gradually removed from the old cemeteries and reburied in Greenwood and Forest Lawn cemeteries, both outside the town limits. In 1880, Bethel Presbyterian Church was closed and the site sold to a group of local businessmen. The now empty Presbyterian cemetery on Broadway was proposed as a site for a new post office. Public "war" erupted again. A number of people were opposed to the idea of building on the old cemetery—it just didn't seem right. Others suspected the new owners of the property (a group of Presbyterians) of collusion, graft and any number of other crimes. Ultimately, the federal government decided it would use the space, paid for by the town, and a large stone post office was built on the site of old cemetery in 1886. In 1962, when the present post office was being constructed, on the site of the old one, work came to a halt when bones were discovered. Workmen suspected a murder. Historians recalled the "Resurrection" war of the 1880s, and the fact that the place had once been a cemetery.

Almost every small town had a furniture factory around the time of Confederation in 1867. Prime local woods were available, a labour force was eager to work and a growing population was in need of furniture as their families and fortunes grew. Tunstall's Cabinet Shop opened early in 1862, "it is needless to describe the many machines—all of ingenious and modern invention and construction—which the Messrs. Tunstall employ in their trade, suffice to say that they are all of the best and of their own manufacture, and like the first-class furniture of all descriptions that their establishment turns out. The Messrs. Tunstall served their time as apprentices to Messrs. Jacques & Hayes of Toronto, the most celebrated cabinet factory in Canada, if not in America, and all that we can say is that Orangeville ought to be proud of such an acquisition of first-class mechanics within her border, and the appreciation ought to find its vent in an immediate rush of customers to the shop of the gentlemen named."[16]

An interesting article appeared in *The Sun* later that year to further indicate the 1860s as a period of tremendous growth and a testament to the abilities of many of our early manufacturers and entrepreneurs. "A MAMMOTH LAMP during the past week, one of the largest and best designed lamps we have ever seen, was manufactured by M.K.E. Cowles at Mr. Sepha Donner's tin establishment in this village for Mr. J. McDonald of the Grand Trunk Hotel, Brampton. It is nearly five feet high, about sixteen inches square in the middle and surmounted by an ornamental top on which much care and skill have evidently been bestowed. It is designed to be set in a metal frame in front of Mr. McDonald's hotel and is so constructed that the upper half may at any time be taken out and cleaned without much inconvenience by moving three or four small bolts of very ingenious construction. The glass in the under half is beautifully painted and lettered in colours and shows well either in daylight or when the lamp is lighted at night. The lamp reflects great credit on the skills and ability of its constructor, and we think it speaks well for the progress of Orangeville to now be in a position to furnish the more presumptuous Town of Brampton with such a superior article."[17]

The Ontario Marble Works of Georgetown and Orangeville opened in July 1869 with E.N. Orr as proprietor. Located on East Broadway, they offered "monuments, headstones, tombstones, mantle pieces, table tops or anything wanted in marble as cheap as can be got in the Dominion."[18] William Sutton and H.B. German opened their marble works on First Street in February 1871. This business continues today as the Orangeville Monument Works, now relocated on Broadway.

Early Industry: Enterprise and Entrepreneurs   65

In 1870 a new business would open on Broadway, namely the Montreal Telegraph Company. It had extended its line from Toronto to Orangeville via Weston, Bolton, Ballycroy and Mono Mills. With this new firm, the world of quick communication was opened up to town for the very first time. Messages could be sent or received from around the world in a matter of hours.

In 1871, Mr. A. Papst fitted up a billiard parlour in the Brick Block opposite the Paisley House on Broadway, and "furnished it with first-class billiard tables. Played in accordance with the rules adopted by Mr. Papst, the game of billiards is a harmless amusement, and as such it affords abundant entertainment, with mental and physical exercise to those who engage in it, we have no doubt it will become as popular here as it is elsewhere."[19]

Lumber was still readily available and a second furniture factory opened in town in 1873, "Mr. J.W. Kennedy has opened extensive furniture warerooms in the brick building adjoining the Bank of Commerce on West Broadway. The stock is large and varied, embracing plain and ornamental furniture of every description, and is offered at the lowest remunerating prices. To those who may want anything in Mr. Kennedy's line, we can unhesitatingly recommend his stock."[20]

Many women had businesses before the turn of the century, although traces of their existence are hard to find. In 1875, two women were listed among the local shops that had been burned out in a fire downtown and were in the process of rebuilding, "Mrs. Lloyd with commendable energy is erecting a two-storey brick shop on the premises occupied by her, and meanwhile is carrying on the confectionery business in the Elgie Block. Mrs. Carroll, who was erecting a frame structure immediately west of the Union Block when the fire occurred, is replacing it with a handsome two-storey building with a basement for her business as milliner and dealer in fancy goods."[21] Mrs. Mary Ketchum, widow of Jesse Ketchum, was also an astute businesswoman and owned several buildings and businesses.

Businesses create jobs. Jobs keep people in town. Many of our early businesses provided services to the nearby agricultural and lumbering sectors. Taverns served anyone coming into town as well as acting as meeting places and providing entertainment. The pioneer settlement strove to became a town where business flourished. But the fate of local entrepreneurs was not always in their hands. Government policies and the general economy were always subject to change.

6

SUDDEN GROWTH, SUDDEN DECLINE

As Orangeville grew towards the end of the 19th century, the surrounding communities in the new Dufferin County (created in 1881) and in Caledon Township looked to the town as their commercial centre. The railway had arrived and good roads gave good access. Lawyers, doctors and other professionals were moving into the still expanding town. Church congregations were erecting large church buildings capable of holding rapidly growing congregations. The two other key towns in Dufferin, Grand Valley (formerly Luther Village)[1] and Shelburne (formerly Jelly's Corners)[2] were becoming more prosperous as well. Much of the growth of all three towns could be attributed to the railway and to the road improvements.

One enterprise that contributed much to the emerging urbanity of Orangeville was the local newspaper, *The Sun* (established in 1861). Any entrepreneur could readily reach the local population by simply placing an ad or card in the newspaper. New businesses were given lots of editorial comment (if they advertised) and art for ads was a specialty of the paper's printer, Patrick Meany. Political information and opinion was current and editorialized with fervour. Political events could be published quickly and distributed to a broad audience. The other nearby towns producing a weekly newspaper by the late 1880s, included Bolton, Shelburne and Grand Valley. Newspapers also acted as printing houses to supplement work and income by producing broadsheets and posters, another inexpensive and effective way of advertising.

The pioneer period in Orangeville can be considered as ending in the 1870s. Post-pioneer times must have been exciting. New sciences were bringing new ideas. New inventions such as the mechanical cream separator, the milking machine and glass milk bottles were making

Sudden Growth, Sudden Decline

The distinctive CPR station building with its conical roof over the waiting room was built in 1906. It was the second station on the site; the first burned.

both agricultural practices and domestic life easier. Nestle's Infant Milk Food and the commercial production of margarine were just being introduced, and new ways of communication increased the speed by which world news reached town.

The sons and daughters of the Orangeville pioneers were becoming well-educated and either staying in town and taking over family property or businesses, or they were getting post-secondary education and returning to town. Quality livestock was being brought into the area by such well-known individuals as William Henry "W.H." Hunter, who was breeding purebred Shorthorns and Herefords. The Thompson family of Mono Township raised champion Clydesdale draft horses. As well, many others in the area purchased excellent stock. These gentlemen would offer prize bulls or stallions for stud services in the area, thus generally raising the overall quality of local stock.

The town had begun to develop in earnest. The number of merchants had increased from fourteen in 1864 to thirty in 1871. That same year there were thirteen hotelkeepers and by 1891 the number had grown to eighteen. Specialty stores such as dress and mantel (capes and coats for the ladies) shops or fancy goods outlets were coming into vogue. These were stores that dealt in non-necessities and as such were indicators of increased purchasing power. Rural women were now permitted to keep the egg and butter money, as that income was no longer needed for survival on the farm. Bank barns and brick houses along the concession lines needed to be filled with new furniture. The ever-increasing array of appliances designed to "save time" such as harvest binders, agitator washing machines, vegetable choppers and dust mops were all there to be purchased.

As noted earlier, it was a combination of the railway and the improved roads that spurred on the sudden commercial prosperity in Orangeville. Until the arrival of the "iron horse" growth had been slow, but now Orangeville's location was truly en route to many other destinations. From the town, the railway went both north and south to the larger centres and east into the productive farmlands of central Ontario.

In 1871, the population of Orangeville was 1,500 persons, and, within five years, the population had risen to over 2,000. With this growth came prosperity, which, interestingly, was opposite to the general economic state found across Canada. At the time the country was suffering from the recession of the 1870s that followed the end of the Crimean War. With the increased wealth in Orangeville came new commercial banks, now interested in opening branches in a growing community.

The new railway terminal on Town Line led to new growth in that area. The first surveys of new lots in that section were completed by John Corbit of Orangeville. W.H. Hunter, who owned the land, named William Street after himself and John Street after the surveyor. These lots filled up quickly and led to the laying out of the streets south of Town Line, surveyed in 1871 by Kenneth Chisholm. He was a Brampton grain merchant who also ran a general store in Orangeville from 1864 to 1892. He, too, named a street after himself, Chisholm Street, which runs parallel to Town Line. Green Street was named after John Green, also from Brampton, who had come in 1864 to manage Chisholm's store. A Mr. Elliot, Chisholm's business partner, also named a street after himself, but it was never opened. This survey of lots in 1871 marked the end of the early development of the historic street system in Orangeville. Few streets were added in town until the growth spurt of the 1950s, almost a century later.

In 1873, the Toronto, Grey and Bruce Railway published an advertising handbook that contained the following:

No village has prospered by reason of the direct operation of railway facilities as Orangeville. About the period of the commencement of the railway survey of the village [1863], the population of the village was scarcely 1,000 and since then it has doubled that number. Village property will now realize twice its former value and farming land around has increased in price 25 to 30%. The village is situated on an elevated plateau with well-cultivated country around, rising on the west and north with a gentle slope, and

Sudden Growth, Sudden Decline   69

fringed here and there with narrow strips of woodland, which give a pleasing effect to the background of the landscape.

Orangeville is an incorporated village fast rising to importance and, being the junction of the line from Bruce with the main line from Owen Sound, is bound to become one of the leading inland towns of Ontario. It has at present flour mills, woollen factories, two foundries, steam planing mills, two saw mills, two wagon and carriage factories, one cabinet factory [steam power], one pump-making establishment, two brickyards, a large tannery and several smaller works. There are several handsome brick blocks, with spacious stores, some substantial and commodious brick hotels, and the churches are tasteful brick structures of Gothic design.

As a grain market Orangeville has risen to considerable importance since the railway has opened. For about four months during last winter twelve to sixteen car loads of grain were daily shipped besides large quantities of other produce being cordwood, cedar posts, fence rails, and timber. Four to five carloads of store goods also reach here daily form Toronto for supplying the stores in this place. The railway will have a heavy traffic from this place ever increasing with the rapid development of the resources of the surrounding country, the land being not only excellent for grain, but admirably adapted for grazing purposes and the rearing of fat cattle by reason of the number of fine water springs in the district. No place appears to have a brighter future than the plucky Town of Orangeville.[3]

It was during this period, the result of the combination of commercial growth with its corresponding prosperity and the destruction by fire of early frame buildings, that many of the beautiful brick commercial blocks of Broadway and the stately Victorian homes of the Historic District were built. The homes of the businessmen and professionals sprang up along York Street and James (lower Mill Street) Street. As noted, the railway boosted development in the area surrounding the railyards. Today, very little remains of the pioneer period, mostly because of the frequent fires. It is the Late Victorian architectural style that is seen today on a walk through town beneath the stately maples. They were planted by the Orangeville Horticultural Society in 1881, with money donated by the Ketchum family, and a premium offered by the town to property owners who planted trees.

The growing community could no longer be considered a hamlet. In 1863, Simcoe and Wellington counties passed consenting bylaws, and in January 1, 1864, Orangeville was incorporated as a village. The new village opted to join Wellington County. Ten years later, on January 1, 1874, it formally became a town by act of the provincial government. The busiest era of the town's history was about to begin with the unprecedented growth of the 1870–90s. By 1891, the population had exploded to a new total of over 2,961 people.

Paralleling the growth of the town was the expanding influence of the church. By 1867, the Anglican, Methodist and Presbyterian churches were well established. Reverend Alexander Henderson was in charge of the Anglican parish, known as St. Mark's. The Episcopal, Wesleyan and Primitive branches of the Methodist church all had well-organized congregations, and carried on their church and Sunday School work with energy and zeal. In 1868, the Episcopal Methodists built and dedicated a new roughcast church, Centenary Church, on the southwest corner of First and Zina streets. Reverend Thomas Argue was the minister at the time. The Wesleyan Methodists worshipped in an edifice situated on the north side of First Avenue, just east of Second Street, on land donated in 1857 by Jesse Ketchum. Reverend Richard L. Tucker was minister of this congregation from 1866 to 1872, and it was under him that the new church was constructed on First Avenue in 1872.

The Primitive Methodists, in 1867, were busy building a new brick church on the northwest corner of Zina and First streets on a building site donated by the late John Green (Chisholm's store manager). This edifice was opened and dedicated to the worship of God in February, 1868. Reverend H.S. Matthews appears to have been pastor of the Orangeville station at this time and the name of Reverend T.W. Jolliffee appears on the records as Junior pastor. The new church was used by the Primitive Methodists until 1886, when they united with the present First Avenue Church, and afterwards selling their building to the Baptists. There were two Presbyterian congregations in the village—the Old Kirk congregation (Church of Scotland), who worshipped in Bethel Church, which stood on the ground behind the cemetery on the site now occupied by the Orangeville Post Office, and the Canada Presbyterians, who met in a church erected near the site of the present Town Hall. Reverend W.E. McKay was the Old Kirk (Bethel) minister and Reverend H.D. Steele appears to have been minister of the new Canada Presbyterian Zion church in 1878. Later it became the St. Andrew's Church. Religion began to assert its way into daily life in Orangeville. Liquor was no longer available on Sundays

The Dufferin County Courthouse was designed by architect Cornelius J. Soule of Guelph and built during 1880. Today, it is designated under the Ontario Heritage Act. Currently six courtrooms are housed in the facility, along with many additions including the Dufferin County administrative offices and other county departments.

and most businesses now closed on the Holy Day. Rather than calming down the town. however, it seemed that the factions of the Temperance Movement and those who preferred the more open pioneer times would often come into conflict.

The choice of Orangeville as the county town for the newly formed County of Dufferin was also a tremendous boost in 1881. The courthouse and jail building itself was considered one of the finest brick courthouses in Ontario. It was designed by Cornelius J. Soule of Guelph and built in 1880 (Soule had also designed the Zion Church). The jail served many purposes but was usually busy as a home for the insane, the indigent, or even for orphans. The new registry office brought precious land records "home" for the first time. Courts now had a permanent home and the courtroom itself was grand. The whole complex brought a certain prestige to the town, and now Orangeville was included in the decision-making of the entire county through its representatives. Local historian Steve Brown dispels the ongoing myth that there was fighting between Shelburne and Orangeville for the right to be the county seat. "Orangeville was the only incorporated town when the County of Dufferin Act was passed in 1874 and Shelburne was an incorporated hamlet. There was only one choice available.[4]

The process of the formation of the county had been a long struggle. As early as 1861, there had been agitation for a new county to be called Hurontario and to be composed of most of the current Dufferin, as well as Adjala and Caledon townships. The idea for a new county had started in Mono Township when one of the township councillors decided Mono would get a better deal if it seceded from Simcoe and joined Peel County. Their taxes were lower, after all, and Mono wasn't getting much from Simcoe. The ambitious citizens of Orangeville seized on the idea and started promoting the idea of a whole new county to be called Hurontario. Competition arose from another group proposing a new county based on Mount Forest as the centre and to be called Lorne.

The Hurontario group persisted for about 12 years, and the plan eventually evolved into Dufferin. A private member's bill was passed in the Ontario Legislature in 1874, clearing the way for the new county.

It took the local municipalities another five years to vote on the idea of separation and another two years for Ontario Premier Oliver Mowat to get around to issuing the proclamation. Dufferin County became official on Monday morning, January 24, 1881. The citizens of East Garafraxa played a prominent role in the agitation for the new county. On voting day they did their bit, voting more than 99 per cent in favour of the new county as did Orangeville and Mono. Amaranth was a little less solid at about 90 per cent. The rest of the townships were as adamantly opposed to separation. But the south carried the day, and Dufferin was approved.

The county had been formed with Mono and Mulmur townships leaving the County of Simcoe, Melancthon Township and the village of Shelburne leaving the County of Grey, and East Garafraxa and Amaranth townships and the Town of Orangeville leaving Wellington. East Luther Township also from Wellington County joined in 1883.

The night that the votes came in on the creation of the county in 1879, the residents of Orangeville celebrated in style with bonfires on Broadway, First and Mill streets and behind the Town Hall in the market square. It is reported that the whole town stayed up until the dawn of the next day. Orangeville had won the vote. Other municipalities had voted against the formation of the county, but the majority ruled.

Nothing brought the attention of Canada to Orangeville more than a well-timed visit to the town in 1886 by Prime Minister Sir John A. Macdonald. Orangeville was growing and prosperous and a well-known Conservative stronghold. The town was the epitome of small town Ontario success stories:

> It was a great day in the village, and in this Conservative area, when it heard of the forthcoming visit of Canada's outstanding statesman, Sir John A. Macdonald. Several weeks were devoted to preparation and arranging for a huge demonstration to welcome him, and that every resident would see and hear this great man, known in his day as 'The architect cause for which he had vigorously worked and had seen accomplished,' he has gone down in history as one of the most outstanding of Canadians. The historic day of November 29th, 1886, became the day of the visit. The demonstration, it was said, was one in point of magnificence and enthusiasm that surpassed any other held in Dufferin County. Broadway and several other streets with public buildings were gaily decorated with flags, bunting and evergreens. The main street was graced with a large decorated arch.
>
> Commencement of the program of this great day was the rendering of several patriotic selections on Broadway at 10:30 a.m. by the Citizen's Band. Following this they marched to the station where an enthusiastic crowd had gathered to welcome Sir John A. Macdonald on the arrival of the morning train. Such was the interest that it estimated that the crowd that had gathered numbered around 3,000 people, and as the time for the arrival of the train drew near, many more people were added to the crowd and Mill Street and adjoining streets were a dense mass of human life. Sir John's arrival in town was delayed over fifty-five minutes, owing to the fact that his visit attracted the residents of the various municipalities, who had crowded to their respective railway stations to cheer the Prime Minister and his accompanying ministers. It was said that great crowds had gathered at Brampton.
>
> On the approach of the train into Orangeville station, the local band struck up the air 'See the Conquering Hero Comes,' and cheer after cheer rent the air from thousands of throats. Owing to the dense crowds that had gathered, it was fully five minutes before Sir John

and Honourable John Thompson and Dr. [George Turner] Orton [the local Conservative MP], who had accompanied the Prime Minister's car, "The Jamaica," were able to descend from it to the platform and amidst the most enthusiastic cheering and handshaking and the words of welcome, the honoured guests were escorted to their carriage. A gala procession was then formed to give Sir John a real welcome to the village, consisting of twenty-four outriders, the Citizen's Band playing the stirring marches of the day and looking smart in their bright uniforms. The regal and stately carriage that carried Sir John, the Honourable Thompson, Mayor [Thomas] Henry and [Falkner C.] Stewart was drawn by four very beautiful high-stepping grey horses. Another carriage followed with Dr. Orton and the reception committee and a parade of one hundred loyal Conservatives from Caledon, who carried a large banner 'Caledon was gerrymandered by Mowat, but always Faithful.' They were followed by a score or more of carriages bearing prominent residents of the district.

It was around two o'clock in the afternoon when the luncheon was ended and the party arrived at the Skating Rink where they were greeted by a monster gathering of 5,000. When the Prime Minister and his party, who were accompanied by the Citizen's Band had arrived, the building was packed to capacity. F.C. Stewart, the President of the Liberal Conservative Party, was in the chair and on the platform were the many prominent citizens with their fine ladies of the Town and surrounding districts. The Chairman, in his opening remarks referred to the wonderful welcome of Sir John and the interest and enthusiasm shown by the residents and the tribute of their honoured visitor, by their presence at the meeting. He assured the Prime Minister of the loyalty of Centre Wellington County [Dufferin wasn't recognized as a federal riding until 1904] of which Orangeville was a part and they would do their duty manfully in the then forthcoming elections and stated that it was his hope that the Conservatives of Canada would be thoroughly organized and would work with a will and the result he felt confident would sustain the overwhelming majority for the Government headed by Sir John A. Macdonald.[5]

At the election, which followed soon after, the Conservative Party rallied around Sir John. The organization of the political party was quite solid and results of 1886 were favourable. He was again elected as the prime minister and served the country until his death in the year 1891.

Another new national pastime brought people, even tourists to Orangeville. Lacrosse, traditionally an aboriginal game, was increasing in popularity, first in Canada, then world wide. Orangeville managed to develop some of best teams to the level of provincial champions. These teams brought visiting opponents and their fans from across the province. Championship games could bring thousands of people into town. The first team formed was The Mechanic's Club circa 1874, followed by The Dufferins, The Young Canadians, The White Elephants and The Clippers. In 1897, The Dufferins won the provincial intermediate championship and the next year defeated Seaforth for the Canadian Lacrosse Association championship. They won more championships and played Ottawa for the world championship but unfortunately lost:

> "Yes, the good old days [of lacrosse] furnished more excitement and enthusiasm. The game was played for what glory was in it—not for the money," spoke an old lacrosse sport the other day, who has followed the game for years. Many will agree with him. Those were the days when there were no gate receipts. The games were played

Orangeville was lacrosse mad and proud of it, winning several national championships. One of the first teams organized was The Mechanics, shown here in 1877.

on the town lot with very little financial backing. In the '70s, lacrosse was at its height in a little Town of Orangeville. That place, as is well-known, has developed more experts in the Indian pastime than a good many more twice its size. They played it there for fun. It was good advertising too. The town became well-known through that noble sport. When the name Orangeville was approached, it was usually answered with: "Oh, that's the place where all the lacrosse players spring from." Well, to be precise, so it is. Names of stars of the gutted stick who played their first game in Orangeville can be run off very simply on your fingertips.[6]

No business indicates the progressive nature of the Town of Orangeville in the period of growth more than the Turnbull Binder. Binders, a new type of reaper replacing the hand-powered scythe, were changing the way that grain was harvested. This new machine was one of the first pieces of mechanized farm equipment that truly revolutionized farming life not only in this area but across Canada.[7] The story of the Turnbull binder and the McMaster binder is also, sadly, a story of what might have been.

William Turnbull manufactured binders in Orangeville in the year 1894, and was faced with opposition to his venture in 1895 by the McMaster Implements of Orangeville, which had also patented a binder. This enterprising firm on East Broadway started first in the manufacture of ploughs, bits, etc. in 1893. Two years later they manufactured a steel binder, known as "The World Beater," and it had proven to be very satisfactory. That first year over 115 binders were made and sold, in addition to 50 hay mowers. Their product was considered one of the finest binders made, although at that time they encountered pretty stiff opposition from the Massey Harris binder and the Peter Hamilton binder, which were sold in Orangeville by agents Beatty & Company out of Fergus. If only our Orangeville binders had reached the popularity of the Massey Harris Company, the names of Turnbull and McMaster would be as well known as the name Massey[8] is today.

This period of growth and change, however, was not without some social troubles. The gap between the rich and poor was widening and there were still very few rights for women and children. In January 1, 1886, a count at the Dufferin County Jail on Zina Street showed twenty-six prisoners in the facility, seventeen males and nine females. Twenty-two of the prisoners were confined for vagrancy and two were incarcerated for insanity. Two of the female prisoners were blind, three were

Sudden Growth, Sudden Decline

dumb and one was afflicted with deafness. The oldest inmate was 90 years old and the youngest a one-year-old infant, whose mother and two other children were imprisoned as vagrants.

The Temperance issue raged across Canada, resulting in the passing of The Scott Act in 1885.[9] Local supporters of legal drinking were at constant odds with those who felt that liquor was destroying the nation. Things became pretty heated and led to Police Magistrate Fisher Munro's residence being bombed. Several of the new liquor inspectors who had been brought into the area were being threatened, including Thomas Anderson of Second Street:

> It was hoped that Orangeville had seen the last of the terrible dynamite outrages that disgraced and made its name a byword throughout the length and breadth of our broad Dominion. Since the introduction of the Scott Act now something more than two years ago, this town has been the scene of a series of outrages such as no other town or city, we venture to say, on this continent. At exactly 8:30 p.m. on Tuesday evening a terrific explosion accompanied by a bright flash shook the town to its very foundation, The glass in the windows of the stores and houses shook and in many cases shattered. The news quickly spread that the residence of Mr. Thos. Anderson, liquor inspector, had been wrecked by dynamite. The veranda of the house upon which it was evident that the dynamite bomb had been placed, was completely demolished, with little vestige of it remaining. The windows, doors and walls were shattered and lath, plaster and timber lay in all directions. The greater portion of the furniture such as pictures, glassware etc. was broken into a thousand fragments, which were strewn upon the floor in the direst confusion. Mrs. Anderson was seated in the dining room at the time and received the full force of the shock which rendered her unconscious. Her face bore a dazed stony look and fears are entertained that her mind will give way under the severe shock her nervous system has been subjected to.[10]

The problems continued for some time, yet no one was ever found guilty of the offence, although the local "Liquor Party" members were suspected. The rift between the factions continued and caused trouble in town for some considerable time.

It was the final years of the 1890s that ended the innocence of the Town of Orangeville. Most of Canada had already slipped into an economic slump. Although many of the general causes of the depression

McDonald's Planing Mill, at Second Street and Second Avenue, provided lumber and trim for most houses built in Orangeville during the late Victorian period. Donald McDonald's fortune was made when he expanded his business into another line and operated as the Orangeville Casket Factory.

were political and complex, and affected most of Canada, here in Orangeville the economic depression was caused by several localized key factors.

Most importantly, local raw materials were declining. The forests were disappearing as well as the related industries of potash, tan bark and logging. "The resulting loss of available raw materials such as lumber, contributed to the rising cost of finished products. A furniture manufacturer in Orangeville raised the cost of his merchandise 30 per cent in 1903. He reported that the scarcity of local timber was the principal reason for this increase."[11] There had been no attempt whatsoever in the Orangeville area to replant any of the forests. In nearby Mono Township, the hills were bare of any natural growth. Without protection provided by the trees, the farmland was susceptible to both wind and water erosion. A second factor was that, despite attempts to refertilize, the soil was becoming depleted and the rich humus of the virgin forests had been stripped of its nutrients.

Horsepower had replaced the oxen of the pioneer, and the blacksmith shop became the centre of town instead of the gristmill. Mixed farming had replaced the wheat crops of the settlers, and much of the cash produce became meat and poultry products instead of grains. The diversity of milk and beef production did allow for some freedom from the very unstable price of wheat. However, it was the American McKinley Tariffs imposing trade restrictions that caused the decline in the market for Canadian agricultural produce and the subsequent drop in price.

The slow "death of growth" had brought the progress of Orangeville to a standstill by the turn to the 20th century. For decades

Sudden Growth, Sudden Decline 79

after there was little new industry and many businesses actually closed. The coffin factory was one industry that suffered from the depletion of lumber, and with it went over 200 jobs. Although Orangeville was well-established as the commercial, banking and legal centre of the county, it was feeling the pressures of cheaper competition from products produced less expensively in the larger centres. But it did have the county buildings, courthouse and gaol. The railway still sustained the economy of the town, but the population was declining. A migration to the western provinces of Canada where land was being opened up, was underway. Local historians feel that at least 20% of the residents of the area moved at that time, some to the northern areas around Parry Sound but most of them to the West. Some from town went off in search of gold in the Yukon in 1897, while others went off to South Africa to fight in the Boer War.

The economic decline that had begun in the 1890s was particularly hard on merchants. From sixty-three in 1891, their numbers dropped to only forty-nine in 1901. The depression, which had reached its full extent at the end of the 19th century, reaped a human toll as well. Many of the community's bright young citizens had to leave Orangeville as jobs were limited, and even with jobs there was little chance of advancement. A photograph taken in 1885 at the Orangeville skating rink shows a group of ten young gentlemen posing together. All were members of a musical club formed under the leadership of Roxy Romano, a skilful harpist and violin player, the son of Italian immigrants. An article written 50 years later, shows how many of these young men were not able to stay in their hometown: two moved to California, one being killed there in a traffic accident; one went to Sudbury to manage the King Edward Hotel situated in that city; in the Toronto area two became successful businessmen, and one in each of Edmonton and Cleveland. It becomes quite obvious that many of the younger generation left town, leaving Orangeville with an aging population.

By the beginning of the 20th century, Orangeville had lost its hustle and bustle and was a quiet rural town. In ten years the population had dropped almost 1,000 persons and in 1900 barely reached 2,000.

The big excitement of the month was Fair Day, the second Wednesday of each month, when farmers would gather from all over the district to buy and sell horses on the main street. Cattle, formerly sold at the stockyards beside the Town Hall, were now herded to the CPR station on Town Line and shipped by train to the Toronto markets. The town hired men to sweep the board crosswalks to keep them as clean as possible from the by-products of horsepower and passing cattle. Saturday night was the big night of the week. Stores stayed open until midnight to accommodate the rural folk who came to town after the chores were done. The nine hotels in town during that era, and the three liquor stores, did a roaring business. Fistfights and "donnybrooks" on Broadway were not uncommon and provided cheap entertainment.

> Apathy set in, for a long and gloomy period that was probably worse in Orangeville than any other place in the County. There were no new faces on the streets. No new people were coming in—and those who did were quickly and subtly driven out as foreigners. Family farms were passed on from father to son, not sold to outsiders.[12]

Fortunately, three new industries were established as Orangeville entered the 20th century, and brought some lost employment back into town. The Portland Cement Company was built near the railway station, the Orangeville Novelty Works on the west side of William Street and the Dods Knitting Mill on Church Street. The town purchased land and transferred it to the cement company at a cost of 5,000 dollars; the plant opened in 1904. The town also financially assisted in the cost of erecting the knitting mill, which opened in 1913. The Orangeville Novelty Works produced parlour screens, other fancy parlour pieces and rocking horses.

Orangeville Novelty Works built footstools, folding screens and a number of other items necessary for the Edwardian home. It closed at the beginning of the First World War, a victim of a major fire.

Sudden Growth, Sudden Decline

Portland Cement Works had a thriving operation beside the Orangeville Railway Station in the early years of the 20th century. A spur line brought marl from what is now Cressview Lake in Caledon. When the building was demolished in 1954, the stone was used to build Tweedsmuir Presbyterian Church on John Street.

It opened in 1910 and burned down in 1913. Dods Knitting Mill was the last major business to open in town until the 1950s.

Even though the town was on a decline, or minimally at a standstill at the turn of the century, it was certainly not behind the times. A reading of the 1910 Orangeville voters' list, shows some professions that clearly mark a town that still is managing to keep current with the times: W.A. Collister, Bowling Alley; Bert Trotter, Telephone Exchange; T.J. Bennett, Billiards; J.M. Deagle, Electrician; Alex Safer, Billiards. The same voters' list also records an interesting statistic that

Dods Knitting Mill was built at Church and Mill streets in 1913. Dods won the contract to provide woollen underwear for the army during the First World War and, by 1918, had expanded their building twice.

A route march for recruiting purposes reached Orangeville in 1916. The 164th Battalion (Dufferin and Halton Rifles) was seeking recruits for the war.

may also count for a small amount of the population decline. Women who were widowed or spinsters and who owned land could vote in municipal elections. The voters' list recorded 78 homes owned by widows and 51 owned by spinsters. Seemingly the town was becoming a quiet place, appealing to retired farmers and single women.

It was the First World War that finally brought the community back together. There was loss and heartbreak, but when the war was over, the community had once again learned how to pull together and get things done, despite the obstacles.

7

TOWN OF CHANGE, 1900 TO 1914

ALTHOUGH THE POPULATION DECLINED IN Orangeville after the turn of the century, the town was not without signs of progress. Things were changing in the world with innovations in the sciences and technology being introduced almost daily. New inventions improved everyday life and enhanced profits for businesses but had little to no impact on actual growth.

Early in the 20th century, hydro-electric power was coming into its own, gradually replacing the candles and betty lamps, the latter being probably the first type of artificial light used in Orangeville. Betty lamps required bear oil and certainly the early settlers met lots of bears in the area. Evenings, however, were often spent in the dark as candles were scarce. Often the only source of light came from the glow of a fire in the hearth. By the 1880s kerosene lamps had come into vogue. Lamps and fuel could be purchased easily from any number of stores, and were a much safer form of light than candles or an open fire. Canadian glass factories in Nova Scotia and Burlington, Ontario, were producing excellent coloured and clear glass lamps that lined the store shelves beside those imported from the USA or England and brought into town by train.

The first electrical power company in Orangeville was organized in 1882. Donald McDonald had a planing mill and coffin factory on the corner of Second Street and Second Avenue. McDonald conceived the idea of using the shavings and scrap wood from the factory to produce steam to generate electricity. At the time, Broadway was the only street with lighting and there were four Arc-type lights[1] lining the street from the town hall to the fire hall. Lights were on from dusk until 10 p.m. and on special occasions until midnight.

In the 1890s, C.W. Watson had opened a steam-operated power plant on the creek where it intersected Mill Street, south of the present *Orangeville Banner* building. The plant had a tall brick chimney, long since demolished, but at one time visible throughout town. At the turn of the century, John Deagle of nearby Cataract in Caledon Township was awarded a five-year contract to supply power for the town. Next, T.R. Huxtable negotiated a contract between his company, the Pine River Power Company from Hornings Mills, about 17 miles to the north, and the Town of Orangeville. By 1914 power consumption by the town had grown considerably and many of the homes and individual businesses were installing hydro as well. Negotiations were entered into with the newly formed Ontario Hydro-Electric Power Commission,[2] and electrical power became readily available in town as poles were erected to carry the wires.

The telephone arrived in Orangeville in 1887. The first primitive switchboard was set up in Robert Mann's Fruit Market and Confectionery Store on Broadway. The central office was open from 8 a.m. to 8 p.m. Monday to Saturday, from 2 p.m. to 4 p.m. on Sundays, and from 10 a.m. to 12 a.m. and 2 p.m. to 4 p.m. on holidays. The line came from Alton and after the first two years the Bell Telephone had 70 subscribers. By 1891 an extension had been completed to Owen Sound and another to Woodbridge, allowing Orangeville residents to make long distance calls for the first time. Two years later, in 1893, a direct line was opened to Toronto and everyone figured that they had gone as far as they could ever go. In 1900, the 100th telephone was installed, and by the early 1920s the number of subscribers reached 500. Due to the difficult economic times in Canada during the Great Depression of 1930s, the number of subscribers only grew to 655 households.

In 1906, a very modern idea was capturing attention—an electric railway system. The idea was being promoted by Mr. Kilgour of Owen Sound. Actually, the project had been around for a few years, but finally the Huron and Ontario Electric Railway looked as though it might become a reality. The first idea was to run a branch line from Orangeville north to Flesherton, but plans changed to a branch line coming into Orangeville from Toronto and the main line running from Shelburne to Collingwood. However, with money so scarce and the railway monopolies running the steam engines efficiently, the project never got off the ground.

In the early 1900s, the way stores did business was also undergoing change. "Not long ago nearly every store in Orangeville had its own

In 1908, citizens of Orangeville had an opportunity to see their first automobile. By 1920, the car was a staple means of summer transportation in Dufferin County, especially for shopping excursions from the rural areas to the county town. The sleigh remained popular in winter until the roads were improved in the 1940s.

delivery outfit, but a union delivery was started by Peter Marlane about 10 years ago. Today, with the exception of two butcher shops, not a single private delivery remains. The last business house to discontinue delivering their own goods is Wise Bros., bakers, who took off their rig Saturday."[3] In order to survive the hard time, businesses had to look at their operations and make changes to cut costs. Buying a delivery service on a contract basis or as needed was cheaper than employing a driver and keeping horses. It was hoped these savings could be passed on to the customer.

It is believed that the first automobile arrived in Orangeville in July of 1908. It was owned by Jasper Noble Fish, a local lawyer. By September of the same year the local newspaper editor observed, "The horse is here to stay, and the auto makes little or no difference. This town has three livery stables and all are doing a rattling good business."[4] According to at least one local resident, it was the automobile that brought the slow decline to Orangeville. In a letter to *The Orangeville Banner*, signed simply "Farmer's Wife," she comments:

> Dear Sir:—There has been a lot of talk lately about people not patronizing their own Town of Orangeville. Well, what are we going to do? We are afraid to go to town on account of the automobile nuisance. It seems too bad after the farmers have made the good roads that we should be afraid to travel on them. Is it any wonder

we send to Toronto for our household necessaries? We can send for
dry goods enough to last six months and get our groceries from the
country stores. In our neighborhood there are very few women who
will venture to drive out alone. Unless something is done to prevent
the automobiles running one or two days in the week, so that the
farmers can have one or two days they can go to town and not run
the risk of being killed, the towns are going to suffer.[5]

Times were tough and unemployment was high. In Orangeville
some attempts were being made to tend to the needs of the poor. The
most desperate cases received food and lodging in the county jail. The
town was making contributions towards families in need, and individual churches were providing support for the poorer families. Charitable work became a church function as well as missionary work. A
Charity Society was set up in Orangeville in 1909, and, less than a
year later in December of 1910, it was reported, "a number of families have been supplied with bread, groceries, meat, boots, new clothing of all kinds and [home] nurses supplied. This is all being done in
such a quiet way that in many cases the party's benefiting did not know
where the help comes from. The Society is anxious to hear of any family in need for Christmas."[6]

Food was becoming scarce and not everyone in town had lots large
enough to grow sufficient vegetables and fruit. The yards in the newer
surveys were even smaller than the larger older Victorian lots and even
many of these had been subdivided into two sections to earn extra revenue. In 1910, an interesting ad appeared in the newspaper, "The
undersigned will rent her garden containing a number of fruit trees
and an abundance of excellent raspberry bushes, which yield prolifi-
cally. The property is on Amanda Street and will be rented on reasonable terms. Mrs. Orange Lawrence."[7]

With the town in decline, jobs for the young boys of the community
became difficult to find. Many of them opted for the mad rush to the
western provinces, while others went to the city. For young girls, not
only was work harder to find, but the selection of suitable men was
declining. How would they fill their time? In 1911, the following notation on the behaviour of some was noted in *The Sun*:

For quite a long time a number of young girls have been running at
large in town. While some of them are rather young, they are a decid-
edly swift bunch and in their gait have hit all the high spots. These

Town of Change, 1900 to 1914   87

unfortunate girls are generally followed by an equally swift bunch of
cigarette-smoking boys and, of course, when there is such a combination it does not speak very well for the morals of the community. Other
young girls get associating with the swift ones and are soon led astray.

No person has apparently bothered with the wild doves and the
thing became a scandal. Last week Chief [Sam] Ewing took a hand
in the game and with the assistance of the parents, took one young
girl in charge and placed her in a home in Toronto. It is planned to
have a general round-up and all incorrigible and bad girls will be
sent to homes where they have a chance to reform. Some of the stories that are told about the actions of those young girls are simply
shocking. They disclose a state of affairs that are at once a scandal
and a disgrace to the fair name of this town and the effort to wipe
out the blot has not been made a minute too soon.

Hundreds of dollars go out of this town every year to convert and
enlighten the heathen in distant lands and a much more important
work under our very eyes remains unnoticed and undone. We shudder when we read about the white slave traffic, but how many little
slaves are sent forth by allowing foolish young girls to bum around
the streets and public places at all hours of the night. True, ignorant,
indifferent and easygoing parents are much to blame for the
destruction that overtakes their daughters, but when parents cannot
or will not look after the welfare of their children it is the duty of
the state to step in and take charge.

Chief Ewing will have the hearty support of the people in his
decision to stop the scandal.[8]

Although this period of Orangeville's history seems generally
uneventful, two things appeared to occupy the citizens and the local
newspapers—temperance and train accidents. In several cases these
two seemingly different news items were connected. Unfortunately,
too frequently the train engineers were drunk. Once, one of them was
particularly under the influence of alcohol and several people were
killed on the way home from the Canadian National Exhibition
(CNE) in Toronto in September 1907.

The vote for "local option" on Prohibition[9] had long been an issue
throughout Ontario, and, in January 1910, a vote was held in
Orangeville to see if liquor would still be sold or not. Most people in
town held strong beliefs, no matter which side of the issue they were on:

Local option carried in Orangeville on Monday by a popular majority of 133, the votes were 383 for local option and 250 opposed. The temperance people put up a stiff campaign and they had been working on the job for many months. The anti-local optionists had practically no organization whatever and had no workers and they are responsible for running behind in the game. Those who supported the by-law and every local minister worked hard for the cause and hustled voters to the polls. They manned rigs themselves and brought out many women who otherwise would not have recorded their votes.[10]

Although there was a demand for a recount, the decision held.

An unexpected business boom followed for those who sold liquor. The sale of liquor would not stop until the first day of May, so everyone stocked up, even the temperance crowd! " 'See that jug,' said the hotel-keeper to *The Sun* reporter. 'Well, that fair-sized receptacle belongs to a rather rabid advocate of local option and he is loading up for the drought that is expected to overwhelm this district.' We're selling them bigger quantities of the family disturber than we ever did at a single session before. If business keeps up I'll have a deficit of stock when I pull down the blinds and pronounce the benediction at the seven o'clock farewell service on the evening of the 30th of the month. The local option patrons of this hostelry tell me they want it in case of sickness and I think they'll have many good bellyaches while the little brown jug holds out."[11]

It took the town a few months until the drinking in the streets calmed down. By then, local men had started to make their own liquor and bootlegging began in earnest. The law was diligent, however, and "whisky spotters" were sent undercover into town to check on activities. On one visit in October 1910 they laid three charges against the Grand Central Hotel and one against the Dufferin House in a single day. Undaunted, those wanting a drink found it where they could.

Grand Valley had remained a wet town. For the annual Grand Valley Agricultural Show four special rail coaches full of visitors from Orangeville visited town. "It was the first time since the first of May that the multitude had an opportunity to worship at a legalized shrine and their zeal knew no bounds. As a result the day was interrupted by fights and pulling matches. Besides a great display of activities, horse races etc., at the exhibition grounds... downtown there was plenty of booze and bonhomie. The fair closed with a grand display of fireworks, ably assisted by firewater."[12] Until the beginning of the First World War, when the conflict turned everyone's attention elsewhere, the "prohibition" discussions continued. But no one really seemed to change sides, and liquor sales did not stop in Orangeville. They just went elsewhere or underground.

In the early years of the 20th century, the town also seemed to be in a state of turmoil due to the alarming number of train wrecks in the vicinity. To give an example, on November 3, 1910, there was a head-on collision between two CPR freight trains a mile south of Orangeville, resulting in injury to the engineer, fireman and brakeman. The newspapers claimed it was due to the amount of traffic and lack of safety features on the trains. The cars and engines had serious damages and the line was closed for a couple of days. The brave rail men jumped from their trains and sustained most of their injuries in that desperate move. Luckily for them, they were taken to the Commercial Hotel in town to receive medical attention. A few weeks later, an Owen Sound express train crashed into a freight train and demolished three cars at Fraxa Station, three miles north and west of town. The passengers were shaken up, but there was no serious injuries. *The Sun* reported, "the wreck hoodoo is still camped on this line of the CPR and wrecks are becoming alarmingly common."[13]

Apparently, alcohol was still part of the problem. There is nothing

Lord Dufferin Hospital, created and funded by the Lord Dufferin Chapter IODE, opened its doors in 1912. When the county council refused to take on its operation, the IODE ran it on their own for the first twelve years.

like a good accident or a good argument over a jug of liquor to keep things lively in a town with no growth, a declining population and little money.

The establishment of a local hospital was an important addition to the town. The Lord Dufferin Hospital was opened in October 1912, thanks to the direction and fundraising efforts of the Lord Dufferin Chapter of the IODE.[14] It is interesting to note that this same group of women, who accomplished so much with the building of the hospital, had been commented upon in an article by the editor and published in *The Sun* only a few years earlier:

We don't know much about the Daughters of the Empire, but we believe they are going out of their line when they provide a program for the public schools. The Daughters are all right and perfectly harmless so long as they do not meddle with politics or things which they do not understand. It requires a great deal of ability to keep the elements from clashing in public schools and we do not believe that the dear Daughters' talents run on these lines.[15]

In its first year of operation under the direction of the matron, Miss M.E. Barclay, the hospital treated a total of 90 patients and successfully performed 36 operations. In 1915, the hospital graduated its first class of nurses—four students, who for three years had lived at the hospital putting in a twelve-hour day, on a seven-day week schedule. The financial remuneration to the nurses was $5.00 per month.

Over the years, as the need arose, several additions were added to the building, which originally had been the Kearns' residence on First Street. A hospital board was established in 1924, with members coming from both the IODE and local men in the community. A new hospital was opened on the same site in 1954 under the name of Dufferin Area Hospital, but it was now to be administered by a board of directors. The IODE relinquished their responsibilities and surrendered their charter to the new board.

The women of Orangeville were coming into their own. The Women's Institute had been established in 1897 by Adelaide Hunter Hoodless[16] and a branch was organized in Orangeville in 1902. Under the motto of "For Home and Country," the institutes promoted education for women with an emphasis on domestic education. In addition, the local Institute established a full gymnasium in the basement of the Orangeville Library to keep the young men of town off the streets and out of trouble.

But it was the '30s and war was looming. For the second time in the century, young men would be going off to fight, some never to return. Some did come back, but were never the same. During this period, young women found employment at Dods Knitting Mill or went to the cities to work in the factories, replacing men who had gone overseas. The eyes of Orangeville were no longer on Broadway, but were turned towards a much larger conflict across the Atlantic Ocean.

8

ORANGEVILLE BETWEEN THE WORLD WARS

ONE OF THE FIRST THINGS that Orangeville did after the First World War was to erect a memorial to honour fallen Canadian soldiers. Discussions started almost immediately after the war ended, but a statue was not erected until 1923. Originally, one memorial was planned for all of Dufferin County, but many of the smaller municipalities lobbied to have something in the communities where the soldiers had lived. Families wanted to see the memorial on a regular basis and not have to travel to the county town to remember a lost loved one. Ultimately, individual memorials were erected in Orangeville, Shelburne, Grand Valley and Mono Mills.

On Sunday, November 12, 1923, a bronze statue of a Canadian soldier mounted on a marble base was unveiled in Orangeville. Lead letters on three sides of the base listed the names of the local fallen soldiers. The ceremony was attended by town and county dignitaries and the remnants of the local regiment that had served in the war marched along Broadway. Almost the entire town showed up for the ceremonies.

A description of daily life in Orangeville around the year 1925 was recorded in a letter to *The Orangeville Banner*, written by Mrs. B. Moffat who had left town and was living in Callander, Ontario. Truly an article on bygone days, it provides a glimpse of Orangeville between the wars from the perspective of a child—a rare view:

Back about 1925 we had plenty of snow in winter and the cars were few in those days, but the horse and cutter was quite fashionable. I recall when I was about eight years old. My father always kept a couple of racehorses and he used to exercise them almost every

Orangeville Between the World Wars   93

evening. We children used to look forward to going with him. We would pile into the cutter bundled up in the buffalo robe. In those days we wore long underwear and thick-ribbed wool black stockings and high laced boots with rubbers on them and warm woollen caps with big thick scarves tied over our heads. Quite a difference from the young folks of today with their nylons and bare heads. I think if people were to dress fit to meet Old Man Winter, they would not complain so about the weather, but they shiver around in next to nothing and curse the weatherman all winter. As I said before, we would all pile into the cutter and away we would go, up by the Fairgrounds and all around town. Well do I remember the frosty moonlight nights with the snow sparkling like diamonds, the crunch of dry snow under the cutter runners, and the smooth, rhythmical jingle of the clear bells. The sky would be studded with millions of stars—you could almost reach up and pick a handful.

We used to get our milk at Jimmie Duncan's up on Elizabeth St., and you could get a 10 lb. honey pail of good, fresh milk for 10 cents in those days. I'll never forget the rattle of the 10 cent piece in that old pail. We would sometimes walk the whole way on top of the snowbanks piled up beside the sidewalk. There used to be huge piles of snow up around the jail. Mr. and Mrs. Duncan were grand people. They used to come in from the stable stamping the snow off on the back porch and bring their brimming pails of steaming, warm milk into the kitchen. Their kitchen was warm and cheerful and had the smell of fresh baked bread sometimes. Often we would get a large slice of fresh homemade bread with homemade butter on it, and if our mitts were wet, Mrs. Duncan would put them up in the top warming oven to dry, and we would warm our toes at her oven door. We always liked to linger there a while with them…

I remember once in February we all came down with measles and we were all up in bed with the blinds drawn. It was pretty grim. The hired girl read to us from Grimm's Fairy Tales, and there are still times on a cold, stormy night when I can picture Hansel and Gretel lost in the woods on a blustery February night. We had no electric lights in those days, and we used to lie in bed and imagine the shadows on the wall were awful things. When we would get up in the morning the frost would be thick on the window and Jack Frost, the artist, would have been there and painted the most beautiful flowers and trees and all sorts of ferny leaves. We would scrape a little place off the ice to see what the weather was like outside.

Well do I remember the mournful sound of the old fire bell in the middle of the night, of "Joe" Gaines getting the horses harnessed to the old fire cart and opening the big doors of Robinson's Livery Stable, where Roy Bryan's Garage now stands [today the site houses the County of Dufferin Social Services offices], and the horses would bolt out with a great clatter, tearing down Broadway at breakneck speed. Somebody in our neighbourhood had a hound and when the fire bell sounded the old hound would howl mournfully and we would be so scared we would cover our head with the bedclothes.

There was an open air rink at the foot of the hill on Little York St. and we used to go to skate all Saturday afternoon for 15 cents. I remember when we used to get out the snowshoes and moccasins and what fun we had snowshoeing across the fields up behind the high school. The snow would be as high as the top rail of the fence and you could just walk across. Skiing was unheard of in those days, except in the Alps. Charlie and Walter Robinson had a big, long bob-sled and we used to all pile on it up by the high school and come right down the hill past where the arena is now. There were no cars to be afraid of and you could get a wonderful start from the top of the hill.

Of course, as we lived in town, we were not burdened with many chores after school or Saturday, so we had plenty of time to enjoy ourselves outdoors. One thing I liked to do was go skating on the little lake in the swamp down at the foot of Broadway. It is pretty well dried up now, I think. I haven't been there for a number of years but I remember going for a walk with my mother one time down round there and seeing the remains of an old cemetery. Some of the very old flat gravestones were still lying on the ground, partly covered by weeds and grass, but the little old gate still swung on one hinge and wild roses were blooming, the only thing that marked the place where some pioneer had been laid to rest. It's remarkable what changes can take a place in a few years.

It is not so long ago on Broadway two blacksmith shops stood almost side by side. We used to stand at the door while "Bob Ferns" would pump the bellows, and make the fire burn up and heat a horseshoe on a pair of long tongs, then take it out and quickly plunge it into a tub of water sitting on the floor, while the steam hissed. Then while we stood there watching, he would take up the horse's foot, lift it up and hammer on the shoe. Another blacksmith shop stood where Fred Webb now has a beautiful new dairy and

Orangeville Between the World Wars

coffee shop, another one down on Second St., and still another on Mill St. where Ferguson's egg grading place is.

Wise's store was across the street then, where Marshall's harness store now is, and we used to like to shop for our mother in Wise's store. There was always the smell of fresh bread being baked in the back of the store and in those days you could always get ice cream cones for 1 cent. Wises made up bags of candy for a cent and you never knew what surprise awaited you in those bags. Then there was Miss McLachan's store down where Laura McCutcheon's hat shop is, and farther down on the other side of the street, next to Meek's Garage, [today a vacant lot on the south side of the east end of Broadway] in that little store next door, Mrs. Widdis had a little candy store. When you opened the door a little bell would ring and Mrs. Widdis would come out and wait on you. She had so many pretty coloured candies and all for a cent—sometimes it took quite a while to choose.

We hadn't any radio in those days—television was something far beyond the wildest imagination—and on stormy winter evenings, when our homework was done, we would sit around the fire in the lamplight while Mother would tell us stories about when she was a little girl or when she was a young woman and spent a few years of her life working up in Chapleau (which was a wild country)…. Mother sewed and made most of our clothes. It must have been very trying for her sewing by hand by the light of a coal oil lamp.

There was a monthly fair in those days, which has disappeared with the horse and buggy. On this day, which was usually the third Thursday of the month, the country folks all flocked to town, summer or winter. March fair was always the biggest. On this day several strange individuals appeared on the streets of our town. If it was winter they would be wearing heavy coon-skin coats and big fur hats and carrying a heavy thick cane or walking stick. Anyone who had a horse to sell would drive up and down the street, and the buyer, if the horse took his fancy, would stop the driver…he would walk all around the horse, poking it in the tummy with his cane and slap him on the back, open the horse's mouth and look at his feet, lift his foot and look at his hoof. If the animal stood up to his expectations, they would retire to the Dufferin House, where a deal would be transacted. I have known people to come from Toronto on the train just for Fair Day. It was sort of an old home affair. The Sunday School would have a supper in the church basement and a concert afterwards, and in winter there was always a sleigh-riding party, or in the summer the Sunday School picnic at Caledon Lake, or Stanley Park, Erin.

There were no restaurants in Orangeville then, but the hotels provided a real old-fashioned square meal for about fifty cents. We had one Chinaman in town who did up the washing for the lazy people and he was sort of an object of awe to the kids. He used to sit out fanning himself with a big straw fan and we would wonder why he felt the heat, because we had always been made to think that the sun was so hot in China that it blistered the hide nearly off a person, and here was old "Sammy," as we called him, away up in Canada where it was supposed to be cold, fanning himself with a big straw fan and slouching around in straw slippers.

There were no pavements then. Broadway was a gravel road, as were all the rest of the streets in town, and in order to keep the dust down there was a big water wagon drawn by a team of horses and driven by "Jimmie Graham," perched high upon a spring seat. As he drove up and down the streets of the town, the water sprayed out the back of his big barrel-shaped cart operated by pedals that were pressed with the feet. We used to run up the street after the water wagon in our bare feet on the wet road and once or twice got fooled as well as drenched when Mr. Graham pressed the wrong pedal by mistake.

There was a coach drawn by horses owned by J.J. White, and just about train time, at the Mill St. corner on Broadway you would hear him holler, "Board, Board!" and anyone who wanted to leave town by train would make a dash for the bus." If the Orangeville hockey team or lacrosse team was victorious for that season, the players were paraded down Broadway, with Orangeville Citizen's Band serenading them.

Ah, those were the good old days![1]

An interesting little business to open during that era was a fancy hat shop located on Broadway. In 1922, Sadie Little opened Miss Sadie Little Millinery, on the north side of Broadway opposite Mill Street. She had a window display of hats and a large array of her creations in the front of the store. The back part was the workroom where the hats were made and where she also did alterations to hats. Miss Little made trips to Toronto to buy supplies for her creations and to acquire some factory-made hats as well. Her nieces, Della and Ruth Hodgson,

The "bus" (the Union stagecoach) was an important part of Orangeville life in the early 20th century. It ferried travellers from the CPR station to their choice of accommodation among the town's many hotels.

would mind the store while she was away on these trips. At the time, the hats would sell from one to three dollars each, depending on the amount of work and the cost of the fabric. Miss Little hired other young ladies to assist her in the business, including Bertha Lemon and Mrs. Ethel Mills. She also did embroidery work, which she sold from the store. The shop remained in operation well into the 1940s and today some of her family still have in their possession some "Sadie Little" hats with her cloth label sewn neatly inside.

The ethnic mix of Orangeville's citizens changed over the time between the wars. During the period of decline many businesses had been run by local families, but the European conflict now brought a number of new immigrants to Orangeville, many of whom started their new lives by becoming merchants.

"Bright and early Monday morning Mr. Sam Merlina had workmen busy on the vacant property, which he recently purchased on West Broadway, announcing that construction work on the new theatre would commence on May 1. Mr. Merlina informs *The Banner* that the new theatre will cost $18,000 or $20,000 instead of $15,000 as at first announced. We understand that the negotiations with Mr. Moorehead, of Brampton, have fallen through and that there is no likelihood of a second theatre being built on the Mill St. site."[2] Mr. Merlina ran

The Uptown Theatre opened to great acclaim in 1927. Not only could it show movies, it had a stage for vaudeville acts. Best of all, it was equipped for sound for the brand new "talking pictures."

a fruit store in conjunction with the new moving picture show. The family ran the Uptown Theatre well into the 1970s and many residents still remember the family and their friendly nature.

Another newcomer making Broadway home was Harry Klappis. He had arrived from Greece via the United States with little in his possession but ambition. He married Blanche O'Reilly of Ohio, a fiery Irish girl, and had a son, Jimmy. In 1930, when a doctor told them to move to a higher elevation to improve Jimmy's poor health, they moved north to Orangeville and opened Arcadia Sweets, a popular candy store, which later became a restaurant. Harry was a well-liked merchant and often told stories of faraway Greece to many residents who had never been out of Dufferin County.

In the early 1920s, the honour of being the "gossip" spot went to Thomas Hewson's blacksmith shop on First Street, located in the alleyway just north of Broadway. Tom had been the mayor of Orangeville in 1922 and was well enough liked to be returned to office from 1927 to 1929. During his tenure most of the streets were paved and street lighting installed, all of which aided his popularity. Politics, both local and national, were discussed to be sure, but it was fishing that was the topic of the most interest in the shop. Tom was a well-known angler in the region, and claimed to know the best spots in the area's many cold water streams. All the serous fishermen of Orangeville would bring their prize catches in to Tom the smithy, and have them duly measured and recorded on the wall. At the end of the season there would be honours bestowed on the best fisherman of the year. All the gossip did not keep Tom from his work and local legend claims that he and his staff could put over 100 shoes on horses in one

Orangeville Between the World Wars　　99

day. When Hewson closed his shop in March 1945, it was considered the end of an era by many residents in town.

Hewson's building was demolished and replaced by the Orangeville Dairy and the Dairy Bar, operated initially by Fred Webb and then by George and Fred Wilson. This building still stands behind 199 Broadway, across from *The Orangeville Citizen* office on the alley.

In 1920, a terrible Halloween prank rocked and saddened the entire town. The headlines read, "Halloween Prank is Fatal—Man Breaks Both Legs in Fall—Richard Allen, former Reeve of Mono, Victim of Foolish Trick—was pleading with boys when platform crashed to the ground—Dies in Hospital from terrible injuries." The article published at the time told the sad story:

Richard Allen, about 75 years of age, died at Lord Dufferin Hospital at 7:00 o'clock this morning as a result of terrible injuries received at 1:00 o'clock Tuesday morning, when he fell from a platform at the rear of the Henderson Block, corner of Broadway and 2nd Street. A number of boys, some of them from the country, were out playing Halloween pranks. The second flat of the Henderson block is divided into several apartments and Mr. Allen occupied one of them. This flat is provided with an outside closet elevated about fourteen feet from the ground and is reached by a walk or platform guarded by railings. The closet is supported by four large posts. The boys armed themselves with axes and were chopping the posts when Mr. Allen, who heard them, appeared and pleaded with them to go away. They kept right on and before Allen realized it, the supports gave way and he was precipitated to the ground, the platform coming down with a crash.

Mr. Allen was deposited among old wagon wheels and sleighs that had been allowed to accumulate in the space under the platform. The crowd scattered after the crash and left the victim to shift for himself, although they must have known he was badly hurt by a drop of fourteen feet. Mr. Allen dragged himself through the alley-way to Second Street, where he was found by night watchman Sam Ewing, who was quickly joined by Special Policeman T.C. Peavoy. Drs. Henry and Macleod were quickly summoned and the injured man was taken to Lord Dufferin Hospital. It was found that both legs were broken in two places and the bones were so badly splintered that they penetrated the flesh. There was also a slight fracture of the skull. From the first the doctors held out not the slightest hope of saving the victim's life and he passed away at the time stated above.

The police at once secured the names of several boys who were in the crowd and we understand they have since learned who the others are. The case is in the hands of the Crown Attorney L.J. Island and a coroner's inquest will be opened this afternoon. It is needless to say the boys have placed themselves in an unpleasant predicament and have made heaps of trouble for themselves and their parents. Last year the boys went on the rampage and destroyed much property and caused a great deal of annoyance. They got off lightly. Had they been taught a lesson on that occasion Tuesday morning's tragedy might have been prevented.

For many years the late Richard Allen was a prominent figure in Mono township politics. He was a native of the township and lived there all his life until he retired from the farm and removed to town several years ago. He filled the position of Reeve for a number of terms and aspired to represent the old constituency of Cardwell in parliament. His tragic passing has shocked the whole community and the whole affair is deeply regretted.[3]

The entire town forgot about their troubles and the depression for awhile as everyone mourned together for both the Allen family and for the boys who had learned a life's lesson in a very hard way.

In the 1920s, the Ontario government was discussing the creation of provincial highways to be called King's Roads. One of the first to be considered was the road that ran from Port Credit to Orangeville then on to the port at Owen Sound (today's Highway 10) And just like the railway of 50 years earlier, the road would run right through Orangeville. Charles Wheelock, the surveyor and town treasurer, was president of the Ontario Good Roads Association. He used his influence to make sure the highway went through the town. Later, when the east-west highway from Newmarket to Kincardine (today's Highway 9) was designated, Orangeville sat not only in the middle but at the crossroads of the two highways. Many hoped that these roads would bring new prosperity, but they failed to do so. *The Sun* felt the reason was, "there is no organization such as a board of trade or chamber of commerce where the businessmen can meet and discuss matters that would be for the benefit of the community. In union there is strength and only by united action can Orangeville make the progress it should."[4]

The radio had become popular and technological changes were

making them more affordable for the common family. Stores downtown had them and radios were advertised for sale in the popular mail-order catalogues of the period; the 1935 Fall/Winter Simpson's Catalogue was advertising console models ranging in price from $38.00 to $99.00. Many of the early models were run with Delco batteries. The radio provided a contact with the outside world for news, new types of music and popular trends. "Long before 6 o'clock Tuesday morning many people were listening at the radio to hear King George's speech at the opening of the Naval Conference in London, England. They were well rewarded for His Majesty's voice came clear and every word could be heard.[5]

In reality, this was the time of the Great Depression[6] in Orangeville, as with everywhere else in North America. Many people were losing their homes and farms for back taxes. Photographs of the era show school children posing for the class photo in bare feet. Orangeville was somewhat better off than the larger cities to the south where homeless, hungry people were living in the streets. In town most people knew each other and were willing to help. As well, the churches were strong, with a variety of congregations and solid attendance. The Salvation Army was very active in Orangeville, gardens helped and almost everyone had a

Flour and gristmills were staples of Dufferin farm life. The workers in the stone mill on Mill Street produced "Anchor" brand bread flour and "Pride of Dufferin" pastry flour under the direction of mill owner, Henry Watt.

talent or product that they could sell. The stores uptown suffered from bad credit, but the old faithful stores stayed open, although there were very few new ventures started. Prices soared for manufactured products. The front page of *The Sun* in January 1922 had commented earlier on a price change, "It's enough to make the biggest whisky head vote for prohibition. Just when the thirsty were going to it with vengeance the distillers step in and boost the price of their poison. This will be sad news for the man of moderate means."

There was a noticeable rise in crime in Orangeville during the Depression era. Court cases involving many unpaid credit notes at local businesses and petty theft increased. The most common crime involved groceries or packages being lifted from parked buggies and from cars left unlocked on streets. Many of the local rural residents had reverted back to buggies and horse-drawn rigs as gasoline had become too expensive.

There was great concern in the area about the depopulation of the farms. The United Farmers Organization became a strong body and held regular lectures at the Opera House. The farmers were talking about co-operative selling and buying, which made town merchants slightly uneasy as there might be stiff competition for their products. As more and more people moved to town, there was a shortage of affordable housing and the price of rental accommodation, when available, was high. It became difficult to sell a farm and the area auctioneers had literally no business. There were plenty of folks willing to sell, but there were no buyers with cash. "Just now farm property is a 'drug on the market'." For the last two years it has been practically impossible to sell a farm. All the farms that have been put up for sale in this vicinity lately failed to bring a single bid. A few years ago farms would have been quickly picked up at fancy prices but now it appears nobody wants to become a tiller of the soil."[7]

But the "good old" days were soon ended, for as quickly as peace had come in 1918, war was declared again in 1939, and for the second time in the century, the attention of the town was on Europe. The radios that had brought music and comedy a few years ago now would bring news of the war in Europe. Life changed once more. Some of the young boys of the area went off to war, while others on nearby farms were needed at home to grow food for the troops. No longer concerned with domestic issues, the fundraising and charitable work focused on aiding the war effort. Dozens of men joined the forces and the town took on a gloomy air, everyone silent, hoping that bad news

This small parade was held on Broadway during the Second World War to raise funds in support of the Allied Troops. During the war, lights were blacked out in town and a 9:00 p.m. curfew was enforced on the younger residents.

by telegram did not arrive at the door. The plans of many of our young people were changed or lost forever, and mothers once again knew of the loss of a child. Again the Dods Knitting Mill, with a government contract for the production of woollen garments, was running three shifts. Prices started to rise for agricultural products and the unemployment rate dropped as the workforce went overseas.

9

LOOK AT US NOW

LIFE BEGAN ANEW AFTER THE Second World War, marking the beginning of a renewed growth period of Orangeville. The war had inflicted great human losses, but in Canada the human spirit had never been higher. "By God, we will make it" was the unspoken attitude that bolstered the morale of the town.

As a result of the political upheaval in the aftermath of the war, Orangeville, as well as other parts of Canada, experienced a new wave of immigration. Not everyone emigrating from Europe was interested in moving to the larger cities, although jobs were certainly more plentiful in the industrial heartland. Rural sponsorships were being set up in 1946–47 through the Agricultural Labour Act. The federal government placed families on local farms as labour, to replace the male workforce killed or wounded in the war, for a one-or two-year period in exchange for sponsorship to bring them to Canada. Families moved into the area from the Netherlands, Germany, Poland, Latvia, Lithuania and other eastern European countries. Suddenly schoolteachers of the area had to tend to children with little to no fluency in English in the classrooms, as well as their regular teaching duties. Training for English as a Second Language instruction did not exist at the time. Children of Dutch immigrants in particular were filling up the rural schools where prior to the war, attendance had been declining. Several English and Dutch war brides came back to Orangeville with their new Canadian husbands.

As the town grew, the naming of the streets continued to reflect ongoing local history. In 1950, Eugene Reid built several new homes west of Faulkner Street, near the high school and named a street after his father, Mathew. Banting Drive was named after Frank Banting, the owner of the farm where the subdivision was built, and, in 1957, Starrview Crescent was developed by local real estate agent, Paul Starr. In the 1950s, local developer Ed Boyer named two of his subdivision streets after two employees of the town, Shirley Roberts and Marion Haddock of Mono.

The first subdivisions were built in the mid-1950s. Bythia Street was developed south of the railway tracks. Elizabeth Street was built west of Clara Street, beginning in 1955, and new bungalows sprang up quickly. Zina Street was extended northwest towards Blind Line and eventually met up with Banting Drive. Individual local contractors were kept busy, buying land, building a home and then putting it up for sale.

The new larger subdivisions as they developed from the 1960s to the '90s ate up the farms that surrounded Orangeville. Unlike the small developers, these subdivisions involved hundreds of houses and included road, water and sewage requirements. Along First Street, the old Abiathar Wilcox farm, then owned by George Judge, was subdivided. Bredin Parkway was named to honour Gordon Bredin, a local bakery operator who served as mayor of Orangeville in the 1970s after many years on the town council. Along the "C" Line area the Gord Williamson and Fred Rennicks family farms were cut up in 1964. Later Harry and Margaret Brown's dairy farm would be developed. Mr. Brown's main farm of 150 acres to the west of the railway tracks actually is referred to as "Brown's Farm Subdivision." Development there began in 1975. The farms of George Cameron, Howard Black, Lorne Rayburn, Ross Thompson and Murray and Nancy Robinson now provide space for hundreds of homes instead of cattle and crops. These subdivisions started in 1990 when Orangeville annexed their farms from East Garafraxa. The first subdivisions on Purple Hill were developed on the farm of Herman Hayward.

From 1958 until 1983 the Orangeville Royal Canadian Legion sponsored International Hockey Tournaments involving Berlin, New Jersey, and Orangeville. Many Orangeville Jr. NHL'ers (a minor hockey league also operated by the Orangeville branch of the Canadian Legion) got to travel to United States to play hockey and experience new things. In 1967, when it was Berlin's turn to come to Orangeville, not only did the families and teams arrive, but they also brought their 60-member Lamplighter Drum and Bugle Corps, to provide entertainment throughout the weekend. Broadway was closed down for their performances. In Orangeville, even a hockey game is a cause for a celebration. The Legion organized boys' hockey and girls' bowling in the winter season and girls' and boys' baseball leagues in the summer.

Well-named, the Grand Central Hotel was the largest and most imposing of the town's many hotels. Built circa 1875, it provided hospitality for more than 100 years before it was demolished in 1989.

In 1962, the Grand Central Hotel was purchased by Joseph De Haas, one of the many to emigrate from the Netherlands after the Second World War. Several years later, under his ownership, the hotel made history when it was granted a licence to open a beverage room. For over 50 years the residents of Orangeville had consistently voted "Dry" each time the issue was brought forward. Dining lounges were now approved and government liquor stores were opened. Mr. De Haas used the commercial travellers' showrooms for his bar, and decorated and refurbished them into an attractive beverage room.

In 1962, street numbering was introduced in Orangeville in preparation for home delivery. There were no more boxes available at the post office. In 1962, the beautiful old cut-stone post office was demolished to make way a more modern facility with additional boxes and expanded postal services. Despite the public outcry, the historic building was not saved.

A former mayor of Orangeville, Arnold Patterson, stated, "Orangeville once was populated by mostly retired farmers, retailers and railway workers. The railway was our major industry. It was a bleak day when some of the CPR facilities closed. Some of the town's present prosperity [1978] is a result of the 1963 council and the then mayor, Harry Tideman. In 1963 under Tideman, the town bought [Garnet Rawn's] 125-acre farm [on Dawson Road], had it zoned industrial and the industrial park was born."[1] With a lot of determination and with the willingness of council to put up the costs of servicing the new park, new factories started to build in the large industrial lots.

The population of Orangeville boomed in the 1960s. In 1951, the year before I was born, the population was 3,249, ten years later it had grown to 4,593, and in yet another ten years, 1971, it had more than doubled to 8,074. As the population continued to expand, new subdivisions were sprouting up in every direction from the historic core. By the millennium, 2001, the population was recorded as 25,000 people in over 8,000 households.

The 1991 Census, showed 10,000 residents in the labour force, with 1,940 listed as clerical and mainly female, and 1,210 listed as managerial or administrative, the majority here being male. The next largest group was sales, listed at 925 persons, almost equally divided between male and female. Only 185 citizens listed their profession as farming, horticulture or animal husbandry.[2] Gone were some of the professions from 100 years earlier as identified in the voter's list of 1910. Then, there were broom-makers, tinsmiths, stone cutters, a pump maker, lime burner, station master and egg dealers along with a myriad of other professions.

Life along the source of the Credit River had certainly changed in 100 years. In the Credit Valley Conservation Report of 1956, it was noted, "There are several sources of industrial pollution in Orangeville, including two dairies and a woollen mill and the waste from various residences enter the stream. Following heavy rains the treatment plant is overloaded and apparently raw sewage enters the stream. Even with considerable dilution from an unpolluted tributary there is remarkable pollution of one of the chief headwaters of a famous trout stream."[3]

Beginning in the early 1960s, Orangeville experienced an industrial boom, which created hundreds of jobs over the 1950 to 1980 period. One of the first to locate here was J.C. Adams from Toronto. He built a factory to manufacture and distribute automobile parts on Third Street. In 1967, the company relocated to the empty Manning Biscuit Co. building, which had been the former Dods Knitting Mill. Acrow Canada Limited, which made aluminum auto parts, opened in 1959 and located on John Street to be close to the railway. Some of the new industries would

108   ORANGEVILLE

choose the new industrial park while others located in various empty lots scattered around town. Many of the industries cited the dependable, steady workforce as the motivation for coming to Orangeville.

Monarch Master Manufacturing opened a factory in 1961, producing coin-operated laundry equipment, but they went bankrupt, and, in 1964, the building was taken over by Fisher Price Toys. This was the first Canadian plant for Fisher Price, but four years later after an eighteen-month strike, they closed as well. Other plants included Greening Metal Products on Third Street (later moved to Commerce Road) and Canadian Westinghouse, which, in 1969, built a large factory near the bypass at Fourth Street. Filtro Electric made electric kettles and popcorn makers and Lilliston Canada made parts for farm machinery.

Polyethylene Bag Canada, which manufactured polyethylene film, opened on John Street and later became Union Carbide Limited. This is one of the very few industries to have survived over a long period. Operating today as Clorox Limited, the management credits the strength and dedication of their employees as the foundation of their success.

Many of these early factories brought their administrators in from out of town. The men brought their families and quickly settled into the community and became involved in local service groups. Hundreds of the families that relocated to work in these industries stayed here long after the companies moved away. They form a strong link in the backbone of the "older" residents of today.

The current industries provide a great service to the community by offering employment opportunities and contributing to various community groups. Although many of Orangeville's residents do commute to work in larger centres, many also dream of getting a job closer to home someday, so they can spend more time with their families and in their town.

Changes to the telephone system were another indicator of technological growth. In 1961–62, dial telephones were introduced and Orangeville schools held lessons on their use for the students. In the year 1968 alone, there were 503 new phones put into service. Another advance occurred in 1966 when Consumers' Gas Company brought a pipeline in from Brampton and installed gas mains throughout the town to serve homes and businesses with natural gas. Coal furnaces and wood-burning stoves were on their way out.

In 1971, the town made a huge financial commitment and decided to erect a new recreational centre, which would accommodate hockey in winter and box lacrosse in the summertime. An indoor pool was planned to replace the existing outdoor pool in Idlewyld Park. Backed by the Lions Club, a fundraising committee (Mike Flecker, Roy Dyer, Irwin Scott and Les Cartwright) raised over $143,000 from the local community. During the early 1970s modern recreational facilities were in vogue across Ontario, the belief being that such centres would attract new business. Orangeville would not be outdone.

Downtown Orangeville was responding to the challenges of changing markets across North America. New businesses started up and left, others changed hands. Interestingly, several of the older shops stayed on and became the mainstay of the downtown, stores such as: Marshall's Men's Wear, the Clover Farm Grocery Store and Jeffers and Sproule's Pharmacy. With many of the new store owners on Broadway wanting a more modern appearance, a number of the older buildings had their storefronts radically altered or were torn down. Patterson's Furniture Store refitted the entire face of the old *Sun* building with a solid modern front. Other buildings were simply removed. "Why would an august institution like the Royal Bank want to move in on sleepy little Orangeville, knock down three old buildings on the main

The old and the new met along Broadway in the 1970s. The Grigg Company was a five-and-dime store that had been established for many years. Jeaneration was a new store marketing to the local kids and the few town hippies of the period. Jeaneration caught media attention when it sold "hot pants" to local high school students, both male and female.

Part of the original Ketchum Block. This photo of the building's facade was taken in the early 1920s. It later became Torrie's Clothing Store. The girls are unidentified.

street and in their place put up a squat one-storey glass and concrete bank? Urban sprawl, that's why."[4]

In 2002, after years of discussion, what was left of Orangeville's unique character was saved when the downtown area was designated a Historic District.[5] On March 18, 2002, Council enacted Bylaw 22-2002 defining the district, and, on September 18, 2002, the Ontario Municipal Board approved the bylaw. This designation plays an important role in protecting the downtown's diverse and rich heritage of 19th century buildings. It also insures that infill projects reflect the character and architectural styles of the district and give special consideration to the height, massing, and setbacks of neighbouring historical buildings. Since 1995, the town has sponsored a facade improvement program for buildings in the central business district.[6]

Currently, the town has 19 buildings designated under the Ontario Heritage Act in addition to the buildings inside the Heritage Conservation District. One of these buildings, the Jull Mill, was demolished in spite of its designation. This listing includes: twelve residences, the Orangeville Public Library, the Dufferin County Courthouse, the old Dufferin County Land Registry building, one commercial block, a set of Victorian row houses and the Orangeville Municipal building.

Probably one of the greatest success story of modern Orangeville is the formation of Theatre Orangeville. Its cultural antecedent began in 1875 when an Opera House was built as part of the Town Hall. Over the years, hundreds of local entertainments were held there, but plays were always the crowd-pleasers. By 1990, it had been decided that the space available in the old Town Hall was no longer adequate for the use of the town municipal office. The original Opera House itself had been made into offices in 1968. Discussions at council and coffee-shop levels ranged from adding on to the old building, to demolishing it and building something new on the site, to moving out totally to a more modern location somewhere in town. Fortunately, several people remembered the grandeur of the old Opera House on the second level, its wooden panelled walls and dropped ceilings long since lost to view. Could they possibly still be there? Many of the councillors did not see the value of restoring an old structure in a building that already did not meet their space requirements.

Fortunately, Vic Large, a former mayor and councillor, had fond memories of the old Opera House fixtures. Somehow, he obtained a one-month reprieve and permission to remove the new fixtures in order to determine what had been covered in the ceiling. Vic contacted a local builder and contractor, Karl Edelbrock, and myself as an historical representative. The work began. Labourers worked from early morning until the light was gone from the windows, since most of the electricity had to be shut down. The town moved its offices temporarily until a final decision could be made.

One month later, all the interested councillors and interested groups who had been following the progress, were called together for a tour of what had been discovered. Underneath the more modern trappings, albeit rather worn and tattered, was the theatre space, complete with some of the original trim and painted stenciling. Pam Claridge, a local singer and publisher of *The Orangeville Citizen*, put on an impromptu concert. To everyone's amazement, the acoustics were perfect and the music was sweet and true. The public was quickly sold on restoration. Grants were completed and an architect, Carlos Ventin of Simcoe, hired to try to work out the additions necessary to accommodate growth, as well as allowing the rebirth of the Opera House.

Two years later, a proposal to create a company called Theatre Orangeville was put forward. The report suggested, "that a new professional Theatre Company be founded and based in Orangeville...that this new professional Theatre Company offer to become the principle user of the newly renovated Town Hall Opera House."[7]

Local resident, Jim Betts, a well-known playwright and composer whose work included *Colours in the Storm*, a musical based on the life of Canadian artist Tom Thomson, had prepared the report. The idea was accepted and with unprecedented excitement, Theatre Orangeville was born. Since then the theatre has become a major part of the Orangeville scene. Hundreds of performances have been given, world premieres have been launched, the Theatre Orangeville Youth Singers have become town favourites and the townsfolk have been able to enjoy professional theatre within walking distance. The most popular plays remain any of those from the "Wingfield Farm" series written by Dan Needles, a local author who had been raised in Mono Township. Everyone knows that his stories are based on his experiences in Dufferin County and the community comes out in droves each time one of his plays is staged. The Theatre Orangeville Youth Singers (TOYS) choir performed in *Joseph and His Technicolor Dreamcoat* at the Royal Alexandra Theatre with Donny Osmond—a real coup. Today, Theatre Orangeville is central to the identity of the town, carrying on the tradition of local entertainment.

In September 2000, following the announcement that the CPR was going to abandon the rail line linking Orangeville to the Greater Toronto Area, the town purchased 55 kilometres of the line. This was done with the support of several major industries in the community that relied on the freight rail service for competitive transportation costs. The industries also represent over 600 jobs. The rail line, still in operation, is now referred to as the Orangeville Brampton Railway (OBRY), and is a wonderful example of public and private sectors partnering to

The cast of the Orangeville Fan Drill Company posed for this group photograph in 1894. For almost one hundred years, local and travelling performances of all types were held in the Opera House, located upstairs at the Town Hall. These groups brought culture and entertainment to town and created thousands of memories in the process.

save rail service. A town owning a railway in Canada is unique, especially one the size of Orangeville with its current population of 26,000 people. The acquisition process involved Orangeville working co-operatively with communities such as Caledon, Peel, Georgetown and Brampton, with the federal government through the due diligence process, with the County of Dufferin and with the Province of Ontario for the actual purchase. Another innovative feature of this project was the formation of a rail-users group—the Orangeville Brampton Railway Access Group (OBRAG), comprised of manufacturers who rely on the railway for freight service. This group is responsible for capital improvements, ongoing maintenance of the railway and the hiring of a rail operator. Each partner shared in the risks and responsibilities and now benefit from the rewards of the successful venture.

In September 2004, rail services were expanded to provide passenger excursions aboard the Credit Valley Explorer, operated by Cando Contracting Ltd., the short-line operator that provides freight and excursion services to the OBRY. These excursions have proven to be highly popular and typically include a three-hour, 70-kilometre return tour through the Niagara Escarpment and past some of the most outstanding scenery in Ontario. The train passes

The carving of tree sculptures from the trunks of trees that had died along the streets was the brainchild of Mayor Drew Brown. Drew brought many new and innovative ideas into town in an attempt to attract tourists. This particular carving is of A.D. McKitrick, early owner of *The Orangeville Banner*. The carver is Peter Mugensen of Mount Forest. *Courtesy of John Woolner, Orangeville.*

attractions such as the Forks of the Credit Provincial Park and across the spectacular trestle bridge over the Credit River. In acquiring the railway and ensuring continued operation of the freight service, the town has protected the rail line from abandonment and enhanced opportunities for the long-term economic development of the region.

The Art Walk of Tree Sculptures is another creative way Orangeville has of bringing history to life—giving some of the dead trees new life as carvings of some of the town's historical figures. The unique project has also put the spotlight on art. The sculptures have attracted a lot of attention from residents, visitors and other municipalities. After visiting Truro, Nova Scotia, one summer where he saw some historical figures carved out of stumps, Mayor Drew Brown decided Orangeville could rejuvenate those trees that had been declared beyond hope by the municipal arborist. The project was initiated in 2002. Carvers were eager to be part of the project, and residents and visitors alike enjoy viewing the new creations. The most popular sculptures are the ones depicting bears—but everyone seems to have a different favourite. The town, with its broad artistic community, has made "art" a centrepiece.

It seems that most of the controversy surrounding the growing transportation problems was not aimed at the town roads but rather at the roads that go around town. In 2005, a road bypassing Orangeville was finally completed. An earlier bypass had been built around the east end of town in the 1970s, amid its share of controversy. Merchants deplored the loss of Highway 10 from the centre of town, but the bypass was built despite protests. Its completion effectively opened up the old fairgrounds to commercial development. Some unexpected problems arose when the contractors found they were excavating through not only a sensitive wetland but also the site of the old Orangeville town dump. Bottle collectors clambered through the mud each night and much of Orangeville's history came alive one more time.

The area south of Broadway was recommended to have a bypass as well, leading traffic to the west of town to rejoin Highway 9. The first report by the Town of Orangeville on the subject dates back to 1978. At least six reports followed until finally the environmental assessment was completed in 1991. It was not until 2001 that the County of Dufferin got the project underway. Everyone was in support since the combination of transport trucks rolling through town and the overall volume of traffic had become a major problem. Trucks roaring through residential areas were shaking the foundations of several of the historic buildings downtown.

The project cost just over 14 million dollars, with more than seven million coming from the Ontario government. Premier Ernie Eves was the Dufferin-Caledon MP at the time. The size and scope of the Tom Lockyer Bridge that carries the new road across the Credit River is a far cry from the causeways built through the Credit Flats some 170 years ago by Seneca Ketchum. (Mr. Lockyer had been a local contractor and a relentless promoter and supporter of the area, a man much respected. He passed away in 2005.) The South Arterial Road has proven to be a real benefit to the town already. Not only is it effective as a route, but it but provides pleasant scenery as it passes through the ecologically sensitive wetlands.

A new 2006 town project showcases Orangeville's evolution, from a natural forest to a mill-based village, and ultimately to an urban centre. Depicted in a unique and prominent landscaping project located on three medians in the middle of Broadway in the downtown core, it was designed by second-year landscaping students and Professor Harry Chang, program coordinator of the Horticulture and Landscape Program at the Humber Institute of Technology and Advanced Learning. The project was paid for through community donations, "The funds have been raised in the community,"[8] Mayor Drew Brown said. The most westerly median highlights the natural forest, with the planting of native species of varied heights. A waterfall (made out of natural stone and measuring just under three metres in height), with water falling in four directions, represents the fact that Orangeville sits at the headwaters of four river systems. The water goes into a pool at the base of the waterfall and is recirculated. Some water runs along a chute to the top of a symbolic waterwheel (a little over two metres in height), representing the emergence of the mill and its energy source—and the village that became Orangeville. Water cascades down the waterwheel and into a stream that flows eastward in the median to a point where the water is again recirculated. The median has a flagstone walkway in the centre with a circular flagstone feature and stone benches.

The central feature of middle median is a clock tower. The clock was originally built and installed on the old post office in 1936 where it remained until the post office was demolished in 1962. Fortunately, the clock was rescued by John Vandendam, the town works superintendent at the time. It sat atop the town hall from 1980 to 1993, until the hall was renovated. Now the marble timepiece, which weighs about 2,000 pounds, has a new home in downtown Orangeville.

The most easterly median, positioned in front of the Town Hall, accommodates a pergola with stone columns and a white cedar roof structure. A wrought iron railing is in place where required to provide a barrier protecting pedestrians from traffic. There is a circular feature opposite the main door of the Town Hall/Opera House made out of flagstone, along with two stone benches. As one proceeds east, there

Left, the old clock, rescued from storage by Deputy Mayor Jim MacGregor, now stands in the middle of Broadway, reminding us that we have lots of time to enjoy Orangeville. The clock was originally in the post office tower, rebuilt on top of Town Hall and, finally, its faces look up and down Broadway for the third time; *right*, created by local artist Peter Turell, this statue of Orange Lawrence stands looking down the middle of Orangeville towards the flats. The statue forms part of the town's new meridian parks that take advantage of the width of the street. The project caused much controversy in 2006. *Both photos courtesy of the Town of Orangeville.*

are more benches and a statue of Orange Lawrence, the founder of the town, created from magnesium phosphate. The almost three-metre high sculpture stands on a base and towers above street level to welcome those coming into town. The statue, created by Grand Valley artists Donna Pascoe and Peter Turrell, has the town's founder with his coat over his left shoulder, sleeves rolled up, and working plans in hand, symbolically ready to build his mill on Mill Street. Mayor Drew Brown sees it as a "celebration of Orangeville. It is a representation of all we are. We have community values that very much mirror our history, and growth hasn't take those things away. When people come up from the flats, up the hill, and see Orange Lawrence, it has a tremendous impact."[9]

Perhaps one of the biggest and most economically influential recent events was the announcement that Humber Institute of Technology and Advanced Learning, in partnership with the Town of Orangeville, would develop a campus to be built on Veterans' Way. Currently in the planning process, the school will provide needed post-secondary programming for the growing population in the area as well as access to an increased skilled labour pool for our local businesses. In fact, over the next ten years, the campus could accommodate 2,000 students on the 28-acre site. This partnership will create new and expanded academic opportunities as well as bolstering economic growth.

Orangeville has become a place of choice to live. The town has all of the modern services and conveniences of a larger city. But it is the surrounding natural environment that attracts many new residents and is the reason that many stay. The river still runs through town and a walking trail is being constructed to follow it where possible as well as becoming a trail to connect the town with the Island Lake Conservation Area. There are parks, a wonderful theatre and great food available at all price levels and of different varieties. It is a healthy place to live and to locate business. The downtown is currently experiencing a facelift as several local businesses are restoring their storefronts in heritage styles and colours. Orange Lawrence's home still stands at the end of the street I live on, shaded by the trees planted over a hundred years ago by the Horticultural Society.

The challenge to the future of Orangeville will be to assist in the protection of the amazing natural environment that surrounds the town. It

Orangeville resident, Lyn Jelly, stands in front of the second Lawrence house on the corner of York Street, where he currently lives. Mr. Jelly is a direct descendant of Orange Lawrence. Incidentally, he is also a descendant of William Jelly, the founder of Shelburne. *Courtesy of John Woolner, Orangeville.*

will also have to find sensitive ways to protect the built residential and commercial heritage in the downtown core. Although protected now by the Ontario Green Belt and Niagara Escarpment plans, the pressures to expand are great. It is the hope of present politicians and residents that the town will not grow any larger than a 35 to 40,000 population, although Ontario government estimates are higher. One of the strengths of Orangeville is the integration of "old" and "new" residents; another is the reputation of being one of the friendliest towns in Ontario. But can this lifestyle be kept that way? Only our history, in time, will tell.

10

MUNICIPAL HISTORY:
GETTING THINGS DONE

FROM THE VERY BEGINNING OF its history, the movers and shakers of Orangeville have had big, big plans for the village. It was in the Fall of the year 1863 that a bylaw to incorporate Orangeville as a village, was passed by the Wellington County Council after having appointed Peter McNab, an Orangeville resident, to take a census of the population. He counted 1,200. The residents were tired of being attached to the townships of Garafraxa, Mono and Caledon. Getting work completed in the settlement was next to impossible.

Before the incorporation of the village some roadworks were underway, authorized by the township and county councils. "Several important improvements have been made in the appearance of our streets during the last few days. Broadway has been gravelled, and the old bridge over Mill Creek, where it crosses the street, has been replaced by a new one. About 30 or 40 men are yet employed in excavating and gravelling some of our leading streets. We do not remember having ever before seen the public money and labour so advantageously expended."[1]

It may be assumed that in the early days, matters pertaining to the welfare of the settlement had been subject to the advice of Orange Lawrence, the Ketchums and other qualified prominent men. In reality, three different officials represented the town on three different county councils and their influence was negligible; often the representative did not even live in Orangeville but on a farm or in one of the other small hamlets. However, upon reaching the status of a village, the community now could nominate its own village council. *The Sun*, the village newspaper, complained that there were only a very few ratepayers in the community assessed with enough wealth to qualify for the office of councillor. "It would appear," it said, "as if special pains have been taken in assessing to leave only the privileged few to aspire to the office of Councillor."[2] The newspaper featured a front-page editorial about Orangeville becoming a village. It is likely that Mr. Foley summed up the feelings, frustrations and future plans of the village well, although his population figures do not agree with other reports:

Located at the convergence of three counties and as many townships, the position of Orangeville renders the management of its judicial and municipal business both inconvenient and unsatisfactory. It is no longer desirable that deeds and other legal documents, affecting the conveyance of village property, should be registered in different countries, or that a community whose interests are identical, should be compelled to attend on juries and county business in Barrie, Toronto and Guelph. Nor is it consistent with our interests that the village should continue to form a part of three different townships, having little or no influence in either. Such a position we conceive to be humiliating to a place having about two thousand inhabitants, and annually contributing upwards of one thousand dollars to the revenue of three different municipalities. Of this large sum not more than forty dollars are yearly expended on improvements in the village—a result due to the fact that we are unrepresented in the councils of the counties of Wellington, Peel, and Simcoe, and but to protect our own interests, Orangeville should be erected into a corporation by itself and attached to some *one* county.

The steady, yet rapid progress of Orangeville is really surprising, and the consequent increase in the value of village property quite marvellous and unprecedented. Its unparalleled prosperity during the past 12 months is almost lost sight of in the gigantic preparations which are being made for the erection of new buildings; and it is not till one reflects upon what has been done in this short interval, and compares the extent of the business done here with other towns and villages, where less briskness in all trade is easily discernable, that the mind can be brought to bear upon the magnitude of the improvements taking place in almost every part of the town.

Though landed proprietors by charging an exorbitant price for village lots have materially retarded the growth of Orangeville, yet not even this barrier can stay the rapid advance of the progress the town is making. New stores, private dwellings, foundries and artisan shops

Municipal History: Getting Things Done

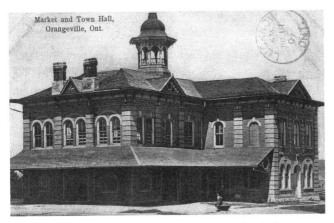

The Orangeville Town Hall was built in 1875 and included a market on one side and council chambers on the other. Originally, striking porches shaded the market area, helped to keep the meat inside cooler and away from direct sunlight.

of all kinds, are being erected this summer; and the noise of the anvil, the sound of machinery, the click of the trowel and carpenter's merry song, are to be heard wherever we turn our steps through the town. Amid all this din and bustle there is no pause—not time to think. Everybody is busy in some enterprise or other. Should this rate of progress continue, as now, even without further increase, a few short year will make Orangeville one of the most flourishing towns in all of Canada. We might well pause and ask how long such an industrious intelligent and enterprising community will be compelled to submit the injustice and inconvenience of going to Guelph, Barrie or Toronto to transact County and Judicial business. What better argument for a New County than the self-evident fact, that the wealth, intelligence and enterprise of this section of country entitle it to the pre-eminent right of a County town and Judicial Court of its own—Who can deny us this right as a people and portion of this Country?[3]

An exciting election for the first members of the new council took place on January 4, 1864. There were eight candidates for five seats: Falkner C. Stewart, William S. Thompson, Thomas Jull and John May had previously served as councillors in Mono and Garafraxa's municipal affairs. Following the election meeting in the Bythia Street Public School on January 18, 1864, F.C. Stewart was the first reeve. J. May, a newly elected councillor, gave notice of a bylaw to appoint village officers and to arrange their salaries. The meeting was adjourned to meet at Kelly's Hotel a week later.

This photograph of Thomas Jull, miller and son-in-law of Orange Lawrence, would have been taken circa 1880. He was an inventor, as was his son Orange. It was Orange Jull who created many devices including the Rotary Snowplough.

Falkner C. Stewart, a merchant of this small community, was the first local representative to attend the meetings of the Wellington County Council in the year 1864. However, he was defeated by Thomas Jull, son-in-law of Orange Lawrence, in the elections the year following only to regain the position after a successful election campaign when he defeated Jull at the polls in the year 1867. This did not discourage Thomas Jull. He came back to win a year later and once again became the reeve, and was elected successively for the next two years.

In the year 1864, the proposal for laying sidewalks brought vigorous debate. Constructed of wood, these walkways were an improvement over the deep mud that came each spring and after each rainfall. But the actions taken by the village council did not please all the citizens of Orangeville. When the sidewalk along Broadway was completed, it enabled pedestrians to finally get out of the mud and manure, but as the newspaper noted, "we must confess that its usefulness will be considerably neutralized to children attending our Common School unless a branch sidewalk of about one hundred yards be made along Bythia Street to the school room. We feel assured that the parents of children attending the school, if called on, would subscribe a few cents each to have the sidewalk continued."[4] Some of the roads needed work as well and Jesse Ketchum made an offer to council to excavate the turnpike and gravel Second Street at cost of $50.

In 1864, the town council passed Bylaw #3, regulating the licensing of shops and taverns in the Municipality of the Village of Orangeville. Regulations included:

—that the applicant is a fit and proper person to be entrusted with a licence to keep a tavern and is of good moral character;
—he, she or they must have in addition to what is needed for the family, not less than four bedrooms and good beds therein with a sufficiency of good bed clothes and furniture for the same and a good stable sufficient to contain twelve horses in addition to what

Municipal History: Getting Things Done   123

may belong to the owner or his family;

—that the applicant have a driving shed sufficient to contain six horses and to have one month's feed for the same, say one ton of hay and twenty-five bushels of oats.

—that every tavern keeper shall exhibit over the door of such tavern house in large letters the words LICENCED TO SELL WINE, BEER AND OTHER SPIRITUOUS AND FERMENTED LIQUOR.[5]

In 1864, the village treasurer issued his annual statement and reported income from tavern licences as $104, and store licences as $95.

The 1869 municipal election for the village was plagued with problems. Like an old time soap opera, it was one that revolved around status, power, and accusations. It also provides a perfect example of the political culture of its time. The election for reeve and councillors took place on December 21, 1868; Thomas Jull Esquire was elected as reeve, and John Anderson, Thomas Jackson, Peter McNab and Joseph Pattullo as councillors. John Corbet, a local farmer and land developer, and a list of petitioners wanted the election deemed invalid and void on the basis that it had been organized improperly. From the petitioners' perspective, candidates were not proposed and seconded correctly. They placed the majority of blame on the returning officer, Francis Grant Dunbar. All candidates, however, stated in their affidavits that the nominations were made openly and audibly, and confirmed Dunbar's interpretation of the order of events.

It does appear, nonetheless, that there were very few people in attendance at Bell's Hall during the time the actual nominations took place. It was argued that the low attendance was not due to lack of community interest, but rather many deponents argued that they were misled by Returning Officer Dunbar who, they said, openly favoured some of the candidates, thus influencing their votes. Justice John Wilson, from Wellington County, was called in to rule and he made note of the one-hour grace period, that was supposed to follow the nominations. Wilson noted that the one-hour clause was used against the electors rather than in their favour. Mr. Wilson decided that it was the returning officer's duty to improve and create a more openly conducted nomination, as well as to inquire whether or not there are any more nominations before closing the meeting. The defendants were found not guilty of a criminal offence, but guilty of immorality. Their acceptance of a seat in the 1869 election, which they knew was improperly

124   ORANGEVILLE

conducted, contributed to an immoral act. Dunbar was also found guilty of immorality, as he conducted the election in a biased and manipulative manner under the Municipal Institutional Act of Ontario. Justice Wilson determined that the governing parties were occupying invalid seats, and ordered them to vacate their positions in order for a new election to take place.

Following the judgment, the ensuing election turned into an open battle between the first elected council under Thomas Jull, which sat from January 1869 to March 29, 1869, and the second slate of candidates. A newly elected council, consisting of Falkner C. Stewart, Samuel Henry McKitrick, Benjamin Fountain, George Wilcox and John Corbet, came into power on April 12, 1869, and sat for the remaining nine months. Joseph Pattullo was the only member of the first council to be re-elected, proving that the new elections were necessary to satisfy the village electors. Loyalty and connections with the right people helped to cement a position in early Orangeville politics, but consistently led to accusations of corruption.

Maitland McCarthy, a successful lawyer of the district, was elected as reeve from 1870 until 1874, at which time he was elected as the first mayor of the newly incorporated town. The first official town council was comprised of Maitland McCarthy as mayor, Mannaseh Leeson, reeve, with John Green, Falkner C. Stewart, William Parsons, Robert Hewat, James Henry, Benjamin Fountain, William Campbell and John Fletcher as councillors, being two from each of the four wards. Orangeville was divided into East, West, North and South Wards with Broadway as the centre line separating north from south, while John Street and First Street provided the other axis.

In February 1874, the council placed $200.00 at the disposal of the Finance Committee to defray the expenses of promoting a new county. Even before the town had been incorporated as a village in 1864, there was much talk of a new county being established in the area, to be called Hurontario County. Many Orangeville businessmen were eager to make their town the county seat. At a political dinner held in 1861, local resident, Samuel Montgomery, remarked that "there are as many good and loyal lot of men in this neighbourhood as can be met with in any other part of the Province, and that Orangeville is entitled from position and wealth to be made the county town of Hurontario County [that is to be]."[6] Finally, the County of Dufferin Act was passed by Ontario legislature in 1874 setting up a provisional county, not to be officially proclaimed until 1881. The new county was named Dufferin

Municipal History: Getting Things Done   125

after Lord Dufferin, the Governor General in 1874 when the legislature was passed. George McManus from Mono introduced the bill and "Dufferin" was the name adopted.

In 1874, Councillor John Fletcher gave notice that at the next meeting he would introduced a bylaw for the erection and maintenance of a "Public Weigh Scales." This was badly needed to ensure accurate weighing of rural produce and commercial products. That same year, J. Polley and a number of others requested that council secure the construction of a road from Orangeville to Hockley along the valley of the Nottawasaga River. There was also other important matters to deal with to keep the municipality running smoothly:

A disagreeable stench, emanating from the putrid carcass of a horse, permeates the atmosphere in the vicinity of the Central School. No one thinks it his duty to remove the nuisance, and anticipating its continuance till exhausted by the process of natural decay, people in the neighbourhood are beginning to wear clothespins on the nose. Council should deal with this matter immediately.[7]

Falkner C. Stewart was elected reeve again in the year 1875, with James Allen as deputy reeve, and James S. Fead, a noted local lawyer and banker, became the mayor. It was in this year on April 28, at 3:00 a.m., that a tragic fire broke out on the Jackson Block. The Council Chambers fell victim to the flames. The local paper described the fire:

On Tuesday night, or rather on Wednesday morning about 3 a.m., a fire was observed in the small room in the rear of the Town Hall, and in spite of all efforts of those who assembled on the alarm being given, the building was destroyed, nothing being saved with the exception of a few of the seats. By hard work the lock-up was saved. The fire was without doubt the work of an incendiary, who had evidently obtained entrance through the window; but so far no clue has been obtained to the guilty party or parties, although a reward of $200 has been offered. The loss is estimated at $2,000....[8]

The town, now needed a new place for its municipal meetings, so the councillors voted for the erection of a town hall and market. The market would contain butcher stalls for the sale of meat.

Three lots were purchased from Mrs. Mary Ketchum as a site for the town hall and five thousand dollars was allocated for the project.

Part of the stonework on the Orangeville Town Hall has carvings of heads of cattle. When built, the Town Hall was the only place where meat could be sold legally. The cattle heads adorn the arches of the old butcher stalls. *Courtesy of John Woolner, Orangeville.*

The land was surveyed by C.R. Wheelock and the contract for its construction was given to Clow & Foster. Francis G. Dunbar of Orangeville was named as the architect. During that same year $6,000 was spent for a new Waterworks and Fire Hall, $2,000 for the improvement of Broadway and a $1,000 grant to the Mechanics Institute, which was set up in rented space. This was the year in which things really began to take shape in Orangeville.

In 1876, after years of complaints from residents about the health conditions, the new town got its first Health Committee. For years the medical doctors in town had maintained that the open refuse from animals and human waste was causing health problems for the citizens of Orangeville. "The Health Committee went its rounds for the first time this year on Monday, and found the atmosphere in many of the backyards fetid with the exhalations arising from the decomposition of refuse matter [manure piles] deposited in them during the winter. The parties were allowed three days to remove the rubbish, so that the town is likely to get a thorough cleansing. We trust the Committee will continue to apply itself vigorously to the work of purifying the town."[9]

Also, in 1876, the council voted $1,000 for the creation of a Public Cemetery, citing health and space concerns resulting from the overcrowding of existing cemeteries. The old burial ground of the Bethel Presbyterian Church near John and Broadway was full, as were both the Methodist and Anglican cemeteries. The town bought a site in Lot 1, Con. 1 Amaranth, but there was much discontent over this proposed location. Several private citizens were resolved to have a cemetery on Lot 3, Con. 1, WHS, Mono. Ultimately the town acquired a cemetery named Greenwood (only the third public cemetery in Ontario) while Forest Lawn Cemetery was organized as a private company. The interred bodies were moved from the old cemeteries to the new ones, which were located outside town.

Municipal interest was certainly in the news when John Foley, editor of *The Sun*, became the reeve and represented the town in the County Council in the year 1878. Joseph Patullo, a controversial lawyer and justice of the peace and later a police magistrate, was elected the mayor. The council of that year took action to beautify the town. By then most of the forest had been cut off for lumber or consumed as firewood. The town was bare of shade:

> The bonus of twenty cents a tree offered by the Council, has induced our townsmen to beautify their homes, and improve the appearance of our streets and town, by setting out shade trees. Care should be taken in planting to box the trees properly, so as to protect them from cattle. Last season quite a number were set out, but many of them perished for want of proper protection.[10]

John Foley, however, was defeated the following year. By 1881, James Henry was the reeve. It was during that year that Orangeville became the county seat, attracting new county officials and other professionals into town. Orangeville now had a seat and vote on the new county council.

In 1882, a decision was made to erect a new two-storey high school. It, too, was born in the usual welter of controversy one has come to expect around the erection of public buildings in Orangeville. But perhaps the school board got off easier than some others, as no concerted attack seems to have been mounted against the decisions made by members of the town committee. After all, in that same year, the

A rare interior photo of the Orangeville Town Council in progress in 1896. To the left in the photograph, on the opposite side of the bar to the council, are the representatives of the local press there to record the proceedings of the meeting. Henry Endacott was mayor at the time.

post office site controversy was well underway, as was the controversy over building the town bell tower on the fire hall. Everyone apparently acknowledged the need for a new high school in Orangeville, yet it would be two years or more before plans, site discussions and tenders could be agreed upon. Orangeville High School opened in 1884.

In 1885, Orangeville shifted from coal oil lamps to electric lighting for the illumination of the streets. The Orangeville Electric Light Co. had erected a plant to supply lighting for twelve street lights on central Broadway and shortly afterwards for a few stores. They burned sawdust from the casket factory to generate the power.

William L. Walsh, a noted lawyer, was the mayor in 1890, followed by Johnston Lindsay for 1892–93. In 1893 Orangeville Bylaw #396 was passed, stating, "The town constable or other person duly authorized may from time to time enter the shop or premises of any person in which bread shall be kept for sale and there inspect the bread and seize and take away any bread which shall be of bad quality or under blight."[11]

It was during 1894, when William T. Bailey was mayor, that the proposed waterworks system, which had originally been used for fire protection, was changed to supply drinking water to the residents. Some of the wells in town were proving unfit for human use. The matter was discussed in council, and several months were taken to decide the best place for the well and reservoir. After several properties were inspected and the water tested, the McKinney farm of West Broadway was chosen as the site. Mayor Bailey and the council called for tenders, and the construction contract was awarded to Shields & Gowanlock whose bid was $39,499. The clerk was authorized to advertise debentures for $45,000, which were completely sold in a week. Some of the citizens disagreed on the location because of its nearness to the Greenwood Cemetery, but it was proven that steps would be taken to prevent any contamination from the graves.

A succession of mayors were elected in the years that followed. Henry Endacott, one of the town's largest dry goods merchants and whose store was in the block where the Canadian Imperial Bank of Commerce is now located, was the next to be elected mayor.

After Endacott came Thomas Stevenson, the local druggist, in 1897, followed by William L. Walsh. The next mayor, William Still, a photographer, died of a heart attack while still in office in 1901. The fatal seizure was believed to have been brought on by the shock he received when he was trapped in a fire in T.W. Chapman's store a few days before. He had

The Public Library in Orangeville, supported by funding from Andrew Carnegie, was built during 1907 and 1908 on an L-shaped lot around the then Bank of Commerce. Toronto architect Beaumont Jarvis created the "double front" design.

had considerable municipal experience, having served twelve years on the council as a councillor, deputy reeve, reeve, and finally, the mayor.

Frederick J. Marshall served two terms as mayor in the years of 1902–03. It was in the summer of 1903 that the dispute between the school board and the council took place over the heating system in the public school. Both groups had different ideas on the choice of a furnace and the new system proposed, whether it should be hot air or steam. However, after heated discussions, and a lengthy legal battle, the board installed the system they wanted—steam.

The lovely park surrounding the Town Hall was created on the site of the old cattle-market pens and suggestions for its name were given to the council. Alexandra, the name of King Edward VII's consort was chosen. It was officially christened as such by Miss Hazel Marshall, daughter of the mayor, at its formal opening on August 3, 1903. It is reputed to be the first park in Canada to be named after the new Queen.

Marshall Green, a leading dry goods merchant was proclaimed mayor by acclamation in the year 1904 and again in 1905. Plans were made to build a public library to replace the Mechanics Institute, and a bylaw was passed to purchase a site and to commence the construction at an estimated cost of $15,000. After much debate, it was decided to send a letter to Andrew Carnegie, the American philanthropist,[12] for a donation of $10,000. The financial support came through for the proposed library and an agreement was signed between the Carnegie Foundation and the municipal council.

130 ORANGEVILLE

At this time there also were plans to establish a furniture factory, to be run by Disney & Hertell of Hanover, which would employ fifteen employees year round for at least fifteen years. The town, anxious for industry, passed a bylaw to authorize a loan of $15,000 to the promoters of the proposed Orangeville Furniture Factory. An agreement was signed and the bylaw authorizing $15,000 payable to the company was passed. Ten thousand was to enable them to buy the site and erect a factory, with the remaining five thousand to be for installing a plant. In return, Disney and Hertell were to have the plant ready to operate on November 1, 1904.

Two years later, Charles R. McKeown, a prominent lawyer, was nominated for mayor and was proclaimed without a contest. The following year, 1907, he was not contested for a second term. However, in 1908, Alex D. McKitrick, editor of *The Orangeville Banner* ran a very successful contest against McKeown and became mayor for a two-year term. Dr. W.H. Riddell, a prominent racing man and veterinarian, succeeded him in 1910, also for a two-year term. During this period J. Dods applied to the council for permission to open a branch of his textile business in the town. He asked for a loan and council approved. In 1913, the brick building was built on Church and Mill streets. For many years this was the town's major industry until 1966 when it closed, after having expanded twice during the Second World War.

Dr. G. Harold Campbell was the mayor from 1914 to 1916. It was during his term that the Hydro-Electric Power Commission introduced their system of lighting to the residents, the illumination of the streets. In former years, the Dufferin Light and Power Company operating from Hornings Mills in Melancthon and the Cataract Electric Company operating downstream on the Credit River in Caledon Township had supplied the town with light. Both companies went out of business with the creation of the Ontario-based company.

Thomas Henderson, a local blacksmith of Second Street, was mayor in the years 1917–18, followed by George O. Lewis (1918–20), then Telford S. Parkinson, a prominent dry goods merchant (1920–21). Thomas S. Hewson, a blacksmith on First Street, came to the role in 1922. During his term, the paving of Broadway began. The next mayor was C.V. Jeffers, a druggist, in 1923–24, then W. Gillespie in 1925, and once again Thomas S. Hewson was returned for a two-year term in the years of 1927–29. During this term as mayor, Tom had most of the streets paved, had new sewers laid, and finished the paving of Broadway.

Municipal History: Getting Things Done

Top, in 1921, Broadway was paved for the first time in 1922, finally eliminating the dust and the mud. A central strip of concrete was laid down the street from John Street to Wellington. The area on both sides for angle parking was still gravel; *bottom*, this photograph of the historic paving of Broadway shows the original storefronts on the Jackson Block of buildings at the corner of Mill Street. Gillespie's Hardware was located in the corner store.

Sometimes the town became involved in various service groups. The first Boy Scouts organization in Orangeville was formed in 1919 and disbanded in 1921. In 1929 it was revived again, this time under the sponsorship of the municipal government. The town fathers apparently believed that the local youth needed clubs and activities to keep them occupied and out of trouble.

James D. Arnott, shoe dealer, became the next mayor in 1930–31, followed by T.S. Parkinson who completed a two-year term from 1932 to 1934. Next came J.R. Hoare, from 1935 to 1936. T.S. Parkinson returned in 1937 and occupied the mayor's chair for five years in succession from 1937 to 1942. Historian Sidney Dickens commented, "He was a good mayor and it seemed that during those years, he was the only one qualified for the job."[13] Richard McCullock, a fuel oil dealer, was a young man for the political scene, but he became very popular in the town. People felt he had modern ideas together with executive ability. After serving on the council in the various offices, he was elected mayor in 1943 and held the position for four years. It was Richard who spearheaded a new crest for the town, with a windmill pictured that never existed in Orangeville's history! Doug Fendley, a florist, succeeded him in 1948, but Richard McCullock, known within the town as 'Dick,' had proved to be an able mayor in the previous council and was returned in the year 1950, to be followed by W.A. Richardson in 1952–54.

It was during the mayoral terms of J.A. "Mac" Maude (1955–62) and Harry Tideman (1962–64) that Orangeville came to life industrially. Several new firms built their factories here, the population expanded and an economic boom resulted. Over a few short years the town changed from what seemed to be a place for retired farmers to a busy, bustling community alive with industries.

An industrial park was opened. New subdivisions were built to house the new citizens coming to work for these firms as well as for the commuters who were willing to drive down the road to Brampton

Boy Scouts were organized in Orangeville by the town council. There was one troop for the entire town.

Municipal History: Getting Things Done 133

to work in order to live in Orangeville. Two of the new industries were Acrow Canada Limited, which opened in the year 1959, and Manning Candy Co. Limited, which built a large factory in 1961 and operated there for three years. In 1964, a manufacturing plant was started by the Polyethylene Bag Co., later purchased and operated as a division of the Union Carbide Corporation. Greening Metal Products opened as well as the McCord Corporation, which had started as a radiator firm in Detroit and had opened its first Canadian plant in Walkerville in 1912. The company chose Orangeville as an ideal town for its operations, and, in 1962, built a large factory and employed many local residents. In 1966 they had a mammoth opening, but unfortunately in April 1967, they closed their doors.

In the early sixties, transplanted urbanite and author Max Braithwaite served on town council bringing a whole new perspective to the council, particularly more modern views of growth and planning. He was one of the first politicians who was not raised locally or working in a local business. The year 1963 was the centennial year, marking the anniversary of the date when Orangeville was incorporated as a village. Harry Tideman had the honour of being the mayor during this historic time, and Orangeville had a celebration that was remembered for many years to come. After two years he was succeeded by Sam Lackey, a painter and decorator and the proprietor of the large department store on Broadway. Although it was still a prosperous period for the town, industry ceased to locate here for a time. The boom had slowed down and Orangeville returned to its normal sedate life.

Sam Lackey provided solid leadership and would have done more for the town had he enjoyed better health. In the memorable year of Canada's Centennial, Arnold Patterson, who had served the community well as the reeve, became the mayor by acclamation. Orangeville, like the rest of Canada celebrated its history throughout the year. In all, Mr. Patterson served a total of 22 years in various capacities as well representing Orangeville at the County of Dufferin as its warden. He had the uncanny ability of representing the needs of urban Orangeville while also understanding the importance of the rural municipalities to the town's economy.

Women finally entered Orangeville municipal politics in the sixties and seventies. The first woman to serve on council was Johanna Malouk (1966–68), followed by Phyllis Clarke (1968–70) and Jean Hamlyn (1970–72). The daycare centre is named in the honour of Mrs. Hamlyn, and Johanna Drive was named after Mrs. Malouk.

In the year 1967, a new public school was erected in response to the rapid growth of the population. Upon completion the school was named Parkinson Centennial Public School to recognize Boris Parkinson's long-term service with the board of education, and in honour of the Centennial year. The first Roman Catholic Separate School, St. Peter's, had been opened in 1961. The town project for the Centennial year was the renovation of the Public Library, which was formally reopened by Mayor Patterson and the town's Centennial Queen—100-year-old Mrs. Sophia Rayburn.

In 1968, the employees of Fisher Price Toy Company went on a strike that lasted for several months. The result was that no settlement was reached, and the firm closed its doors, packed its machinery and left town. The town council seemed to always be involved in negotiations to attract and keep industries and would offer tax and water benefits if businesses would locate in the industrial park.

It was in this year that the new St. Timothy's Roman Catholic Church was formally opened for worship by Archbishop Pocock of Toronto. The cost of construction was $125,000. The former church, St. Peter's, which had been erected in 1876 inside the town limits but south of Town Line on John Street, was closed. This location had allowed the church to be in Orangeville yet remain within the Toronto Diocese and to serve its mission, St. Mary's in Brampton.

In the year 1969, a new industry, United Extrusions Limited, makers of plastic tile, was seeking to locate in Orangeville. It was the year when the future of Orangeville seemed uncertain. The Honourable Darcy McKeogh, Minister of Municipal Affairs, had proposed the scheme of Regional Government that April. Had this scheme been instituted, Orangeville would have become a part of the Peel-Halton District, and cut off from the Country of Dufferin. There was much talk both for and against the idea and finally it was decided to postpone the issue to a later date. Discussions about restructuring would surface periodically for many years and still sometimes comes up in political discussions.

The Maxi Taxi, operated by the Georgetown Transportation Co., was the first public bus service, though in a small way, Later it was renamed the Orangeville Bus Service. In the fall of 1969, the giant electrical firm of Westinghouse built a factory on Third Avenue and opened for business. Mayor Gordon Bredin was a chief negotiator for this firm's locating in Orangeville. In 1970, the local paper, *The Orangeville Banner* purchased a lot on the site of the old creamery on Mill and Armstrong streets, and built a new, modern newspaper plant.

Municipal History: Getting Things Done

That year, Victor Large, who had served on the council in the various offices for many years, became the mayor. Under his leadership, a new recreational and sports complex was introduced to replace the old wooden arena that had served the town for almost fifty years. Tenders were let for its erection, and the cost found to be in the range of $100,000. It was later named the Tony Rose Memorial Arena after the manager of the facility who had lost his life in a car accident.

During this period the old Fire Hall that had been a landmark for many years on Mill Street and John, was put up for sale, the bell removed and a new building erected on Dawson Road. The Orangeville Town Hall was renovated with a modern drop ceiling and wood panelling and its interior modernized. This is the same interior that would later be removed to reveal the original splendor of the Town Hall and Opera House. In 1969, office space was rented in the building for the new Dufferin County Board of Education that had been created with the closing of the rural school sections.

The years 1970–82 marked the long reign of Victor Large as mayor. Vic was obviously well liked by everyone in town. A local business-man, he was one of the town's greatest supporters of lacrosse since Dr. Campbell. Vic was on county council when I was hired as curator of the Dufferin County Museum, so he is also obviously a man of good judgement. During that period, Councillor Pat McLeod (1974–85) was instrumental in establishing the Local Architectural Conservation and Advisory Committee (LACAC) and lobbying for the preservation of our historic buildings.

Gordon Courtney was the mayor from 1982–91. Mr. Courtney was a popular quiet man, effective in his role. His wife Jessie was equally famous in my eyes for her lemon pies which were a legend around town.

For six years (1991–97), women took over the running of Orangeville. Mary Rose served as mayor and Janice Gooding repre-sented the town at the County of Dufferin. These were years of unprecedented growth for Orangeville and the accompanying prob-lems were complex. These same women ushered in Theatre Orangeville and the downtown farmers' market as well as many other cultural and social projects.

Citizens of the "old" Orangeville returned to the front. Rob Adams, the son of a local lawyer, was mayor from 1992–2000 and Drew Brown, whose family have lived in the area for four generations, has been mayor since then. In 2005, as part of the heritage projects initi-ated by Mayor Brown, plaques were placed on street signs of streets that were named after former mayors such as Still Court, Fead Street and Walsh Crescent, as a tribute to many of our former government leaders. "It is a town's municipal history that gives the town its direction, right or wrong. These people deserve to be written about and remembered,"[14] said Mayor Brown, when unveiling the project, a very popular one with local residents. For older residents the plaques provides a link to the past, and for new residents the signs give them welcome knowledge about their town's heritage.

I I

BROADWAY: STREET OF DREAMS

IF ORANGEVILLE WERE A BODY, Broadway would be its soul. Broadway was the first street and today is the centre of the town. An unusually wide street, it has wonderful views that combine business, entertainment and opportunities to socialize and be friendly, a place to meet friends and a place to make friends. Over the years Broadway changed from being a dirt path to a street in a town of sidewalks full of inebriated Irish, living life as they had back home. It changed from fronting wooden buildings to being home to more lavish brick structures. It changed from being a quiet main street to becoming the hub of traffic nightmares before the building of the two bypasses. Its growth was inevitable, having been named after Broadway in New York City by Jesse Ketchum the Younger. Likely he dreamed that one day it would be as busy and as popular as its namesake.

Broadway had the lure; it brought business into town and it brought me into town. Broadway was the wide street in the area that reflected a bigger world than the farms that surrounded Orangeville. When I was a kid, I would count the days until I could come in again, to Broadway—the theatres, the stores, the fashions and the fads.

One of the stories told to explain the greater width of Broadway has been that the surveyors had made an error, causing the surveys of Mono and Garafraxa not to meet, and Broadway was widened to make up the difference. Another story is that Orange Lawrence and Jesse Ketchum both decided to give the required width for the street from their respective properties, but chronology indicates that this would have been impossible, as Orange Lawrence gave it its first name—Main Street. I believe that Broadway's width is due to the foresight and planning of Jesse Ketchum, who knew that such a wide

For many people, it was shopping that brought them into town to explore what Broadway had to offer. There was a choice of goods and specialty shops to please everyone's taste—if you had the money. Margaret and James Sanderson's store was located on the south side of the main street, postcard dated 1911.

street would serve a multitude of purposes for a prosperous growing town—the town that he envisioned but never got to see.

The streets north of Broadway that Ketchum laid out on his property follow a neat orderly grid pattern with Broadway as their starting point. The streets to the south were much less rigorously planned and seem to have been created as the need arose. Orange Lawrence also sold lots, but with no apparent plan for streets (a survey was made after most of the south side of Broadway was sold off). One problem was that the creek kept getting in the way. Bridges were expensive to build and to maintain, and in the early years frequent flooding washed the wooden structures out on a regular basis. While commercial activity spread out up First Street and down Mill Street, the heart of the town was always Broadway. Its generous width made it easy for travel and parking teams of horses. The north side of Broadway is the sunny side and the businesses there tended to be the shops and more specialty stores. The south side, made shady by the tall buildings that developed, tended to attract the businesses of the rural consumer such as feed and grain stores and the larger hotels and their liveries. The last farm business to survive was Marshall's Harness Store that operated from the early 1920s until the 1970s.

The early buildings, all of wood, were always at risk of fire. In October of 1873, a fire burned down many along the south side of Broadway.

Broadway: Street of Dreams 139

But the businessmen were energetic and resourceful and immediately started to replace them with beautiful brick Victorian-style stores, many of which remain today. It might be mentioned that it was the same businessmen who, after the fire, were the strongest lobbyists for the creation of the waterworks system.

The section of Orangeville west of First Street and north of Broadway was originally laid out by Jesse Ketchum. The land was purchased as a development site in 1870 by local businessmen James S. Fead (pronounced as 'fade'), and brothers Maitland and D'Alton McCarthy. Fead Street is named after James Fead, who was also a private banker and the local magistrate. Zina Street in that area is named after the McCarthy brothers' mother, Charleszina Hope Manners McCarthy.

The McCarthys have an interesting family history. Maitland opened the first law practice in Orangeville in 1861 and was the town's first mayor in 1873. In 1881, he became the first judge of the newly formed County of Dufferin. Although D'Alton never lived in Orangeville, he represented the Cardwell Riding (Mono, Adjala, Caledon, Albion and Bolton) in federal parliament from 1876–78. In 1896, he left politics while representing North Simcoe over the issue of extending French language rights outside Quebec. He was against any extension. The issue led in the defeat of the Conservative Party in 1896. Faulkner Street was named after Falkner Cornwall Stewart (1832–1897), the brother-in-law of the McCarthy brothers. Stewart operated a general store and was the first warden of Dufferin County in 1881. He had two sons, Maitland and Harry, who were nicknamed "Dime" and "Silver." "Dime" fought in the Boer War, and "Silver," one of the early residents of Vancouver, became a successful miner.

What follows is an extensive excerpt from *The Sun,* printed in 1869. It provides an authentic and colourful "word tour" of early Broadway:

Before completing the pace that carries us forward from the old year to the new, let us cast a retrospective glance, and note the progress our village has made, in the way of new buildings, during the year of 1869…for there are certainly many speculating eyes turned to the principal village on the TG&B Railway line that have never yet seen the limits of our incorporation, and to those we can safely vouch that few villages in the Province have, within the same space of time, multiplied their buildings, public and private, more rapidly than has the flourishing village of Orangeville, and still the prospect brightens.

...so, let us go westward on the north side of Broadway, and immediately our attention is arrested by a newly painted sign board, bearing the very cosmopolitan inscription of "The People's Store." You notice it projects from a most substantial two-storey red brick building, 22 by 55, recently competed and fitted up and is a trim and attractive place of business, costing upwards of $1,500. Elbowing our way further westward, we pass several buildings, remodelled, tastefully fitted up, and occupied as stores, and find ourselves on the corner of Broadway and First streets, confronting that magnificent red and white brick structure on the verge of completion erected by Messrs. Chisholm, Elliot & Green, of Brampton and Orangeville, and from the large embossed letters on the ornamental segment ,which crests the coping of its walls, we are reminded that it shall henceforth be known as the "Commercial Block"—a very appropriate inscription, for every outline of this fine edifice has the unmistakable dash of a place of business; this building has a frontage on First St., of 45 feet, and on Broadway of 65 feet, and is three storeys in height, with flat, galvanized iron roof. The ground floor is divided into two splendidly finished stores, with offices and fire-proof vaults in the rear; the second storey is elaborately finished off, conveniently laid out, furnished with vaults, and admirably adapted for offices, etc. and accessible by front entrance and commodious stairway; the third and upper storey is divided for warerooms or public purposes. It cost upwards of $7,000...

A little further west you notice the hydra-gabled frame cottage, built by Mr. Armstrong, and the brick on the opposite side of the street is a substantial wagon and blacksmith shop. Still westward, is the new residence of Dr. Carbert, a two-storey frame, 22 by 36, with back kitchen, etc., and immediately beyond, with placid modesty, Mr. J.S. Fead has planted his cottage, a 24 by 30 frame rough-cast. The storey-and-a-half red brick dwelling opposite was built by the Rev. Lewis, of Mono, and is a very comfortable tenement, and yonder on the hill is a neat frame, storey-and-a-half dwelling, T–shaped, with steep roof, the property of Rev. R.L. Tucker, of Bath, beyond the precincts of which we will not ask you to strain your visionary powers; but make a right half-face, and accompany us up First St., where, on our left, is the double brick building, erected two years ago by Mr. Wilcox.... The "smoke that so gracefully curls" up First Avenue, is from a neat brick cottage, 24 by 30, built by Mr. Buyers, and here, under the shade of this

St. Mark's Anglican Church on First Avenue, pictured here, is the third church built for the congregation. The first was a log building on Purple Hill. The second was a stone building on the present site, followed by this brick building. The spire, however, was altered when it blew down in a windstorm at the turn of the century. The image of a man on top of the spire was put there by overprinting the photograph, a popular photographic trick of the time. The man shown was the builder of the church. The photo would be from the early 1870s.

stately primitive Methodist Church, is a very tidy tenement, 18 by 24, built by Mr. L. Brown.

Another right half-face, and we turn down First Avenue, where the congregation of St. Mark's is vigorously battling with the late season in rearing a magnificent red brick church, with white brick abutments in the modern Gothic style; the nave is 35 × 55, chancel 20 × 35, and vestry 12 × 14; it has a spacious basement story the full size of the building. The windows are of stained glass, from the manufactory of the famous McCausland of Toronto; it will be impossible to complete the spire this season, which will be over 120 feet in height, but when completed will be an ornament, and credit to our village. This building will cost upwards of $7,000. The design is by Mr. Robinson of London, Ontario.

Looking north westerly towards Third Avenue, there is a handsome brick cottage, 25 × 36, built by Mr. Stevenson, and a large frame Gothic residence by Mr. Milloy. On the corner of Second Street and Second Avenue, Mr. Nicholson, and Mr. Dunbar have each added a new wing to their residences, and Mr. Menry has built a large double tenement costing upwards of $700. Let us double Dr. Hewat's corner back towards Broadway, and steering to the left, we see the large brick belongings to Mrs. Galbraith, and which was two years ago partly demolished by fire, raising itself up as in an entirely new dress, having undergone a complete repair from the flat roof to a pitch roof, the various tenements entirely fitted up a-fresh at an expense of over $1,300. The bevy of workmen you see in the distance are just finishing up the construction of an immense new water wheel for Mr. John Parsons' sawmill, which will cost something in the neighbourhood of $500.

We will cross Broadway and walk up the south side by the "Paisley House." This very fine three-storey hotel with its double row of front balconies, was commenced last season, and is now completely finished from cellar to attic in the very latest style, and comprises all the most modern improvements, conveniences and appliances necessary for the comfort and entertainment of the travelling public, or boarder. Besides the Bar-room, which is large an handsomely furnished, it contains on its first flat a very large dining hall, public sitting room, and commercial men's sample room. The second flat has two elegantly furnished parlours, and with the third flat, contains 24 bedrooms. The rows of stables and sheds in the yard, many of them built this season, look like a new settlement.[1]

Early life along Broadway however was not always pleasant for every one. The conflict between the fun loving and the more serious minded often reared its head. Such is evident in a letter to *The Sun* in 1875, signed simply by "Merchant":

Sir, Will you lend your valuable assistance towards doing away with a dangerous nuisance, and one that would not be tolerated in any other well regulated town. I allude to the practice of training and racing trotting horses through the main streets at a time when they are frequented by passengers. No good can possibly result to the community by permitting these petty sportsmen, with their sorry horses and skeleton cutters, to openly violate the law by driving without bells, at full speed, two and three abreast, through streets devoted to trade and business traffic and the danger to young children and old people is most imminent. Should this practice be allowed to continue, any accident happen to me

Broadway: Street of Dreams

Orangeville held monthly cattle markets or fair days starting in 1848. The trading took place on the main street as this photograph from 1890 shows. The popular straw hats of the period were often made at home using flattened wheat straw.

or mine, I give warning that I will take the law into my own hands, and shoot dead the horse that has been driven to the commission of the injury."[2]

Another resident also wrote to complain, "We direct the attention of our City Fathers to the number of half-starved cows which infest our streets, to the greatest annoyance of farmers and others visiting the place. A farmer cannot leave his load of grain five minutes without having some half a dozen short horns nibbling at his bags. If the people of Orangeville will keep cows, they ought to feed them at home and not allow them to go about poaching a chew."[3] It was a happy day in town when finally, in 1863, a bylaw was passed to prohibit cows and pigs from running on the streets. There was no mention of the hens.

And the unpleasantness of Broadway was not always restricted to the emotions; sometimes it even extended to the nose. A report appears in 1869, "An intolerable nuisance exists on Broadway, to which we would direct the attention of our town fathers. Drains crop out at different points along the street, emptying the nauseous slush and filth of cellars in pools which emit sickly and disagreeable exhalations. If cellars are to be drained on the street, surely the drains should be carried under cover beyond the fronts of residences."[4]

But for all its trouble, animals and bad smells, Broadway has also always been a place of fun. To this very day, when you want to celebrate in Orangeville, the first thing done is to close down Broadway. "A trained bear was exhibited on Broadway, last Wednesday, by two Frenchmen. Bruin appeared to comprehend his masters' orders thoroughly, and walked, danced, tumbled, and even mimicked the girl of the period at their bidding. The motley crowd who witnessed the performance, rewarded bruin and his masters with a few coppers at the close of the entertainment. The worthy trio started for Mono Mills in the evening, there to repeat their free exhibition."[5] But such fun can also cause trouble on the main street of town, "A company of strollers with bugles and dancing bears passed through Orangeville the other day. K. Chisholm and Co.'s horse became frightened and ran away, breaking the wagon in pieces. All such nomads should be arrested."[6]

Even in my lifetime there is always talk about the widening of Broadway or the paving of Broadway or of the snow on Broadway. Orangeville's main street has consistently received the attention of council who seek ways to change it or improve it. How to deal with traffic frequently has been a topic of discussion. A novel way of traffic control at the turn of the century was two amber lights set on short standards in the pavement of Broadway, one near John Street and one near Second Street. In the good old days, they divided horse-and-buggy traffic into two lanes. The young swells of the day would take their fast horses up and down the main street around the lights to show off before heading out of town. In the early 1900s, this constituted "fast driving."

The first electric lights in Orangeville were on Broadway. There is nothing more appealing than Orangeville "all lit up." Improvements for lighting were constantly being made. In 1929, "new lights, which have been placed along both sides of Broadway, were turned on for the first time one night last week. To say that our citizens are pleased with the improvement is putting the matter mildly. They brighten Broadway up wonderfully. When the lamps are lighted on both sides of the highway the street is just as light as in daytime. The globes are white, quite large and give off a soft, white glow, that lights the street thoroughly and yet is not dazzling. When painted, the standards, which are of the ornamental type, will present quite a pleasing appearance and will be a pronounced improvement on the old wooden poles... The members of the local Hydro Commission have shown good judgement in their selection of standards and lamps. The work of the Commission has gone far to beautify Broadway and make it one of the finest thoroughfares in the province."[7] Incidentally, when replaced in the 1970s, these light standards were purchased by a local ski resort and other private citizens. Today, they light the driveway entrances to the Hockley Valley Resort in the Hockley Valley and Mulberry Farm Antiques at Mono Mills.

It is time to take another stroll down Broadway, but instead of looking at the buildings as presented in the 1869 "word" tour, this early 1900s "tour" will introduce many of the local businesses. Anyone who reminisces about the main street where they lived always remember the merchants who sold their wares along the sidewalks. Each owner had his character and history. Each clerk had a story:

At the turn of the century, Broadway, our proud main street, is the heart of the business and mercantile centre of Orangeville. During the years, it has undergone so many changes. Few are living today who remember the original setting. Wooden buildings and log houses have given place to the fine brick, stone and roughcast houses of today. From the time of Robert Galbraith, the first merchant who conducted a business, to the fine chain of stores of various commodities that comprises the business mart of the present time. Even in the last twenty years, many new storefronts and modern buildings have been erected. The purpose of this article is to recall some of these early business ventures and to give a graphic description of the proprietors and their early beginnings.

W.C. Dahl & Co.

Although this business was not established until 1890, it became one of the most prominent in its line. Its patronage extended the limits of the community. The value and quality of their dress goods attracted many from the rural areas, and they did business on a large scale. W.C. Dahl, its proprietor, was born in the village of Erin, coming to Orangeville in 1881 to enter the employ of Bookless & Reid, General Merchants. After ten years in their employ, he purchased the business that had become then Bookless & Haley, dress goods and clothing merchants. The business prospered to the extent that in 1895, he bought the bankrupt stock of Crozier and Fleming dry goods at 55 cents on the dollar, together with its book accounts. In addition to the fine store in the Ketchum Block, he branched out and had stores in Grand Valley and his hometown of Erin. In order to have complete co-operation among the employees of the three stores, he had a desire to get them acquainted. He invited them to a gathering at his fine home on West Broadway, which included a supper, followed by parlour entertainment. After this event, the members of the [Orangeville] staff would not meet as strangers to the out-of-town staff, and the business would benefit.

In 1898, the firm, then known as Dahl Brothers, dissolved partnership leaving W.C. Dahl to carry on the business alone. A year later, owing to ill health, he was forced to retire. Armitage & Company of Lindsay purchased the business at the rate of 80 cents on the dollar. W.C. Dahl succumbed to his illness at his lovely home on West Broadway on August 20, 1899. In private life he was a valued member of the Canadian Order of Foresters, The Ancient Order of United Workman and The Harris Lodge. No. 216, G.R.C. and A.F.AM.

Ritchie Brothers

A year after W.C. Dahl & Co. had been purchased by Armitage & Co., who operated the store and built up a large business, the firm was sold to Ritchie Brothers. Messrs. F.W. and E.W. Ritchie were local men and well known, both had spent their boyhood days here and attended local schools. They were the sons of R.W. Ritchie, who for many years lived on First Street. On Wednesday, June 20, 1900, Ritchie Brothers made their debut on Broadway at the corner of Mill Street with a gigantic and financially successful sale. The store, later operating under the name of "The Maple Leaf Store," prospered and after six years they opened a similar one in Dundalk with F.W. Ritchie in charge. This store also prospered and became one of the better class stores in the village. However, F.W. Ritchie suffered from ill health. His mother arrived in Dundalk to carry on business and to nurse her son. In 1906 he suffered a severe attack of quinsy, and although he put up a great fight for his life, death became the victor. After his death the store was managed by his brother Harry.

Thompson Brothers

Since the day of opening their doors to the general public in 1894 with a sale, they carried a good line of dry goods and ready-made clothes. This firm enjoyed a very good business and were widely known for the best values in clothing. Not only did the firm serve the populace of Orangeville, but also had branch stores in Mount Forest and Durham.

In 1903, they enlarged the store by adding millinery and a women's wear section, a large stock of groceries and a well-lighted carpet room. This made it the largest store in town at the time. John Thompson became one of the area's best known and most successful businessman. He was a senior partner in the firm that he and his brother conducted. Born near Bowmanville in Durham County on March 23, 1860, he spent his early years and received his education there. His business career began when in 1883, he went to the village of Alliston. For six years he conducted a very successful business and it was during this period that he met Miss E.A. Reilly and made her his wife.

Coming to Orangeville in 1894, he, with his brother, founded the firm of Thompson Brothers. It was in 1896 that Thompson Brothers fell victim to the tragic fire that also consumed a number of other stores on Broadway. They suffered a loss of $4,000 to the store and its contents. In the social life of the Town, John Thompson took a great interest. His contribution to the business life of the community was unequalled. However, in 1899 he was claimed by the Grim Reaper, and was laid to rest with so many distinguished men in the pretty Forest Lawn Cemetery.

The business of Thompson Brothers then passed into the hands of his brother Edward, who operated under the name of Ed Thompson and Company. For many months during the illness of his brother John, Ed had managed the store successfully. Ed Thompson built a new store on Broadway after the fire. It was a two-storey building, 25 feet by 23 feet, with a basement and a spacious upstairs. Built of stone, it had a front of cut stone, supported by two iron pillars. It was a very handsome building. At the same time he built a fine brick house next to the store and a stone house on Wellington Street. In 1902, the business was sold to D.H. McBride and Emerson Gillespie, who were then employees of Marshall Green & Co., dry goods and millinery merchants. They assumed control of the store in August 1902.

Marshall Green & Co.
For many years, Orangeville's largest dress and dry goods store was on the corner of Broadway and First Street. Marshall Green & Co. started in business in 1880 on Broadway. Eight years later this firm moved into a large store on the south side of Broadway, formerly the home of Gilchrist & Kent, where they did a large business for fifteen years. In 1903, the store was sold, forcing them to move.

In 1904, Marshall Green bought the business block on Broadway and First Street from H. Turner of Saskatoon. The price was in the neighbourhood of $5,000. The building, at this time, was made into two stores. One was occupied by F.J. Lawson, a dealer in boots and shoes and the other by William Erskine, a druggist. As these merchants had a lease, Marshall Green carried on the business in a large store he rented on south Broadway, opposite First Street.

Shortly before 8 o'clock one morning a fire was discovered in the store. The fire was coming from a stairway on the east side of the building and was leading from the rear of the store. It happened that at this time two of the clerks arrived to open up the place for the day's business. They fought the flames until the firemen came and for forty minutes they battled the blaze. For a time it seemed the whole store would be enveloped, but it was saved, although the stock was severely damaged by the smoke and water. Mr. Charles King who lived in the apartment above, suffered a total loss. His home was gutted. After the fire, the store was cleared out and the stock moved across the street to a store that had just been vacated by George Endacott. Marshall Green had his stock covered by $10,000 fire insurance, but Charlie King had no insurance and lost everything.

When the firm moved to the new premises on First Street and Broadway, the name had been changed to Green, McBride & Co. The old firm had dissolved and D.H. McBride, who had formerly been a partner in the firm of McBride & Gillespie, was made a full partner of Marshall Green. Orangeville now had two large stores; Green & McBride on the east, and Henry Endacott on the west. Each on opposite corners of First Street.

Sometime later, McBride retired and for many years the firm reverted to the old name, Marshall Green and Co. Mr. Green, in addition to his large business interests, was very active in municipal politics. He was elected by acclamation in 1904–05 as the Mayor of the Town. At this time the question of building the new Public Library was being discussed by both the Council and the general public. He fought very vigorously for it's erection. With the death of Marshall Green, the business was sold out. The building was outfitted for a supermarket by the Great Atlantic and Pacific Tea Company.

Henry Endacott & Co.
The firm of T.W. Chapman general store that had done business on Broadway for a number of years, was purchased by Henry Endacott in 1898. Business then increased and it was evident that the firm had need of larger premises. A large store that had been occupied by K. Chisholm had become vacant. The premises, which were easily the

largest in the area were on the corner of Broadway and First Street. It had been built in 1867 by Chisholm & Co., on a lot they purchased from McCarthy & Fead, who had been two prominent lawyers, for the sum of $2,200. Commanding one of the best business sections of the Town, it then became the new address for the Endacott firm.

Henry Endacott was a shrewd businessman, although his other interests were in the service of community municipal affairs, he served in the various offices of the council and in 1896 was elected as mayor. A year later he was appointed to the Board of Health for a term of three years. He made an unsuccessful bid for the position of sheriff of the county in 1906. However, after the death of Sheriff Thomas Bowles, the first sheriff, Endacott was appointed the sheriff of the county in 1913 and held the position until his death in 1943.

After Henry Endacott retired from business, the store was removed and out-fitted for the Bank of Hamilton.

Ernie Daniels, Jeweller
Ernie Daniels, the popular Jeweller in the small store near the Post Office. Ernie started in Orangeville in 1890 and at the age of 23 bought the store and stock of $800. He said at the time that he had only 15 cents left in his pocket, however, he had many good friends in the Town and his business prospered. Sixteen years later he married Miss Minnie Morrow, a well-known Orangeville lass. They made their home on Zina Street.

In 1848, Mill Street ran from Main Street (now Broadway) to Jull's Mill on the Mill Square. From the Mill Square it ran south to Town Line and was named James Street. Several businesses lined the street and, with the coming of the railway, a number of shops and hotels appeared at the south end. The entire street was named Mill Street around 1880, photograph taken circa 1910.

150   ORANGEVILLE

He set up his business in an office that had once been occupied by W.T. Bailey in 1886. His business was in the Pattulo Block on West Broadway. It consisted of a watch-repair service and a stock of jewellery. He was very much in the public eye for his part in the minstrel shows that were very popular in those early days. Many were held in the Opera House. It seems that Ernie, though a great entertainer, was quite proficient in the playing of the bones. It was said that he would have been a better entertainer, had he chose that profession, than a jeweller. For fifty-six years he was a successful merchant on Broadway.[8]

To come up to more modern times, excerpts from the writings of Orangeville historian, Alan Rayburn, will continue the tour of a more recent Broadway. Mr. Rayburn wrote feature articles for many years in *The Orangeville Banner* about the history of Orangeville. His columns were eagerly read by residents and former residents alike. Many were kept and glued into scrapbooks for future reference:

From 1929 to 1950, the anchor of Broadway at First Street was the A&P Store. In 1952, the Bank of Toronto built a new structure on the site. Four years later it became known as the Toronto Dominion Bank, through the merger of two of Canada's largest banks. Beside the bank was the D.J. Torrie Clothing Company, where Doug Torrie had located his men's wear shop in 1934. Next came Bob Allen's grocery and butcher shop, but I recall the store better as the electrical supplies shop of Moote and Hodgson. J. Kearns & Son was a dry goods store on Broadway for nearly a century, having been opened in 1876 by John Kearns. In the '40s and '50s, you could count on pleasant service from Will or Graham Kearns.

Jeffers Drug Store was operated by Carson Jeffers and his son, Grant. Carson Jeffers had managed Dr. A.J. Hunter's pharmacy from 1910 to 1912, and then bought the business. Above the drug store, Dr. G.H. Campbell ran his dentistry office from 1902 until his death in 1972. The Chainway was a variety store opened in 1946. Following it came *The Banner* office and George McLean's barber shop. A man of imposing girth, McLean started his tonsorial business in 1902. After that came the drug store of Allan Marshall, which he had bought from N.T. McWilliams in 1927. Following that came Ed Wild's shoe store. Wise's bakery was started by Alf and Jimmy Wise. After they died, it was operated by Jim Meek. I

Broadway: Street of Dreams 151

In the late 1930s, chain stores started to appear in Orangeville. Atlantic and Pacific Grocers (A & P) occupied this First Street corner of the Ketchum Block.

have fond memories of Faith Wise, who showed a strong interest in the town's young people while selling fresh baked loaves of bread.

Next came Bill Irvine's jewellery store, which ran from 1898 to 1953, when he sold to Don Gibson, Adjacent to it was Harry Shiff's Fashion Wear dress shop. Merve Henry opened his confectionery in 1908, and ran it until 1954, when he sold to Harold Reid.

The Dominion Store was managed by Maurice Davidson in the '40s. For over a century, Sproule's Drug Store has been the site of a pharmacy. In the early '40s, it was known as Weaver's Drug Store, and was operated by Herb and Mabel Brooks. In 1944, it was acquired by the popular and pleasant Albert Dunn. Harvey Curry was a partner of Fred Falconer from 1919 to 1932, and later operated Curry's Hardware with his son Lloyd.

Next was the small tailor shop of Alden McGowan, who ran his business from 1929 to 1957. From 1914 to 1956, Mrs. T.S. Parkinson ran a ladies-wear shop on Broadway. Until 1941, James A. Arnott had a shoe store on Broadway next to Parkinson's store. Morley McLean then operated an electrical supply shop there, and later ran a snack bar and bus terminal at the site. A.J. Grigg opened the popular Grigg's Department Store, a 5 and 10 variety store in 1920. I have a clear memory of Miss Mae Young, the rather stern manager of the popular store and the store's bright red front.

The next building housed the Bank of Toronto until 1952. It then became the IGA store of Veryle White and Keith Hunter in 1952. Norman Frampton opened the Canadian Tire store on Broadway in 1944. Adjacent to it were Ken Alexander's Haberdashery and the small fruit stores of Sam Merlina and Jimmy Cancilla. Russell Morrow bought the jewellery business of A.M. Harkness in 1914, moved it to Harry Shaw's store circa 1952 and operated it until 1954, when it was taken over by his sons, Bill and Myr. After that came Harry Klappis' Arcadia Sweets.... The next store was Dalton Patterson and Sons furniture store, where Dalton and his sons, Arnold and Don, catered to the home furnishing needs of a large area surrounding the town.

Next was Don Watt's feed supply store. Following that came Hughes and Norris Men's Wear, which was run by Norris Hughes. After A.H. Woodland's licensing and real estate office was the very popular Three Star Inn, which was run for many years by Walter

The Dominion Store created a sensation when it introduced self-serve grocery shopping to Orangeville in the 1940s. The company renovated a store on central Broadway, under the tenure of the manager, Maurice Davidson.

Smith, and then by Frank Island, followed by Albert Thompson. The next two stores were W.C. McMillan's ladies wear shop and Charlie Reid's drug store. Then came Maher's Shoes, operated by Ernie Gray. Finally, there was the Superior Store, later called Carload Food Market, where the happy Scot, Bill Stirton, was the butcher, and the austere Carm Davison was the grocer.[9]

Broadway is a street of dreams in more places than New York. Orangeville's main street continues to be the one that lures residents and tourists downtown.

The farms that surround Orangeville are fewer in number but prosperous. Replacing the farmers is a population of permanent urban refugees, and part-time residents that locally are called "weekenders." The surrounding hills have attracted residents who appreciate not only the Orangeville and area's arts and culture scene but are also very interested in preserving local heritage and rural customs. Recently there have been many new businesses opening on Broadway for an upscale market. The owners are carefully renovating the buildings, bringing back their Victorian beauty and adding some modern panache. Broadway has also developed several fine restaurants such as The Bluebird Café that has been in business for many years and Sherri Irwin, the owner, has the biggest and best smile on Broadway. The 199 Restaurant produces a fine menu that rivals any city restaurant but in typical Orangeville style, the owner Rodney Hough, never turns anyone away based on dress. One might be surprised at the number of rich and famous spotted there. The owners of both these restaurants were raised in Dufferin County and both of them remind me of the stories told of the hosts of the dozen hotels that once stood along Broadway.

The Mocha Berry Coffee Shop is one of Broadway's favourite meet and greet spot and is known for its friendliness. One of the owners is a descendant of Judge Walter T. Robb, who was Dufferin County's judge for many years, keeping the town and county in strict moral form, as well as being chair of the Ontario Liquor Licensing Board of the time. The area has a healthy mix of people who were born and raised here and people who have chosen to make the area their community.

Broadway with its wide vistas still attracts the crowds in Orangeville and will continue to do so long after we are unable to take these tours together along its sidewalk.

12

LANDMARKS IN TOWN

ORANGEVILLE, LIKE ANY TOWN, HAS had buildings that represent its heritage, some because of architectural style, some because of the people who lived in or used them and some because of events that happened within their walls. The effects of time and change often render some buildings useless, while others are restored or retrofitted for new uses. Some buildings have disappeared and others have remained in place. Orangeville has few architectural traces of our pioneer period, but many of the Victorian commercial buildings and homes still stand proudly.

Unfortunately, however, too many structures have been lost to progress. As early as 1864, a local resident, Robert Huston, a local Purple Hill brickmaker, placed and ad in the local paper, "WAR PROCLAIMED AGAINST LOG HOUSES, farmers, pull down your log shanties, the subscriber will sell brick at three dollars and a half per thousand. He will also sell large quantities of brick for cash, or 2 years credit, on approved endorsed notes."[1]

As noted, many of our important architectural landmarks have disappeared. Among the more notable ones are the original cut-stone Post Office that was constructed in 1880, The Grand Central Hotel, the old CIBC building and Jull's Stone Mill constructed 1857. The town still has the original date stone that was above the main door of the mill. It has been stored at the public works yard for over ten years! The Grand Central Hotel was erected in 1876 and for years was considered by travellers to be one of the best hotels in the province. Allowed to deteriorate, it was demolished in 1992. (Its immediate past as a strip club possibly hastened it demise.) The Post Office was torn down in 1962 and the CIBC building was lost circa 1984 during the

The home of Dr. William Hewat, Orangeville's first doctor and second postmaster. It was built in the late 1850s by J.M. Smith as an escape to the suburbs. It was later Orangeville's first bank. The house, on the corner of First Avenue and Second Street, is still in use. This drawing is from an early Wellington County atlas.

push for modernization by large corporations during the boom of the 1970s. These decisions to demolish were made in corporation headquarters by people outside of our town, and thus beyond the control of the local people.

However, instead of concentrating on lost buildings that can only be remembered by older residents and will never be seen by our new residents, here is a little history on some of the wonderful buildings that remain. Orangeville has always been a great town for walking tours. The historic districts, both commercial and residential, are located on tree-lined streets and have a wonderful mix of architecture. Look up at some of the detailing on the Victorian homes and notice the craftsmanship of some of the older stone buildings that remain. Take a walk down a quiet alley and take in the backyards. Orangeville's history can be accessed easily by getting out of your car, putting on your runners and enjoying the town's beauty—street by street and building by building.

Lawrence/Reid House 1856
One of the last reminders of the town founder, Orange Lawrence, is the last house he lived in and the place where he died. Located at 8 John Street, it is hard to recognize its age under the existing more modern covering. The house is designated under the Ontario Heritage

Act. It is not known if it was built by Mr. Lawrence, but it is known he and his wife Sarah were living there by 1856. The building, one-and-a-half storeys high, has always been used as a residence. The structure behind the house, now a residence, was a Methodist Church built in the Lawrence's backyard in 1867. Across the corner, the residences of two of his children still exist as well. The one on the corner of John and Little York, built circa 1858, was home to John Reid and Rhoda Lawrence. A little further down Little York on the north side, is the small cottage where Thomas Jull and Mary Lawrence lived. This street corner is still rich in built history.

Greystones Restaurant 1854
This stone building was constructed at the corner of Third Street and Broadway around 1854. It, too, has a connection with Orange Lawrence as he once operated a tavern here, but gave it up to go back to general storekeeping. Through the years, there has been little alteration to the building and the stones in the building are a match to those found in nearby Mill Creek. In 1920s, the addition to the end was used as a skate-sharpening shop, and, in the 1960s, you could go there to have your fortune told. This is probably the most well-known historic site in the town.

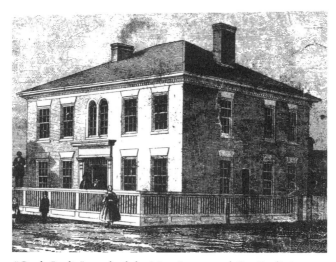

"Castle Leslie" was built by Mary Legate and Guy Leslie in 1858 in classical Irish Georgian style. Leslie was justice of the peace, clerk of the division court and the postmaster during his career in Orangeville. This drawing is from an early Wellington County atlas.

Landmarks in Town

Castle Leslie 1858

The two-storey home of Guy and Mary Leslie was built in 1858 by Mr. Leslie, an Irish immigrant from County Wicklow. He had farmed in Garafraxa then moved to Orangeville. Located at 260 Broadway, the house has a wonderful Georgian-style reminiscent of the old country. This is reputed to have been the first two-storey residence in Orangeville, so the name "Castle" was adopted by the locals.

Brought to Canada by his parents, Leslie had been raised in Garafraxa and was involved with Wellington County politics, including being the clerk of the Ninth Division Court. He was later appointed commissioner of the Queen's Bench, a justice of the peace. He was also postmaster at Reading, before moving to Orangeville.

Guy Leslie became the third postmaster in Orangeville and the first treasurer of the village after it was incorporated in 1863.

Orangeville's First Bank c.1870

There is a small brick house on the southwest corner of Second Street and First Avenue, facing Alexandra Park. It was built by J.M. Smith in 1850. His wife had found life on Broadway too busy, as their store was attached to their home. Their brick cottage would have seemed quite elegant when erected, since most of the buildings at that time were log and some had pea-straw roofs. When one of their children died suddenly, they sold the house to Dr. William Hewat, an Orangeville doctor.

As well as having succeeding Orange Lawrence as postmaster after his untimely death, Dr. Hewat was very involved in municipal affairs and was on the village council when Orangeville incorporated in 1863. He also had a lighter side to his personality. Many early residents in letters to the editor would remember him playing a little melodeon and singing to local children. After his untimely death in 1870, his widow rented out part of the house as a branch of the Merchants Bank. This was Orangeville's first bank, arriving in town the year before the railway.

Colonel Preston House 1870

This home typifies the flights of fancy found in the Queen Anne Revival architectural style, when local builders were indulging in something different and picturesque. Located at 12 Faulkner Street, the house has a turret and verandah and balcony at the front and bow windows at the rear. The decorated gothic windows on the third storey are a modern addition. While the home was built circa 1888 by Alexander and Elizabeth

Dr. Hewat's house as it looks today. Formerly, it was the location of the first bank in Orangeville. *Courtesy of John Woolner, Orangeville.*

McGowan, it is one of the subsequent occupants that deserves our attention—Charlotte Preston, who purchased the house in 1909.

Charlotte was the wife of Colonel J.A.V. Preston, the local registrar of the Supreme Court, registrar of the Surrogate Court and clerk of the County Court of Dufferin. A lawyer, he first practised in Grand Valley. Having joined the Canadian militia when he was only 13 years of age, Colonel Preston served as an officer in the Dundas Regiment in the Riel Rebellion of 1885, and in 1914 was appointed to command the 39th Battalion of the Canadian Expeditionary Force. He went overseas in 1915. His son John F. Preston (later Brigadier) joined him and Mrs. Preston moved to England during the war to be close to her family.

Colonel Preston was a member of the Canadian Military Institute and organized the first Cadet Corps at Orangeville High School in 1907. This fanciful old house is a must see on any walking tour of the town as it and the Park Manor apartments further up the street are the only remnants of the huge homes that once were on what was always called "Quality Hill."

Orangeville Town Hall 1875.
The Orangeville Town Hall, completed in May 1876, is a fine example of a government building of the late nineteenth century. It was designed by a local part-time architect, Mr. F.G. Dunbar, who was responsible for

other early buildings in the town, and elsewhere in Dufferin County. Local craftsmen using local materials, such as the brick from Springbrook Brickyards and stone from a nearby quarry, provided the building skills.

The style, while defying easy classification, can be described as utilitarian but incorporating Georgian elements. The wide entranceways, multiple fenestrations and generously proportioned interior spaces give it a spacious feeling suitable for public use. A low-pitched roof topping decorative polychrome brickwork walls, and raised quoining to provide vertical elements evoke the Georgian era, enhanced by the interesting groupings of windows and chimneys. Other significant details contributing to the building's external appearance are the carved bull's head keystones over the lower floor windows, and the old provincial crest adorning the south doorway.

Colonel J.A.V. Preston from Hastings County practised law in Grand Valley before moving to Orangeville. He held several county legal positions, as well as being active in the local militia.

Historically, the building functioned as both the Public Market and Town Hall. Housing butcher's stalls, council chamber, offices for the mayor and market clerk, and town hall under one roof, it became the focal point for the political and social life of Orangeville. The Opera Hall was upstairs. Today, it is restored and is the home of Theatre Orangeville.

This building was almost demolished in 1964 when councillors agreed to consider the sale of the building to make way for a mammoth Dominion Grocery Store on the side. The plan was to build the grocery store on the first floor and the town hall would rent the second story space. When a public meeting was held the feelings of the townsfolk was quite evident. Local lawyer James Wardlaw stated, "to my way of thinking we are selling our birthright for a mess of pottage."[2] Martin Leskey, who had arrived in Orangeville from Europe agreed stating, "The whole council is selling our souls down the river."[3] The building was renovated in 1993 again after almost falling under the wrecking ball. The renovation and restoration was directed by Carlos Ventin Architects from Simcoe. The Town Hall is now designated under the Ontario Heritage Act.

Forest Lawn Cemetery 1876

One of the most picturesque areas of Orangeville, from my perspective, is Forest Lawn Cemetery. The cemetery has a geography of small rolling hills, reminiscent of the hills of Mono, surrounded on two sides by Island Lake. Wildlife abounds. The sound of the hundreds of birds and the wind in the pines quickly makes it easy to forget that one is still inside the town limits. A small tributary of the Credit meanders by the edge of the grounds, on its short journey from Monora Park to the Credit River. The cemetery follows what is called a park plan, similar to the layout of Central Park in New York City. The roads have wonderful curves that offer views of the lake through the wooded perimeter.

The cemetery was designed by local land surveyor Charles Wheelock in 1876. The property was owned Mary Ketchum and the cemetery was set up as a private company with a board of directors. It was not attached to any religious denomination, and burials from all churches took place there, giving us early Anglican, Catholic, Methodist and Presbyterian family names on the tombstones. When the cemetery first opened in 1876, bodies were relocated here from the older cemeteries in the centre of town. Some of the stones bear death dates that predate the cemetery. From the beginning, it was described as being, "finely situated, being of easy access from town, the ground is high. With the fine situation of this cemetery, the good taste with which it is being laid out, and the improvements contemplated, we feel satisfied that in a few years Forest Lawn will be as beautiful a resting place for the dead as any to be found in this section of the country."[4]

When walking the grounds, one is in very good company. The first stone that is seen upon entering the gates is the Ketchum plot, which lists Jesse Ketchum, his two wives, and eight of his grandchildren. Ketchum's remains were moved here when the cemetery opened. Alexander McLachlan, the poet, rests beneath a stone erected by his admirers in Orangeville. On his tombstone is written, "Untutored child of nature wild with instincts always true. Thy voice did weave songs consecrate to Truth and Liberty." His remains were moved here from Greenwood by the Sons of Scotland. There are several pioneer doctors, such as the two Dr. Henrys, Dr. Frederick Lewis and Dr. R.W. Rooney. And, if, one has been naughty, do be careful while walking by Dufferin County's first judge, Maitland McCarthy, and Dufferin sheriff, Henry Endacott.

A cemetery in a small town such as Orangeville is full of history, each inscription telling the story of someone who has lived in the area, who

Landmarks in Town 161

remains here forever as part of our past. If possible, do read some of the emotional verses that abound on the stones of the older sections. On the headstone of Samuel McClelland, who died at age 21 in 1855, it is written, "Remember man as you pass by, as you are now, so once was I, As I am now so must you be, prepare for death and follow me." Change is inevitable in Orangeville, but this cemetery, one that has been for years well-maintained by the Williams family, remains a tribute to those who have left to make room for us who now call Orangeville home.

Westminster United Church 1879
This is the grandest of the old buildings of Orangeville. It was built at a time when both money and religion were at a peak. Built in 1878, it was designed by C.J. Soule of Guelph. Two years later he would also design the Dufferin County Courthouse. Originally, the building was Zion Presbyterian Church. It has almost every fanciful Victorian Gothic feature known; the spire is sheathed in slate and the original finial is affixed to the front of the building as it kept attracting lightning. The spire, a landmark for the town, can be seen from many points when entering town.

Dufferin County Courthouse and Municipal Building 1881
C.J. Soule of Guelph proposed a brick building with stone facing for the courthouse and stone for the jail, the buildings that were required when Orangeville became the county town for the newly formed County of Dufferin (created in 1881). While the estimated cost was $26,500, the town provided the site for the buildings on Zina Street.

The contract for construction of the courthouse and jail was awarded to the Guelph firm of Dobbie and Grierson, the fee to be $23,000. At the same time, Mr. Soule was hired to superintend the construction, agreeing to inspect the work in progress once a week. Work on the courthouse and jail began in the spring of 1880 and the courthouse was in use by November 1881.

The courtroom itself is a large and spacious room with a high ceiling. One end of the room is dominated by the judge's chair that sits in an apse set into the wall. Opposite the judge and across the room is public seating. Above these seats is a gallery supported by pillars of turned wood with a protective railing of wrought iron. The room is well lit by natural light and has a painted ceiling, decorated with heavy moldings.

Architect Cornelius J. Soule designed this building in 1878 for the Zion Presbyterian congregation, which merged with Bethel Presbyterian Church in 1881 to form St. Andrew's Presbyterian Church. St. Andrew's joined the United Church of Canada in 1925. The town's two United Churches merged in 1948 and chose the name Westminster for the new congregation.

Although the courthouse is essentially a two-storey rectangular block, Soule disguised the predictable interior arrangement with an inventive exterior. On the face of the regular brick exterior, he superimposed three towers that project slightly from the main facade. These tower forms have no corresponding interior space, but they are central to the general massing and exterior effect. The ornamentation is equally flamboyant. Although the courthouse is mainly constructed of red brick, Soule used white brick for a polychromatic effect, employing it for decorative purposes in window heads, ornamental bands and in such places as capitals of red brick pilasters. Soule also used some stone for decoration, albeit sparingly. The main use of stone is around the two front doors and the large round-headed window of the central tower. The building was restored in 1994 by architect Carlos Ventin, and is designated under the Ontario Heritage Act.

King House 1888
The King Bros. Furniture Factory was located on the east side of the corner of Wellington and Armstrong streets strategically close to the source of power from the river. They sold the factory to the Armstrong Foundry in 1894. The building is gone, but the home that they built on Wellington, just south of their factory, remains. It is an unusual house, architecturally different from the other homes in town.

Located at #16–18 Wellington Street, the home was built circa 1888 by one of the brothers, Thomas Theophilus, and his wife, Eleanor. Thomas and Charles King were local builders as well as furniture makers. They

The "Second Empire" style of design owed much to the popularity of Emperor Napoleon III and his empress Eugenie. The rounded bays, long windows and mansard roofs would have been more at home along French boulevards than on Wellington Street in Orangeville. This home was occupied by the King brothers who operated the furniture factory just down the street. *Courtesy of John Woolner, Orangeville.*

would buy a lot, build a home, sell and move on. Over the years they had established a reputation for attention to craftsmanship and fine detail. The King House was built in second empire style, a style introduced in France in the 1870s by the architects of the time of Emperor Napoleon and the Empress Eugenie. The house has the only residential mansard roof in town and unusually large attic windows trimmed with delicate Victorian gingerbread. The windows are all rounded on the second floor and flat on the first. The front bows out no less than three times and the original door was located in the centre bow.

It was build on land that became available when bodies from the cemetery of the Methodist Episcopal churchyard were moved to the larger cemeteries in the 1870s. Certificates from three different judges attested to the fact that all the bodies "that could be discovered" were moved. The old cemetery was surveyed into lots and homes built there, this one being, from my perspective, the most interesting of them all.

Fire Hall 1891
The hall was built by the town in 1891 to replace an earlier fire hall that had been destroyed by fire on May 1, 1891. A two-storey structure with a frontage of 22 feet along Broadway, and a depth of 75 feet along John Street, the fire hall is constructed of brick, featuring white monochrome trim detailing. Originally, the hose tower above the Broadway front was 62 feet high. The hose reels were housed in the front of the building, with the doors opening on Broadway. The engines were housed in the centre, with doors opening on John Street, while the hook and ladder truck was in the rear, with the doors opening out on the south side of the building. The second floor was occupied by the town engineer who used it as a residence.

The fire alarm was the town bell that hung in the tower. It was also used to sound curfew at 9 p.m. for anyone under sixteen. The 2,150 lb. bell was cast at the McNeilly Bros. Foundry in Troy, NY, with the names of the mayor and council engraved on the side.

Over the years the building was modified to meet the changing needs of the fire department, with the west door and several windows being stopped up. However, much of the original architectural detail is intact, except for the section where the Broadway front was altered to accommodate a storefront circa 1982. The tower was also lowered during the 1960s. The bell was removed in the late 1970s and installed in a cairn at Alexandra Park. The upstairs apartment remains, although divided into one large and one small apartment.

Landmarks in Town 165

This building is also representative of a particular period of style of construction in Orangeville. The utilitarian lines of the building are softened by the brick trim, eave brackets and multiple fenestration. Built in a style that might well be dubbed "Orangeville vernacular," it finds an echo in the design elements of many homes in the town built during the late 1880s and 1890s. A familiar part of Orangeville landscape, the building is an anchor clearly delineating the boundary of the old central commercial district.

Alexandra Park 1902
The park and replica bandstand presently behind the Town Hall have a wonderful history. The creation of Alexandra Park and the original bandstand started with the community wanting a concert venue for their own Orangeville Citizens Band. Many small towns in Ontario were presenting public concerts as part of their cultural responsibilities. With all citizens and local councillors jointly recognizing the need, its creation was quick, and tasteful, as the process outlined in the local newspaper recorded:

May 23, 1901: A committee was set up to turn the present cattle ground behind town hall into a park.

May 30, 1901: The council decided to go ahead with the park scheme right away. The old wooden fence that has been an eyesore for so many years at the cattle fairgrounds beside the market will be removed at once and the ground levelled and seeded. A plan has been prepared and every improvement made will be in the line of permanency so that not even a cent will be wasted. A bandstand will be erected on the market square.

July 25, 1901: A pair of fountains will be installed at a cost of $75 each, one to be placed at the market and one at the fire hall. The fountains will be handsome in design and can be used by man, horse and dog.

Sept. 19, 1901: Work on the bandstand is being rushed ahead at breakneck speed so that it would be readiness for the Dufferin Old Boys reception. We understand there is a hitch about lighting the stand.

Oct. 24, 1901: Names suggested for the park include Queen's, Princess, Edward VII, Alexandra, Lorne, Victoria, Minto, Cornwall, Dufferin, York.

April 10, 1902: They are levelling and seeding the park.

May 22, 1902: The first outdoor concert was held in the bandstand.

July 10, 1902: The park presents a melancholy spectacle indeed. Last fall ten evergreen were planted, but they have all yielded up the ghost except two. The place was seeded down a couple of months ago and now there is the thickest crop of weeds you ever saw in your life, but there is very little grass.

Aug 6, 1903: The Dufferin Old Boys Reunion christened the park Alexandra and presented the town with a 100 foot flagpole.[5]

Today, Alexandra Park is a quiet, cool, restful place lined with mature shade trees and home to the cenotaph erected by the County of Dufferin. In summer people are often found there, enjoying a peaceful moment or reading quietly. The replica bandstand is used for weddings and is the site of the very popular Orangeville Jazz and Blues Festival put on each summer by founder Larry Kurtz.

The name of the park has not changed. It is interesting to note that originally only the names of British nobility were suggested. There was no mention of the Newtons who once farmed there in the 1840s, the Presbyterian church that once sat on the site in the 1850s, or the cattle market of the 1870s, or any of the local politicians who had already left their mark on town.

Orangeville Public Library 1908

The Orangeville Public Library as seen today is actually two historic buildings, combined and modernized. The old section of the library was built with a grant from Andrew Carnegie in 1908. It was an open-concept space with lots of high windows for light. Previous to that time the town had had lending libraries and, in 1878, a Mechanics Institute had been created. Mechanics Institutes were administered by the Department of Agriculture and were charged with providing lectures courses and library services to better the intellectual climate of their community. In 1889, they opened their library to the public, not just members.

But it was the town who applied for the Carnegie grant and chose the site at the corner of Mill and Broadway, which had been vacant since the Gordon House hotel had burned in 1903. The architect, Beaumont Jarvis, made good use of the L-shape of the lot, and two entrances were made into the building.

The street corner of the lot was later sold for what became the Bank of Commerce. In the renovation of 1984, local contractor and community supporter, Karl Edelbrock, did an excellent job of incorporating

This Gothic-style home was built by William Morrow on Amanda Street circa 1880. Still standing today, it has been renovated a number of times and none of the original fancy features remains.

the two buildings as well as retaining much of the historic character of the building. The library continues to meet the challenges of a modern growing town. In 1998, "the Orangeville Public Library has joined the Internet age with the installation of six computer terminals with access to the World Wide Web. With the world-wide explosion in information technology, libraries today must provide more than just books," said Library Board Chair Sandy Edwards.[6]

Stop and look up at the structure, it still carries the classical air of the turn of the century and you can also still view much of the typical style that Carnegie used to build his libraries.

Dods Knitting Mill 1913

J.M. Dods of Alton was a well-known businessman successfully running mills in the small town. In 1913, he approached Orangeville for a loan of $30,000 to build a knitting mill in the town. It had always been believed that the lack of industry in town kept Orangeville from achieving the aspired-for growth. The town put it to a vote of the residents as to whether this investment should be made. Some 471 residents voted in favour and 15 against. "Several autos were pressed into service by friends of the measure and those who would not or could not hoof it to the polls were given a joy ride to the booths."[7]

The site of the old James A. Mathews' lumberyard at the corner of Church and Mill streets was chosen for the factory. The construction of the impressive three-storey brick building and water tower was finished in less than a year. Mr. Dods insisted that the building be of quality and be seen to be built to last to show that industry was in Orangeville and was here to stay.

On December of 1914, the company received an order for underwear for Canadian soldiers as Canada was gearing up for the First World War. By October of 1915 over 60 employees were working on "drawers" for the war effort. Two additions and an impressive water tower were added as business flourished during the next war. Mr. Dods bought a home at 248 Broadway, but died before he was able to take possession.

This is just a small sample of the architectural treasures and historic landscapes to be found. In the past, Orangeville has been dubbed both "The Town of Homes" and "The Town of Trees." Each of these historic sections have many stories to tell. Take a walk around and discover traces of the past on the streets of Orangeville.

13

JUST FOR FUN

How did "big" town events get started? Was it because of a group of friendly ladies getting together over tea, aware of the need to raise some cash for a noble cause? Or was it just a community's need to celebrate together?

In the early years, entertainment often developed around church gatherings that were open to all, Orange Lodge events also open to all, and political rallies that were restricted to men, as women had not yet achieved suffrage. These events were identified by many names, from soirees and presentations for people to religious messages delivered by travelling lecturers. Food played an important role. Very little happened in town without food, either prepared by the church ladies, or in the case of political events, provided by one of the local hotels. In the 1860s, oysters must have become very much in vogue as they seemed to have been served at every event. There were even church socials dedicated to their consumption followed by a speech or two from someone. Sports clubs were formed almost as soon as the town came into being. It is evident that despite hard work, there was time for socialization and fun.

From the early 1850s the most popular activity in Orangeville was the weekly horse races held every Friday and Saturday on the Queen's Track. This track was located around today's site of McDonald's on Broadway. A straight race course, it ran from a point near the Forest Lawn Cemetery to Broadway. The area was nicknamed "Ketchum Flats" and eventually became the location of the Orangeville Fairgrounds.

The races brought a lively business to town and wagering was hot. Purses ranged from 10 to 50 dollars, a tidy sum in those days. Many local businessmen owned racing horses and names of the horses

Dr. W.H. Riddell was a veterinarian, a town councillor and mayor. He did much to improve the breeding of horses in Ontario. Dave Hogg, a partner in Dr. Riddell's enterprise, holds the halter of one of their horses purchased in the USA. Mr. Hogg operated a coal and fuel business in town.

ranged from Wild Irishman, Yellow Rose, Agitator to Cheltenham Maid. One account shows that while the races were being run on October 28, 1868, the ladies of town held a tea meeting at the Presbyterian Church and discussed the importance of Gospel Ministration. In the evening the church choir entertained until a late hour. One wonders if perhaps the late hour coincided with the end of the racing and thus enabling the ladies to keep an eye on the celebrations of the men, only one block away.

In 1877, racing became a regular feature of the Orangeville Fall Fair. The old track was improved to a half-mile oval track in 1877 on the exhibition grounds. The Orangeville Turf Association was formed and affiliated itself with the American Trotting Association. Now regular races could be held. Admission to the track was set at 25 cents and ladies went in free. For many years racing continued with the Dominion Day Race the most popular, attracting visitors from across Ontario and from United States.

In the 1920–30s, Orangeville horse racing received a boost when local veterinarian, Dr. William H. Riddell, started keeping a racing stable and bred most of the finest trotters in the area. His horses included such notable names as The Bison, Reta R. Riverdale, Peter Dale and Lauderdale. Dr. Riddell drove in his last race at age 70. He was a director of the Canadian Harness Racing Association and close friend of the

Just for Fun   171

Honourable Earl Rowe M.P. Many older horse enthusiasts claim that with his superior breeding stock and by organizing quality race meets, Dr. Riddell single handedly was responsible for saving harness racing in Ontario at a time when racing had become unpopular across the province.

Political gatherings have always drawn big crowds and created much conversation in Orangeville. In 1861, there was a political dinner held in honour of the Hon. J.H. Cameron, the Conservative representative from Peel. Over 600 people gathered at the North Wellington Hotel in a structure erected specifically for the event. The gathering started at noon and the speeches and toasts continued until after 7:00 p.m. Promoting the town was foremost in the minds of the local politicians. One toast was for the "Prosperity of Orangeville," which apparently "was drunk with much enthusiasm."[1] Countless political rallies, meetings and nomination meetings have been held since then. Premiers and prime ministers and many others with impressive titles have visited us. An Orangeville tradition was begun in 1861—any excuse for the "Party."

In pioneer days, Queen Victoria was a much-loved monarch in the little town. The Orange Order held the monarch in great reverence, and loyalty to the country formed the backbone of their organization. So it is no surprise that the birthday of the beloved Queen would be a big event:

> The anniversary of Her Majesty's was celebrated with great éclat in Orangeville on Monday last. The weather, though somewhat sultry, was very favourable, and everything combined to render the day as agreeable as possible. By nine o'clock about fifteen hundred men, women and children had assembled on the grounds in the rear of Mr. Graham's Hotel. The Orangeville Brass Band marched to the grounds, where they performed several field and company movements with great precision, despite a little confusion being caused by the commanding officer giving the wrong directions. In the afternoon the single and married members of the Orangeville club played a friendly game of cricket. There were hurdles, stands and other jumps for men and boys, as well as other foot races. The entries were numerous and the competition heated. The most amusing events were the wheelbarrow and sack races, especially when the contestants were blindfolded. In the evening there was an imposing torchlight procession and a display of fireworks. The brass band headed the procession playing loyal and inspiring renderings to the beloved

Monarch. The amusements of the day ended a half past nine o'clock, by the ascension of two illuminated air balloons. The best order prevailed throughout the day, and all appeared to take a lively interest in contributing to the general rejoicing.[2]

Thus, the Orangeville tradition continued, this time being, "just" any excuse for a party.

The year 1863 must have been a great one for the residents of town and the surrounding area. Later the same fall as the celebration for Queen Victoria was held, a circus came to town, announced by a quarter-page ad in *The Sun*. What an event for a population living far from the larger urban centres! Women and children rarely travelled beyond the home except on family affairs, as most of the commerce was handled by men. But a circus! Well, if you can scratch up the cash, it is open for all to have some fun.

Billed as the "New Monster Equescurriculum," the circus was managed by L.B. Lent. He must have liked to invent new words, because our present-day dictionary does not list 'equescurriculum' but, by looking at the advertisement, one can gauge that it was a very impressive affair. An etching shows a group of six men bearing aloft a beautifully posed horse on a large plank of wood; another depicts "Wallace's Troupe of Acting Bears," all of which are dressed in the most dashing apparel as worn a hundred years ago. Some bears are gesticulating at a human being behind a desk, another is boxing with a male opponent, and yet another is courting a lady bear, complete with crinoline and poke bonnet. A Mr. Kerr, dressed like a matador, leans nonchalantly on the hind quarters of his "Educated Sacred Bull" from, so the advertisement reads, "Hindostan." The newspaper reported that, "From the far west came the 'Wonderful Leaping Buffaloes,' which can be seen jumping over a high fence. Professor Langworthy was there with his corps of performing monkeys and dogs, and Joe Pentland, the veritable and inimitable clown, officiated during the Equestrian scenes and the clowning section."[3] Admission was 25 cents with no half prices, and no extra charge for reserved seats. Two performances were given, one at 2:30 p.m. and one at 7:45 p.m. Apparently it was a new class of amusement such as never before seen or attempted by a private enterprise. And the like of it has never been seen in Orangeville since.

That year also saw the creation of the town's first organized sports club, the Cricket Club, formed in April 1863 at Witter's Hotel. The

Just for Fun   173

president was Dr. Hewat, with other officers and committee men being: Francis Irwin, Maitland McCarthy, Thomas Stevenson, F.C. Stewart, David Youmans, F. McAuley, W. Parsons and J. Foster. Their first games were played on the newly created fairgrounds. This was the first of the hundreds of sports clubs that have been formed in Orangeville. Many teams have brought fame to the area, and many people have been brought into town to watch countless games of sport. They were Orangeville's first tourists.

For those who wished to join more intellectual organizations, these were formed throughout the years as well. A Mechanics Institute and Reading Room was opened in 1864, with the public meetings to discuss current issues held in Bell's Hotel. The Mechanics Institute Board consisted of local businessmen, not teachers or ministers as one might have expected. It was believed that the Institute would "tend very much to the moral and social improvement of the people of this town.[4] In September 1864, a debating society was formed, which also met in Bell's Hotel. At their meetings, as well as the debating, a regular item of discussion was held on "Municipal Improvement." It is interesting to note, from our modern perspective, that the club was only open to "respectable and intelligent young men."[5]

In May of 1867, a notice was received from Ottawa stating that the First of July, the new birthday of the Dominion of Canada was to be proclaimed a public holiday. On Monday, July 1, 1867:

All the stores and principal places of business were closed and the streets were decked in all the gaiety of festive attire. The weather, though somewhat sultry, was favourable, and the "bone and sinew" of the country, flocked in by every avenue to participate in the sports of the day, and celebrate with loyal hearts and joyous demonstrations, the inauguration of the New Dominion. At 9:00 a.m., the Orangeville Infantry Company, led by Captain [Orange] Lawrence [Jr.], marched to Broadway and fired a "feu de joie" followed by a rifle match against Mono Mills. In the morning there were games of cricket and baseball. In the afternoon, foot races, hurdle jumping, sack and wheelbarrow races, including a wheelbarrow race in which the competitors were blindfolded! There were picnic parties…by the churches and games and amusements until 9:00 p.m. Toward evening, the streets presented a very animated appearance. Men and women who had dallied with time, suddenly thought of their homes, and all kinds of vehicles from the heavy lumber wagon to the easy graceful carriage, were called into requisition to bear them thither. For a time all was bustle and confusion, but at length the crowd melted away.⁶

For those of a more gentle nature, there were more elegant events, "A Honey Social will be given by Mrs. A. Wilcox, on Tuesday evening, the 13th of March, at her residence on First Street, Orangeville, on behalf of the M.E. Church. Teas will be served from 7 to 9. All are cordially invited to attend."⁷

In 1871, the activities available in winter picked up with the opening of a new covered skating rink on Broadway, under the management of Oliver Ketchum, son of Jesse Ketchum. Some of his children were growing up, and like Orange Lawrence's offspring, they were staying in town and making their own mark. Some years later another rink was built on the corner of Church and Mill streets. In 1922, the town was asked to take on the responsibilities of running an arena and they declined. To get one going, a private company formed by local businessmen was set up with a board of management, to erect and manage a skating and box lacrosse arena.

The building, however, fell into financial troubles and it was taken over by the Orangeville Rotary Club in 1938. They returned the arena to financial stability, and, in 1956, they donated it to the town. It

Hockey was the winter rage as Orangeville entered the 20th century. Even the young women of the town got into the act, as this 1897 photograph indicates.

Just for Fun 175

became the home of the Orangeville Figure Skating Club and the Legion's minor hockey program. Many great dances were held upstairs. The building burned down in 1973. One of the last groups to use the facility regularly was the local youth when the town decided to allow the Orangeville Drop-In Centre to locate there. Many kids of my generation have fond memories of the '70s and the centre certainly has its stories to tell as well.

From the late 1860s, with the establishment of Orangeville's early Loyal Orange Lodges, there have been Orange Parades. The King William of the day would be set on top of a white horse and the parade would begin. The lodges usually had drum and fife bands for lively music, and banners and regalia for colour. The whole family would come to town to attend the various events and picnics that accompanied the celebration of the "glorious twelfth":

There have been bigger but no better celebrations of the 12th of July in Orangeville than the demonstration on Tuesday. The rain did not prevent the people from pouring into the town and at noon there must have been at least 4,000 visitors within our gates. The morning was devoted to meeting and welcoming the visiting lodges which made their headquarters at the Town Hall. Quite a crowd come up from the Brampton district [and] the Alton Lodge brought the band of that place with them.

At one o'clock a big parade assembled and the procession marched up Broadway to Faulkner Street to J.C. Reid's grove at the high school. Sam Roney of the Purple Valley Lodge was the most artistic drummer in the procession and could easily give the visitors a number of pointers on how to do the trick. The Laurel fife and drum band still improves and the boys were liberally applauded on the march. Mr. Graham of the Brampton district was the oldest Orangeman present at over 92.[8]

One of the parent organizations of the annual Orangeville Fall Fair was the Mono Agricultural Society. It had been organized in 1854. Geographically, the membership included all of Mono, Amaranth, the north part of Caledon Township and Garafraxa east of the 14th Concession (now County Road 125). The first exhibition (or fall fair) of the Mono Agricultural Society was held on Friday, October 16, 1863. Seven years later, Saturday, September 3, 1870, the agricultural society held a raising bee on "The Fair Green" to build an agricultural hall.

In five hours, the seven heavy timber beams were raised into place. The finished building was 75 feet long, 36 feet wide, with board on the outside and lath and plaster on the inside.

It was open for the show fair on October 20. This agricultural hall sat on the site of the current bandstand in Alexandra Park. The building not only served the needs of an agricultural exhibition but also served as the militia drill shed, the local lock-up, and as the site of the "Railway Ball" held when the first train arrived in 1871.

The livestock shows were held on the streets of Orangeville. Exhibitions of agricultural products, handicrafts and flowers were held in some of the stores along Broadway. The fair moved to the present site of Fairgrounds Shopping Mall circa 1878 when Mrs. Mary Ketchum sold land at the north end of Second Street to the Agricultural Society.

Through the years many entrepreneurs have tried to make their living from entertaining the public. For example, Orangeville once had a shooting gallery. "At the Shooting Gallery, adjoining the Royal Hotel, on Saturday night, Mr. J.W. Ferguson made twenty-four bull's eyes out of a possible twenty-six, shooting off-hand. On Monday evening he made fifteen bull's eyes out of possible sixteen, without breaking a straw extended across the bull's eye. Mr. Ferguson is an excellent shot and will, we understand, be one of the Canadian team to shoot at the Centennial Exhibition in Philadelphia."[9]

Of all the sports ever played in town, it is lacrosse that made Orangeville most famous:

It was in 1875 that the lacrosse stick first made its appearance in the home of the Dufferins. From that day until later than 1900, Orangeville held many championship teams. The "Green and White" [colours worn by The Dufferins] captured the shield the first year the Canadian Lacrosse Association put it out for competition. The Dufferins fell to pieces the following year. The reason? Well, when those big promoters of the game—the men with the alluring bundle of greenbacks—appeared on the scene looking for material, they grabbed up as many men as possible. Promoters of the game, when it turned professional recognized the ability of the Orangeville boys and they deprived the rude forefathers of the Dufferins of seeing another real, good contest in fast company. The Dufferins disbanded when rays from greenbacks were seen in the horizon. They left home for places where they could swell their purses. There was no money in Orangeville to hold them, so the town lost its grip. Amateurism went out, professionalism came in.

Some of the old stand-bys stayed at home and are still staying, not enough though to make a stellar team. Besides they are getting older. Of course, they have a twelve up there, but it is not good enough for big company. They're coming stronger, however, and within a few years Orangeville will probably redeem lost laurels. Boys just big enough to handle sticks swarm to "Idylwyld," the old stamping ground where many a game was fought and won, and are developing.

'There were some hot games,' continued Mr. Thomas Mara, of Brampton, who was captain of the first team in 1875. 'Other places in our vicinity started to get teams. We got on a few game with them and we were generally victorious. Some of our men complained of the width of the goal posts. They were then about as wide as those used to football games. However, we remedied that and increased the width of the stick.'...My, but we had the exciting times. Talk about fights! Why we were scrapping continually at every game. They usually finished when it was dark and more than a few were called off on account of fights. That's nothing to boast about, but that's just how it was played.

The "Mechanics" was the name of the first team in Orangeville.

The Dufferins of Orangeville were the reigning champions of the Canadian Lacrosse Association in 1901. Here the team is in action on their home ground, Idlewyld Park in Orangeville.

They hardly left the town, except to go to a few villages around-about. A rival team in Orangeville was soon formed called the Olympians. The Mechanics used to play in Grand Valley, Shelburne and Bolton. Shelburne was certainly a hot lacrosse town. Keen rivalry existed between Orangeville and Shelburne. We always went there with a dread in our minds and a fear of getting broken heads, and vice versa.... One time we journeyed to Bolton and had to walk halfway. We never used trains—just carry-alls. Money was scarce.

In 1878 I think the Dufferins loomed up, after the Mechanics and Olympians amalgamated, a name which has lasted ever since. When the Dufferins were formed, lacrosse started to flourish in real earnest. Nobody was paid and everybody took a hand in the game, barring financial backing. We couldn't get money. That was one drawback. I remember once we had a team up from Toronto during a July 1st or 12th celebration. It was a fierce game. How we came out alive was a miracle! We won by 3 to 2, and, I think, the deciding goal was a fluke. It was thrown into the crowd and an Orangeville spectator threw it to our inside home man and he scored. You know how much we collected that day? Well, just $3.35. There was no fenced enclosure. It was played on the town commons. No gate receipts—the hat was passed around and we secured that sum. So you see we couldn't afford very well to bring teams from other places or go very far ourselves. We got a field with a fence around it later and charged a fee. We got what was due us then from the spectators, except the kids, who used to crawl underneath or leap over the jagged fence.

We just played independent ball—there were no leagues then. Orangeville was the hub of lacrossedom up to a few years ago. The town was a hot-bed of enthusiasm. How the home-brews did fight to win!

Lacrosse games now don't seem to be in it with the hard taught matches of the earlier years. After a win the town players were lionized by the young bloods and older persons. At night every old box, slab or board that could be obtained in the town was thrown in the centre of the roadway on the main street. Oil was carried from the hardware store and was poured on. A match was touched to the shavings. A large flame would shoot up. During the entire night the bonfire would burn. Early the next day it would be smoldering. The whole town would stand alongside and participate in the celebration. The town band would rend lively yells. There's no doubt about it they were good old days—nothing can touch them now.[10]

Just for Fun 179

In the glory days of lacrosse crowds could reach up to 7,000 persons. It is believed that the first team was started with a $25 sponsorship from Lord Dufferin himself. The first organized game was played on a field that was situated on the present site of the Dufferin County Courthouse.

A number of other sports clubs have existed. We know that Orangeville had a cricket club as early as 1862 when a game between the Orangeville and Charlestown [Caledon] teams was advertised. They also played against the Amaranth Cricket Club in June of that year. The Young Men's Christian Association (YMCA) was organized in Orangeville in November 1868. The president was W.E. McKay, with the town's resident minister as vice-president and manager. Other officers included Isaac Simpson, J. Mitchell, John Green and Thomas Stevenson. The association promoted all sorts of sports in the belief that if kept fit and busy a young man would stay out of trouble. Perhaps it worked.

Curling was an other extremely popular sport in Orangeville and the town has produced several championship teams. The game first was played in the early 1890s in a building near the Dufferin Court-house. In 1911, the curling club secured a site on John Street, north of present-day Tweedsmuir Presbyterian Church and built a two-sheet curling rink, which they sold to the church in 1948 for its expansion. In 1958, a four-sheet rink with artificial ice was built on the present site of the old Orangeville Fairgrounds land.

Lawn bowling was introduced to Orangeville around 1903. The first games were played on the lawn of the private residence of Dr. Thomas Henry Jr., on First Street. There was sufficient interest for the Orangeville Lawn Bowling Club to be formed and a few years later a bowling green and club house were established on John Street. Things moved along quickly perhaps because the mayor of the period was Dr. W.H. Riddell, known to be a very avid lawn bowler. The land was acquired from the Orangeville Monument Works facing John Street.

It was in that year, 1903 that the town finally opened up John Street from York Street to Broadway. Prior to that time, residents of the south end of town could only get uptown via either Bythia Street or Mill Street. Games were suspended during the Second World War. After the war, the Orangeville Branch of the Canadian Legion was anxious to erect a Legion Hall and the remaining living members of the club voted to donate the land but maintain the use of the greens. The Legion moved two portable classrooms to the site when the high school burned in 1948 and retrofitted them for their purpose. When the Monora Park Pavilion (on the other side of town) was being built,

Lacrosse for young men and lawn bowling for the older ones. The popularity of lawn bowling peaked just before the First World War. The Orangeville club had its own greens on the east side of John Street, just south of Broadway.

land for a new lawn-bowling green was made available for the club. Early in the early 2000s, the original greens on John Street were paved over to provide additional parking for the legion activities.

Winter was a time of great activity. "The toboggan slide was opened on New Year's Day by the members of the Orangeville Snowshoe and Toboggan Club. The slide is a little north of the cheese factory, near Purple Hill, and is an excellent one. Over thirty of the members and their friends took part in the opening and had a very good time. They enjoyed the sport immensely."[11]

In 1889, William Jelly brought his famous mastodon bones to Orangeville. These bones had become a sensation in the local newspapers. The Jelly family had unearthed the rare find on their family farm at Bowling Green, just west of Orangeville. In the late Victorian era, science and archaeology were very popular and the discovery was the talk of the county. The bones were set up on display for a week that Fall in the front windows of *The Sun* newspaper office. In that week over 600 people had trooped into town to see this natural phenomena, which had been found right in their backyard.

One of Orangeville's long standing service organizations is the Orangeville Horticultural Society. The trees that they planted along many of the town's streets at the turn of the century form the canopies of today along the residential historic district. The society was founded in 1897, and its first exhibit was held in the present Opera House that Fall. And what an event it must have been:

> the seats were removed and decked in flowers and fruits; the auditorium looked like a beautiful inside garden. Large crowds thronged

Just for Fun 181

the Hall and came from the surrounding countryside to view this spectacle of beauty. Six tables were covered with a profusion of plants and flowers whose arrangement was artistic, tasty and symmetrical. Another table was covered with the choicest fruits interspersed with art flowers with a background of tall plants. An orchestra under the leadership of local undertaker, J. Hulse, was made up of his two charming daughters. They were on the platform but almost hidden by flowers and foliage. The stage was gaily decorated with red, white and blue bunting and flags, making a very pretty setting. In the evening of this historic day, the scene was one of animated beauty, with the brightly lighted Hall, moving throngs of people, the chatter of merry conversation, the many handshakes and the artistic dresses of that day worn by Orangeville's fine ladies."[12]

The Dufferin Old Boys Association was formed in 1899 with all former residents of Orangeville invited to join. In 1900, the first executive was set up with such notable members as John McKee, the president of Dods Medicine Co. (Dods Liver Pills), and Earl Whaley of Whaley and Royce, well-known music dealers. Annual train excursions were organized for the group and their wives, the first of which occurred in August 1903. Hundreds of guests would arrive by train and thousands more would flock to town for the events and the picnics. "Anyone who has had the honour of once living in the Town of Orangeville, or for that matter the county, will ever have in their hearts a memory of their life here in the haunts of their childhood days."[13]

The heading, "the spinster's convention 1903," may seem far fetched. But not so, for it really happened in our fair town. This unusual event was held in June 1903, in the Town Hall, and was sponsored by the Ladies Aid of St. Andrew's Church (now Westminster):

On a gaily decorated stage, with the "Old Maids" dressed in costumes of the vintage of the year 1830, it was a colourful sight, and furnished a novel and at the same time a delightful departure from the usual concert entertainment. The affair created widespread interest, and it seemed that the whole population of the younger female set descended and filled the Hall to capacity. So great was the success of this venture, that it was held again the following Monday night, to an overflowing audience.

During the convention, the Old Maids of the Town discussed topics such as "Men," dress reform and other subjects, which drew

Orangeville was a good place to be from and the Dufferin Old Boys knew it. The former residents of Dufferin in Toronto organized an association and held annual rail excursions to Orangeville each year for a picnic. A tug-of-war was part of the fun.

bursts of laughter and applause from the crowded audience. There was a short play in which some of the chronic bachelors came in for appropriate and affective sallies, but they did not seem to mind and enjoyed the whole event. Eventually in despair because of the congested state of the matrimonial market, the convention voted to migrate to the Klondike where women were few, and men were willing. In the play, Dr. G.H. Campbell acted the role of Professor Makeover and entered the stage, and through a machine, the most hopeless Old Maid could be made into a rosy-cheeked, appetizing young maiden, which offered a panacea that surpassed the Klondike.

Miss Winnifred Bennett, who for many years was engaged in the hotel business in the Town, was the President of the convention and used her wonderful voice in solos "Men" and a "Picture No Artist Would Paint." Several addresses were given on dress reform by Miss Netta Marshall, on Women's Rights by Miss Emslie and a solo "No One Loves Me" was so ably sung by Miss Nellie Clark. Many young ladies took part and made the convention the success it was. Yes, [among] the men who assisted besides our beloved Dr. Campbell who had as assistant professor Mr. Harry Ritchie, was W. Bowles the excited photographer in the play who broke his camera in his attempt to snap a picture of the Old Maids.

Just for Fun   183

Choruses "Why Don't You Propose to Me" and "We are Laying Plans to Catch You," were climaxed by a drill that stole the spotlight, of twelve little girls who had been trained by Mrs. R. Irvine and whose names may still be familiar: Netta Golden, Hazel Patterson, Eva Franson, Helen Haley, Birdie Leighton, Alberta Kearns, Audrey McLaren, Elsie Stainforth, Bessie Wellbourne, Fran Dodds and M. Kenny.

Although this convention was in some cases somewhat humorous, it gave some of the diehard bachelors a few pointers as to the value of the female population that they had never before seen, and it proved very enlightening-held since as it is possible that the fair young girls in Orangeville these days don't have the difficulties of those early days to find the man of their choice.[14]

On June 2, 1953, Coronation Day was celebrated royally in Orangeville. The town gave a party that was treasured by citizens and guests alike:

Inspired by the great events culminating in the Coronation of Queen Elizabeth II in Westminster Abbey, thousands of Orangeville and the surrounding community cast business and cares to one side for a day and gave vent to expressions of loyalty and love to their Sovereign in a series of moving events that will long be remembered in this community. Flags bedecking streets, places of business and homes lent colour to the lively proceedings. The Celebration got under way on Monday Night at a grand Coronation Ball in the Rotary Arena Hall, which was jam packed with 450 revelers who entered in the spirit of the occasion. His Worship Mayor W.N. Richardson, wearing his chain of office, was present accompanied by Mrs. Richardson. Also present were Deputy Reeve Bill Stirton and Mrs. Stirton, Members of the Town Council, and it might be safely stated that every walk of life in the community was well represented. The highlight of the evening came at midnight when it was announced that Miss Nan Scott, daughter of Dr. and Mrs. C.I. Scott, Orangeville, had been elected Queen of the Ball. Beverley Hall, of Caledon, and Joan Henderson, of Orangeville, two other students of the District High School, were the elected ladies-in-waiting. Following the announcement, Miss Scott, clad in scarlet cape trimmed with ermine and carrying a bouquet of roses, was seated in a throne chair and crowned by His Worship Mayor Richardson…Coronation Day was inaugurated with a 21-gun salute fired by the members of the Legion. Needless to say, if any townsmen were asleep when the salute started, they did not remain long so.

184   ORANGEVILLE

Following this, over 60 members of the Legion gathered for breakfast in their Hall and around the bacon and eggs enjoyed that comradeship that can only be found only among those who have donned the King's uniform. The Parade in the afternoon was one of the finest witnessed in Orangeville. It was marshalled by Fred Bulley, and proceeded from the Court House down Broadway to Alexandra Park. Leading the Parade was Fire Chief Alvin Holmes, followed by the No. 1 and No. 2 fire trucks and members of the Fire Brigade looking very natty in their blue uniforms. Other organizations parading were the Cubs, the Scouts, the Girl Guides, members of the I.O.D.E., Brownies, the Canadian Legion, the Women's Auxiliary to the Legion, and the St. John's Ambulance Brigade. Music for the parade was capably provided by the District High School Band.

The service at the Park was most impressive and was conducted by the Rev. John Bartlett, chaplain of the Legion and rector of St. Mark's Anglican Church, assisted by the ministers of the Town. The Orangeville Citizens' Band played for the hymns. Following the service those present listened with deep reverence to the inspiring address of Queen Elizabeth II. [broadcast by radio] After the service the parade reformed and passed in review before Mayor W.N. Richardson and members of the Council and others taking part in the service. The concert, provided by the Orangeville Citizens' Band in the evening, was thoroughly enjoyed by the large crowd present. Bandmaster Russell Morrow and his musicians acquitted themselves splendidly for the occasion. After the concert a fireworks display was given showing a portrait of her Majesty, and was in the charge of the Fire Department.[15]

The town celebrated it 100th anniversary with a monumental birthday party in August 1963:

...former Orangeville residents, relatives of some of the early town fathers, and friends from near and far, poured into this town to assist in the celebrations. Centennial races were held at the fairgrounds, a special fashion show was held, where all the models wore gowns that would have adorned the ladies of the town when it came into existence a hundred years before. There were band concerts and fireworks displays and a Miss Centennial Beauty Queen Contest. A daring and spectacular air show was given by members of the RCAF, and the many beards that had been grown by masculine residents of the town for the occasion, were judged for their texture, colour and length. The largest

Just for Fun 185

parade of floats, bands, horses and pretty girls that Orangeville had ever seen was held on the August Bank Holiday Monday. All-Star baseball games were played, street dances and other dances drew crowds of happy people and a galaxy of television stars made their appearance.

The history of Orangeville was printed in a book to commemorate the occasion and the *Banner* published a special Centennial Edition that was sold out within a week, despite the fact 2,000 additional copies were printed. Bronze, silver and gold Centennial coins were minted as mementos of the occasion, and these too, were completely sold out. Orangeville never looked more beautiful. Flags, flowers and bunting decorated every possible pillar, post, storefront and home. Shop windows became museums for the occasion and displayed treasures that had been hidden in attics and family chests for years and years, and to make the old-world air even more complete, the shopkeepers, office workers and waitresses all wore period costumes.

Orangeville's Centennial was an event that is still talked about with wonder, and will be remembered by this town for many years to come.[16]

From the souvenir booklet produced for the event we find an ad for Clover Farm, a downtown grocery store. Instead of peddling the store-wares or offering specials, owner Harman Leader wrote "Progress is not measured alone in material things. Progress is measured in our spiritual growth, our ability to live agreeably and graciously with our fellow man. It is our firm belief that although Orangeville has attained much in physical gain in its past 100 years, its true growth has been in the welfare of it's people."[17]

One of the things making Orangeville such an attractive place to live in is the well-attended and "fun" activities that happen throughout the town and throughout the year. Perhaps it is the ability to express enjoyment that gives the "spiritual growth" that the unknown writer of 1963 was talking about.

14

AND BAD TIMES TOO

EVERY COMMUNITY MUST DEAL WITH tragedy in various ways, and tragedy comes to a community in various ways. Orangeville has long had a reputation of being able to "pull through" when the going got rough and always had a reputation of "pulling together" whenever the need arose. Whether it was flood or fire, neighbour helped neighbour. Orangeville has experienced fires, floods, wind and more wind. The stories that follow tell about the strength of residents of the town. Were they not survivors, the town would not be here.

Fire was always a pernicious threat to early Orangeville, either the threat of fire consuming the wooden buildings of the small village or of forest fires breaking out on the outskirts of town. In 1864, a fire raging in the woods at the present corner of Hockley Road and Mono Sideroad 5 had destroyed several hundred acres of trees. The billowing smoke in the sky kept everyone in town with eyes peeled on the fumes for several fearful days. Buildings in Orangeville of that period were compactly built and were primarily of wood. That same year a fire in the Marksman's Hotel on Broadway was extinguished before much damage could be done, but it made the villagers very conscious of what could happen. As a result, citizens started immediately to petition the town for the purchase of a fire engine. The availability of water from the nearby Mill Creek made the idea more acceptable to the town council from a financial point of view. A hose-drawn pumper was acquired, and was run by William and Eliza Sutton.

In the Fall of 1870, fire struck downtown and destroyed much of the core district. Other disastrous infernos followed in 1873 and in 1874. The replacement buildings, mostly constructed of brick, make up today's historic streetscape in the centre of town. Party or common walls were often used between adjacent buildings in brick construction. This was supposed to save on costs but later proved a fire hazard as well since flames could spread with great ease. In an attempt to deal with the risk of fire, a bylaw was passed in 1875 creating what was called a "fire district" in the downtown area. It required that all buildings be built of brick:

A destructive fire broke out in the stables to the rear of the Wellington Hotel, on Broadway, about eleven o'clock on Friday night, and, despite the most strenuous efforts to stop its progress, spread with fearful rapidity to the adjacent buildings and at one time threatened the principal part of the town with destruction. The stables and their contents…quantity of hay and oats, several sets of harness, and four horses…fanned by a strong breeze, extended to the hotel from which they spread eastward to the residence of Mr. D. Menary, and blacksmith and wagon shops of Messrs. Menary & Bro., the tinsmith shop of Mr. W. Parsons, the dry goods store of Messrs. McCleverty & Eastman, the grocery store of Mr. W.R. Lloyd, the shoe store of Mr. J. Tilt, the dry goods store of Messrs. Longeway & Bros., the saddle and harness shop of Mr. T. Jackson, and the Exchange Hotel and all the sheds attached to it, all of which, with the greater portion of the contents, were completely destroyed. The buildings were principally rough-cast, and in less than two hours from the time the flames were first observed, the whole block west of Mill Street as far as May's saddlery, and as far east of Mill Street as the Mammoth House, was reduced to ashes. The stable to the rear of the Exchange Hotel was several time on fire, but the citizens, with praiseworthy exertions, extinguished the flames, and thus prevented further extension of the conflagration eastward. Mr. May's saddlery shop was saved with great difficulty. At one time it was feared that the fire would extend to the north side of Broadway, but the great width of the street, the watchfulness of the citizens, who extinguished burnings falling on the roof, and a favourable wind, confined it to the south side. There was no fire company, but had there been one it is believed that the fire could have been confined to the premises in which it originated. The origin of the fire, which caused this great loss of property, is unknown, but it is supposed to be the work of an incendiary.[1]

Fires that threatened the residents did not always come from within the town itself. In August 1874, huge bush fires broke out in three nearby townships, Amaranth, Melancthon and Mono, "the air in

Orangeville High School was opened in 1884 and was destroyed by fire in February 1948.

Orangeville has in consequence been thick with smoke. The fires raged with great fury in the vicinity of Orangeville on Monday, and fanned by a strong wind at one time threatened the town and the farms adjoining it. The citizens turned out in great force, and by their aid the fires were prevented from extending to the buildings."[2]

The high school fire of 1948 was called a "major calamity" for Orangeville and district. It's impact is still alive in the memories many older residents have of the event. The old Orangeville High School was gutted by fire at night, eliminating a familiar landmark from the Orangeville skyline. "The inferno that engulfed the school provided the building with a celebrity that has survived over 30 years. While the destruction of the building was a tragedy in itself, there was also a tremendous upheaval in the town, finding temporary accommodations for 250 students and nine teachers."[3] The Orangeville High School had stood at the top of the hill on Faulkner and Fead streets for 65 years.

Space was found in the basements of St. Andrew's Presbyterian Church, Tweedsmuir Church, First Avenue United Church and the Pentecostal Tabernacle. Interestingly, the First Avenue Church congregation finally joined with St. Andrew's Presbyterian and changed its name to Westminster United Church on Broadway, allowing the space in their church to become a temporary school. The fire had accomplished what Church Union of 1925 hadn't, and the two congregations merged. The First Avenue church building was quickly renovated into

And Bad Times Too

a high school and used for four years until 1952 when a new school was opened on Faulkner Street.

The weather in Orangeville is also the source of some interesting tales. Some aspects caused no more than an inconvenience while others caused great damage and loss, and still others just left the residents of town thanking God that they had been spared. Weather in the highest land mass in southern Ontario can be very unpredictable. (Orangeville is 1450 feet above sea level and just a mile to the west, the altitude is 1700 feet.) And it is this habit of changing quickly and drastically that sometimes brings havoc to an otherwise quiet little town.

The month of January 1869 was unusual; it was so mild and springlike that the trees started budding. And such pleasant weather helped the January Fair held on the streets of Broadway. It was reported that, "the event was well attended but the display of cattle was not large. Out of the 47 head on the ground about 20 were in good condition and brought fair prices."[4] In the Fall of 1873, the vagaries of weather were sufficient to warrant this account:

> The weather during the past week has been as "fickle as the wind." Monday was a mild, sunshiny day, but Tuesday was cold and boisterous, with alternate shows of wet, clammy snow, and drizzling hail, while Wednesday was raw and chilly. Today the ground is covered with snow; but the weather-wise—and who don't pretend to

In the mid-1940s, the Gem Restaurant on Broadway caught on fire. The fear of the fire spreading to other buildings along Broadway prompted many local merchants to review the safety features of their buildings.

The cloudburst in June 1890 flooded Spring Brook and Mill Creek. In the west side of town the mill pond dam gave away, creating a wall of water that wrecked the other dams and bridges in its path. Leighton's Shingle Mill near John Street was undercut and destroyed.

have some knowledge on this ever-recurring subject—predict a thaw, to be succeeded by some fine weather. Hopeful prediction! We trust its fulfilment is nearer us than next summer![5]

Early spring and sudden rains often brought severe flooding to Orangeville. Most of the early industries relied on the power of the creeks, and were built right on the riverbank. Many of the early urban residences in the village were built in what today is recognized as a "flood plain of the Credit." Every few years the papers would report a disastrous flood, both in town and down river in Melville, Alton and Cataract as well. Jull's Mill was a perennial problem as the sawdust deposits built up like silt and created flooding right out to Broadway. In 1863, a sudden rainstorm broke the dam at the mill and severely damaged Mr. Wallace's furniture factory. The town constructed breakwaters along the bottom of Mill Creek, but these too washed out when hit with a flash flood.

It is the wind of the area, however, that has always caused the most concern and the most damage in town. In July of 1870, Richard East of East Garafraxa got caught in a storm and took refuge in a log building, which was overturned by the hurricane, and was crushed to death under a log. In Orangeville it was reported that, "the town was visited by a thunderstorm of unusual severity, accompanied by a raging wind. The flashings of lightning were incessant and the thunder pealed without intermission, like the deafening roar of the continual discharge of heavy artillery. The rain fell in torrents and the wind raged with great fury carrying destruction in its path. Accounts of blowing down of stables, barns, houses and fences reach us from all quarters and there is unfortunately little reason to doubt their accuracy. Several buildings were struck by the electric fluid."[6] The next year, the wind came back, this time with even heavier damage in town:

A heavy thundershower, accompanied by a strong wind visited Orangeville on Tuesday evening. The rain fell in torrents, and the wind blew with great fury, levelling trees and fences, and unroofing several buildings, and damaging others considerably. Mr. J. Ferguson's residence, on First Street, was unroofed and part of the wall of Menary Bros.' blacksmith shop was blown down, but we did not hear of any more serious damage being done by the gale in Orangeville."[7]

In December, two years later, the wind came late in the year as everyone was thinking of snowstorms but not wind. One afternoon the fresh snow almost entirely disappeared, exposing naked fields and muddy roads. A warm rain followed for two days, causing a thaw, which was succeeded by a terrible gale that blew down fences, unroofed sheds, and did other damage. "The gable of Mr. House's residence on First Avenue was blown down, and the roof of the Bank of Commerce on Broadway shifted about twelve inches. Currie's Hotel, at Camilla, was unroofed, and the Agricultural Hall at Mono Mills blown down. The M.E. Church at Melville was completely destroyed, and other buildings in the neighbourhood also damaged. Fences were blown down in every direction, and telegraph poles upturned. The gale was the most destructive that has been experienced in this section for a number of years."[8]

The storm that toppled the tall steeple of St Mark's Anglican Church on First Street on July 2, 1887, was long remembered by a whole generation of residents. During an electrical thunderstorm the lengthy spire fell into the street. Many citizens at the time believed the lightning had struck it while others believed that the wind had brought it down. The argument was never resolved. Although the newspaper of the day proclaimed that the spire would be rebuilt immediately, today the low square steeple is what remains of the base. It has been fancied up with cement decorations, the storm is forgotten and long gone is the generation who argued about how the spire ended up lying in the street.

The worst storm ever was on June 15, 1918, when a cyclone hit town. The newspaper reported "CYCLONE HITS ORANGEVILLE":

Orangeville was visited by one of the worst electric storms in its history about ten o'clock on Tuesday night. In places the wind assumed cyclonic proportions and did very serious damage. The south side of the business part of Broadway suffered most severely. A section of roof 24 feet in width by nearly 60 feet in length was lifted off the back part of J.E. Smith & Co.'s. implements, warerooms turned upside down and deposited in the Queen's Hotel yard. Part of the heavy roof fell on the roof of the Queen's kitchen, crushing it in and causing considerable damage. The unroofed portion of Smith & Co.'s building was used as a storage room for buggies, cutters, piano and other stock. A number of buggies were broken by the falling debris and everything was soaked by the rain which fell in torrents for a full half hour.

Part of the roof was lifted off the front of J.H. Hulse's dwelling house and undertaking rooms. The wind carried the roof to the rear of Geo. Fleming's residence to the east. In its flight the mass struck a chimney on the back of Mr. Fleming's dwelling, causing it to fall. The chimney crashed through the roof of a back kitchen, making a sorry mess of the interior. Serious damage was sustained by Mr. Hulse from the rain, which came through the opening in the roof and flooded the greater part of the house. The storm blew in the brick top on the front of Hill & Co.'s store. The mass crashed through the roof and also the ceiling of the storey below. A large quantity of wood, which was stored on the upper floor of the building, broke the force of the falling brick, otherwise the mass would probably have gone right through to the cellar. The plate glass was blown out of one of the front doors of the store and a window at the rear was blown in.

A chimney collapsed and came down through the roof in the back room of Dr. W.H. Bowles' dental office. The plate glass front of Geo. McIntyre's office, near the post office was blown in. A large window in the front of Fuller, Allen & Holmes shop suffered a similar fate. The fire hall smokestack had a narrow escape. Two of the

And Bad Times Too 193

guy supports gave way under the terrific strain and the upper part of the stack was shifted two or three feet out of place. Further east on Broadway a section of roof about twenty feet square was lifted off the south end of the Hotel Alexandra stables. The egg warehouse was partly unroofed and the blowpipe leading from Armstrong & Robinson's foundry to the moulding shop was demolished.

The cyclone seems to have crossed town in a southeasterly direction. Mrs. Whittler's dwelling house in the West Ward was partly unroofed, some trees were twisted off on Zina and Bythia Streets, and fences around the properties of Jos. J. Kelly and J.W. Aiken were levelled to the ground. A section of the north-end wall of T.J. Robinson's livery barn was wrecked, leaving a hole twelve or fifteen feet each way in the upper storey. It is thought the damage was done by lightning, as the wall was strongly built and would have withstood the wind. Windows in the frame buildings east of the livery yard fared badly and looked yesterday morning as if they had been through an artillery engagement. The tops were twisted off a couple of maples on Dr. Rooney's grounds on John St. A number of trees on Mill and Church streets were similarly destroyed. Lawns everywhere were strewn with branches and other wreckage. The storm worked havoc with the electric light and telephone wires. The Hydro and Deagle systems were both put out of commission, and electric power users were compelled to shut down yesterday or else devise some other method of getting along.[9]

Orangeville got a scare when a tornado passed by the town in August 1971. It travelled through The Maples and continued into Caledon. And what may have been the most tragic windstorm in Dufferin County brushed Orangeville on the 31st of May 1985. "In the early evening, a tornado had ripped through Grand Valley and brought homes and trees to the ground. Farm buildings were destroyed and livestock loose or missing. People lost their lives, and the long black funnel was heading straight to Orangeville. The town was narrowly missed, the Mono Plaza, only a mile from the outskirts of town, was completely destroyed. Many local residents such as Arnold Patterson and Jean Turnbull, were at the plaza, and miraculously everyone survived. Although the town was spared, the damage was still considerable. Thousands of Orangeville citizens joined in the weeks of clean up and months of rebuilding."[10] In physical appearance, and in less tangible ways, the community would never be the same.

194   ORANGEVILLE

Despite the fact that Orangeville is far away from the more news-worthy earthquake zones, in 1935 a tremor shook this sleepy little town:

The earthquake Halloween night or rather early Friday morning gave many Orangeville citizens a genuine fright and a rather anxious time until they realized just what had caused houses to rock, china-ware to clatter, tables to dance and plaster to come rattling down the walls. Three distinct tremors were felt here about 1:05 a.m. Friday morning. Most people were abed, although there were still many abroad on account of Halloween merrymaking parties and street celebrations. Some people who were asleep were aroused from their slumbers by the shaking of the bed. For a few minutes the alarm was general and then came the realization that the distur-bance was due to earth tremors. No damage of note was done locally. A few bricks were dislodged from the chimney of Mr. W.C. McMil-lan's residence on West Broadway and came crashing down to add to the alarm of the inmates of the house.[11]

The most talked about weather in Orangeville is always snow. This is the beginning of the snowbelt. As a result of lying between the Great Lakes, the area catches the systems that are created over the lakes. The Niagara Escarpment, just south on Caledon Mountain, causes the wind to shoot upwards and cool quickly, leading to sudden snow squalls and whiteouts.

The abundance and persistence of the snow greatly frustrated the early settlers as it often snowed from November to May. This meant long months of feeling locked inside. During the Victorian era, people were dismayed by the cold trips out to the outhouse privy. The roads were blocked in, but the good thing is that it was easier travelling by horse and sleigh in winter than on the muddy roads of spring. Few residents have died as a result of snow, so the impact mostly was one of inconvenience. However, snow was never an inconvenience when schools were can-celled, but for travellers snow may have been a different experience:

About 75 train passengers had to remain in Orangeville on Monday, Tuesday and most of yesterday owing to the blockade on the local branches. They voyaged to the skating rink on Tuesday afternoon and had a great game of hockey. Some wore skates and some went without. A party from Syracuse, New York, who were on their way to Mount Forest to attend a wedding, could not get there in time and had to return last night. The several blockades this winter have been a regular gold mine for a couple of the hotels."[12]

The same issue of the newspaper noted that an estimated two million dollars had been lost by the CPR and the GTR owing to the severe weather. They commented that "when nature cuts loose man and his works don't amount to much."

My fondest weather memories are of the ice and snow storms of the 1960–70s. Snow or ice would come in and shut the whole town down. The hydro would go out and the roads would be closed. Anyone travelling through the area was stuck in town and would be billeted, sometimes for days, at emergency shelters in the school or at private homes. Schools would close and the fun would begin. In January 1971, I remember that the storms hit before the school buses could get home and over 500 students were stranded in town. Everyone who had town friends stayed over and other parents voluntarily opened up their homes. Bryan's Fuels delivered emergency oil to their customers on snowmobile. But there were many other storms, many much worse, some even lasting several days. Roads around Orangeville still close on occasion, but that night in town with all the other students will remain in my memory forever.

Winter has always been part of life in Orangeville. There is a sidewalk under there somewhere, buried during the winter storm.

Water wasn't the only element to cause catastrophe. The boiler in the Anchor Mills exploded in 1888, blowing out the south wall of the engine house.

There are always tragedies of the human kind as well. There have been a couple of explosions that rocked the town. In the late 1880s, an explosion in a steam engine blew out the entire end of the old stone mill. The force of the explosions broke windows all over town. Although there was plenty of noise, miraculously no one was hurt.

A more recent accident (March 1976) not only shook the town, but also made the townspeople aware of the fact that "things can happen here." "Bricks Blown off House" was the headline from *The Orangeville Banner*. Late one evening, Rick and Gail Woolner and baby Connie were having a quiet evening at their home on Broadway. Unknown to them, below in the basement, there was a hole in a pipe connected to the public sewer system. Seemingly many years before, someone had stuffed a rag in it. An unfortunate series of events occurred because of a leak at the nearby Gulf Station, which drained into the sewer system and then entered the basement of the Woolner home through the pipe. The gasoline filled the basement. That evening when a pilot light ignited the Woolner's furnace, it also ignited the gas in the basement. The result was an explosion that was heard across the town.

It was the couch they were sitting on that saved the Woolner family from certain death. The power of the explosion caused it to flip over in such a way that it shielded them. The over 100-year-old-home had been so well constructed that even though the walls were completely blown out, the structure still remained intact. It is said that on that very evening two strange things happened: the first was that one of the relatives of the Woolners had snapped a photograph of an angel ascending to the sky, the other thing was that a half-eaten sandwich, which Rick had set on the coffee table just prior to the explosion, was reportedly found still on the plate underneath the floor boards with the bite out of it just as it had been left!

And with that, a local urban legend began. In typical Orangeville fashion, that evening a friend of the Woolner's was said to have broken through the police and fire brigade barricades, upon hearing of the accident, to return a box of "Poly-filla" he had borrowed years prior to the explosion. He thought the family might need it.

As noted, Orangeville is a town of weather. The floods have long since ceased and everyone admits that the snow is never as deep as it used to be. But the wind remains and history tells us that it will be back, and the town is situated in an area that has experienced earthquakes. Fires and explosions are a reality of living, both now and in the past. We can only pray that such disasters do not happen to us in our town, but they do.

These are the experiences we share with the pioneers—the realization that we are never in control of some things, neither accidents nor nature.

15

VILLAINS AND HEROES

NEITHER TIME NOR SPACE PERMITS an introduction to every person who passed through the town and whose life in Orangeville would be worth knowning. Instead, here are a few of the town's residents with some brief insights into their lives. Not all were famous, but all contributed to making Orangeville what it is today.

Orange Jull
Orange Jull (1845–1920) was the son of Mary Lawrence and Thomas Jull whose family ran mills in Orangeville, including the landmark stone mill on Mill Street.

> Among the machinery shown at the Provincial Exhibition at Kingston last week was a Grain Cleaner, exhibited by Mr. O. Jull of Orangeville, which was awarded a special premium and the high encomiums of the judges. Hitherto millers have laid great difficulty in properly cleaning grain, the process by which it was accomplished being tedious and expensive; but by Mr. Jull's invention the difficulty is removed, and the cost of cleaning reduced 50 per cent.
>
> The machine, though simple in all its parts, is an ingenious contrivance, liable to no derangement, and very easily worked. It consists of two pans or sieves, a fan, and several spouts, all working in harmony with each other by a number of wheels, cogs and slides. The upper sieve, which first receives the grain has a reciprocating motion, and is so constructed that while the grain passes through the screen to anther pan underneath, much of the impurities which it contained are brought to the surface by the motion of the sieve,

Villains and Heroes   199

and emitted through a bite in the side and carried off by a spout. The grain, partially cleaned, descends through the upper to the lower pan, and being again agitated by the movement of the screen, sand and other impurities pass through the sieve, while the grains shifted from the pan to an air chamber communicating with a fan, and being there separated from chaff and dust, is transmitted through a spout to the smutter. The fan is constructed on the principle of the screw, and is an ingenious contrivance, requiring little power to propel it, and so regulated that the volume of air required may be increased or diminished at pleasure.

The Cleaner has already been introduced into some of the first mills in the country, and performs its work in a most satisfactory manner. It has been patented by Mr. Jull, and is now manufactured in this village. It is as cheap as it is useful, a machine capable of cleaning 140 bushels an hour cost only $110. Mr. Jull is a young man of great mechanical acquirements, a native of Canada, and we hope he will be well rewarded for his useful invention.[1]

Orange Jull was not only an ingenious inventor, but he played a significant role in the life of Orangeville, as can be seen throughout the stories on the town.

Dr. G.H. Campbell
George Harold Campbell (1878–1972), was a sportsman, dentist, commendable citizen and staunch Presbyterian. Dufferin County's first [and so far only] Olympic gold medal was captured by him in 1908. The prestigious trophy was carried home from London, England, by Harold Campbell, an Orangeville dentist, who was a member of the Canadian lacrosse team that year. It was also the only year that field lacrosse was an Olympic medal sport. Campbell was then 30 years old and a valuable member of The Dufferins Lacrosse Club, a frequent contender for the Canadian senior championship.

While his Olympic medal always remained his most prized possession, Campbell had other "boastable" achievements. He was president of the Ontario Dental Association in 1936 and 1937; on the Board of Governors of the Royal College of Dental Surgeons from 1940 to 1949; and served on the executive of the Dominion Dental Council of Canada. He was active in municipal politics, serving as mayor of Orangeville from 1914 to 1916 and on the Orangeville Hydro-Electric Commission from 1917 to 1937. He was a past president of the

Dufferin Children's Aid Society, president of the Forest Lawn Cemetery Company and was one of the first members of the Ontario Good Roads Association. He was a director of the Dufferin Agricultural Society, where he competed keenly with produce from his gardens and was widely known for his prize-winning gladioli. In provincial and federal politics, he was an active organizer and a sometime candidate for the Progressive Conservative Party. Dr. Campbell was also one of the leaders of the "continuing Presbyterians" in 1925, and instrumental in the organization and construction of Tweedsmuir Memorial Presbyterian Church in Orangeville.

In local sports life, he was one of the founders of the Orangeville Arena, the Orangeville Curling Club and the Orangeville Golf Club. He was past president of the Caledon Lake Company and was for many years an official of the Orangeville Driving Club, sponsors of the Dominion Day horseracing meet. But lacrosse remained his first love. He continued to play the game in Orangeville until he was 50. In his graduating year in dentistry at the University of Toronto in 1902, he was captain of the university team which won the World University Lacrosse Championship.

He accomplished all this while carrying on a large dental practice in Orangeville for more than 65 years. He was said to be the oldest practicing dental surgeon on the continent. "Doc" Campbell was still treating patients up to two weeks prior to his death on November 4, 1972, at age 94.

Alexander McLachlan

Alexander McLachlan (1818–1896) was considered by many readers in his time to be the greatest Canadian poet. And although neither born or raised in Orangeville, the town has long claimed him as their own. And he is buried here, beneath a tombstone erected in his honour, made possible by a collection taken up by the citizens of Orangeville.

McLachlan was born in 1818 in Johnstone, Renfrewshire, Scotland. His father died while travelling back to Scotland from his pioneer farm in Caledon Township. Consequently, care of the family was taken over by his grandfather, Alexander Sutherland, a stern and devout churchman. McLachlan went to work in a Glasgow factory to help his family, then at age 14 was apprenticed to a tailor.

At age 22, he and two of his sisters emigrated to Canada and claimed the farm in Caledon, which they sold a year later. In 1844 he married his cousin, Clamina McLachlan, and moved to a bush farm in

Perth County. They next (in 1850) purchased a home in McMillan's Village, a predominately Scottish settlement now known as Erin. During his 27 years there, he made his living as a tailor and through giving educational lectures, usually under the auspices of the Mechanics Institute.

In 1862, through the efforts of his friend, the Honorable Thomas D'Arcy McGee,[2] McLachlan was appointed as the government lecturer and emigration agent for Canada in Scotland, a role that took him back to Scotland on occasion. In 1877, he settled with his sons in Amaranth Township and eventually earned the nickname of "the Bard of Amaranth." It was not until 1895 that he moved to 4 Elizabeth Street in Orangeville. He died a year later.

Alexander McLachlan (1818–1896) was called the "Bard of Amaranth." He published six books of poetry before retiring to Orangeville.

He had several volumes of poetry published. His first published work was a 36-page pamphlet in 1846 entitled *The Spirit of Love and Other Poems*, followed in 1856 by *Poems*, 192 pages in length. Two editions of his one book, a 233-page volume called *Poems and Songs*, were published in Toronto by Hunter Rose. His last publication, *Collected Works*, was printed in 1900, having being assembled by his daughters Mary and Elizabeth. Of his poetry, Orangeville historian and Dufferin County Archivist Steve Brown notes, "McLachlan was a pioneer poet with a simple, straightforward approach to his writing. His work will not overwhelm you with intricate rhyme schemes or subtlety of thought. His work echoes the old heroic ballads and folk songs of his native Scotland."[3]

Miss E.M. McLachlan
Elizabeth McLachlan (1865–1943) was the spinster daughter of Alexander McLachlan. She is one of my heroes. Although unmarried, she was a very successful businesswomen at a time when men thought they ruled the Town of Orangeville. A 1912 biographical sketch describes her in the following way:

> Miss McLachlan has been established here about four years as a confectioner and fruit merchant, during which time she has formed

Elizabeth McLachlan, a daughter of the poet Alexander McLachlan, ran a confectionery and grocery store on Broadway from about 1910 to 1930.

a good connection, and the business has been successful, even beyond expectations. At all times she has exercised great care in the selection of her stock, of which she has a general assortment, everything being the best of its kind, choice and fresh, and prices being reasonable and moderate. She holds the agency for the well-known Empress Chocolate Wafers, the excellent quality of these wafers having developed a growing demand.[4]

Bob Kyle
Several Dufferin boys caught "Gold Fever" and went off to the Klondike to make their fortune. One was Bob Kyle (1841–1916):

> Bob Kyle, who used to run the Orangeville Electric Light here over 25 years ago, arrived in town on Thursday and proceeded to look up all his old friends. Bob has been living in London, Eng., for several years and is interested in a company that controls a process for manufacturing and tanning leather in seven days, producing a much better article than under the old process.
> Bob left Orangeville in 1897 and joined the big rush to the Klondike gold fields, where he engaged in mining for six years. Since then he has travelled all over the world, mining in Russia, South Africa, British New Guinea, New Zealand and Australia. In the republic of Columbia, South America, he constructed the longest ropeway in the world.
> Before coming to town from London, Bob had just spent six months in Finland, where he installed a plant. He describes Finland as a veritable hive of industry where everybody is working. Up-to-date paper mills are turning out great quantities of paper and the country produces much butter. The dairies, he describes, as most

modern and could be copied with advantage by this country. We had a long talk with Bob and he gave us a great deal of information about conditions in Europe. He also left us a large amount of the paper money that is floating around Germany and countries that before the war comprised Russia. The notes are of all denominations, but will probably never be worth much. It requires a whole lot of paper to buy anything in those countries…Upon his return he expects his next jump will be to Brazil.[5]

Mrs. Jane Huston Lalor
"When Orangeville held a patriotic celebration, and Her Royal Highness Queen Victoria was unable to attend, the town's loyal citizens had the next best thing. Jane Huston Lalor, a Queen Victoria look-alike, portrayed the Queen at local entertainments and 'public demonstrations,' such as the celebration sparked by news of the fall of Pretoria in the Boer War. Her likeness to the great Queen was often commented upon. The day after the celebration citizens learned Pretoria still held out. So, three days later, when the city finally fell to the British, the town did it all again—with Mrs. Lalor in an open carriage being her most dignified royal self. Ironically, Mrs. Lalor contracted pneumonia and died within hours of Queen Victoria in January 1901."[6]

Jane Huston Lalor (1821–1901) came from a very theatrical family that ran the local Theatre Company for years, and had a type of menagerie on the present site of Orangeville Golf Course. They used the backdrops from the theatre for their shows and also built a wonderful fairy-tale cabin next to the course. Walter Huston, the famous Hollywood movie actor and director, was born in Toronto (his parents were from Orangeville). Jane Huston Lalor was his great-aunt. Walter also had a sister, Margaret who, after her singing career ended, provided speech training to many of Hollywood greats when they had to shift from silent to talking pictures. Hollywood was influenced by a family whose Aunt Jane played Queen Victoria, right here in Orangeville. Imagine!

Springbrook Ghost
One of my favourite heroes didn't even exist at all. For weeks in 1895, the story of the Springbrook Ghost brought hundreds out to see this eleven-foot spook. The newspapers were filled with the ghosts exploits, séances were held right in the town Opera House, and special train

excursions ran from Toronto each weekend with passengers eager to meet "Mr. Ghost" and get his picture. The name "Springbook" came from the area where he appeared, roughly between the railway crossing and Greenwood Cemetery. He appeared first in the 1880s and was spotted for over twenty years. The following newspaper reference to various encounters give an idea of his character:

Two weeks ago last night, as "Ollie" Perfect, who lives at Springbrook, was driving home from Orangeville, he saw walking at the side of the road, an apparition that caused his heart to leap into his mouth and the horse to jump into the ditch. The apparition looked like a man about eleven feet high, who took a twelve-foot stride and was dressed in black down to his hips, in a white skirt from there to his knees and then in black again. The man, or spook, walked past Mr. Perfect's rig and disappeared in the darkness. Mr. Perfect saw the ghost again a few nights later at the same place, west of the railway track. This time as soon as he reached home, he organized a searching party and started out to locate Mr. Ghost. The search was unsuccessful, and last Friday night Mr. Perfect saw the ghost again.

Mr. John Gillespie, treasurer of Amaranth Township, is also said to have seen the ghost one night last week, although Mr. Gillespie denies the soft impeachment. The fellow peered into Mr. Gillespie's rig as he passed by and then walked on without a word. Mr. Gillespie's description of the ghost tallies exactly with that of Mr. Perfect, and as both are sober, reliable citizens and pillars in the Presbyterian church, there is not the slightest reason for doubting their word. Several other citizens have also seen the ghost during the past two weeks and a year ago Mr. Fred Marshall of Kelly & Marshall saw a similar apparition one night as he was driving along the road.

Mr. Jos. Marshall informs the *Advertiser* that twenty years ago a spook similar to this one was the terror of that neighbourhood. Horses that would leave Orangeville a mile distant would quite often become frightened and heated as they travelled between the "skew" railway crossing and what was then known as Earl's Hotel at Springbrook. One horse dropped dead as the result of fright at this place. The spook had the same habit of peering into rigs and was even said to ride a short distance on the dashboard. At one time it was said to be the spirit of a young woman who had died close by and who was said to have been worked to death. Afterwards it was surmised that the priest had concocted the story of the cause of the girl's death in order to get well paid for praying for peace for her troubled spirit. After a few years, Mr. Harshaw says, nothing more was heard of the ghost....

There are numerous theories as to the cause of this apparition. The railway crossing near which the ghost makes his appearance is a fatal spot, a dozen or more people having been killed there during the last twenty years. Pat McGarvey was one of the last victims and there are those who are superstitious enough to believe that Pat knows something about this ghost business. Others think that the apparition is but the forerunner of a horrible accident that may take place at this crossing in the near future. A tall, gaunt, weak-minded youth named Fletcher lives with his father in a small house west of the railway crossing. The most popular theory is that this young man was in the habit of wandering around at night in a peculiar garb of his own, but it is said that the youth is too ill to leave the house. The latest explanation is based upon the fact that a tramp is said to have been hanging around that neighbourhood for two weeks past and that Saturday morning he was chased out of old man Fletcher's yard. This tramp is said to have worn a black coat over a long linen duster, with a pair of top boots to complete the outfit. This about completes the description of the ghost as it is given by those who had the pleasure of meeting the gentleman. The last that was seen of the tramp was when he was perched on top of an egg-dealer's wagon on its way to Fergus. But the ghost was seen again on Tuesday evening and the mystery remains unsolved...

About 9:30 o'clock a brilliant light like the headlight of a locomotive was seen in the field of Mr. Joseph Ryan, about two hundred yards from the road and opposite the place where the ghost walks. The light seemed to rise from the ground to a height of twelve feet and move rapidly along for about a quarter of a mile. This was repeated three times and then it sank to the ground, turning a bluish colour as it vanished. The height of the spook is estimated at from 8 to 11 feet, so that he could easily have carried this light in his hand. Mr. Jas. Lynn, the photographer went out with a party on Saturday night to look for the ghost. After spending several weary and fruitless hours driving up and down the road, the party finally discovered a strange looking object near the gate of Greenwood Cemetery. Mr. Lynn sprang our of the rig and gave chase. But the ghost was fleet of foot and Jim succeeded only in getting hold of the spook's coat tails. He tore the coat from the ghost's back and secured the stick with which the spook made himself appear several feet taller. This ghost is, however, thought to be one rigged up for the occasion by other ghost hunters to frighten the skeptical Jim. Mack Gray also saw the ghost on Sunday night. It was a bright moonlight night and Mack was driving quietly along the road, when suddenly the spook appeared before him on the road. The horse was frightened and refused to proceed. Mack, so it is said, jumped out and struck the ghost with his whip three times. The spook thereupon disappeared as mysteriously as he had appeared and was seen no more that night.[7]

John Ross Robinson

One of the many Orangeville people to become involved in newspaper work, John Ross Robinson was raised in Orangeville and attended school in the town:

> "Mr. Robinson is among the old Orangeville boys who have reflected credit on the county town of Dufferin and he stands probably at the head of the distinguished list. He has been editor of the *Evening-Telegram* of Toronto for several years, his literary style being pungent and epigrammatic. The editorials in the *Telegram* are remarkable for their vigorous brevity and in this style of writing Mr. Robinson has few equals in journalism in Toronto. He first won notice as a municipal reporter on the *Telegram*, his reports of the proceedings of the city council being always accurate and elaborate, and when the editorial chair of the journal with which he had been so long connected became vacant, the keen and clever proprietor, Mr. J. Ross Robertson, M.P.,[8] had no hesitation in promoting his bright and piquant municipal reporter to the position.
>
> Brilliant success in a field in which success is so difficult has not turned the head of Mr. Robinson, for he is today as plain and courteous as he was in the years when he was climbing the ladder of distinction, and is always glad to meet old Orangeville friends and to say a good word of the old town in which he spent his schoolboy days."[9]

Doctor W.H.Riddell

Dr. William Henry Riddell (1860–1943) is often referred to as the "Dean of Harness Racing" in Canada. He was born in Caledon just outside of Orangeville in 1860. After studying veterinary surgery and graduating in 1886, he opened a practice in his hometown. He was the mainspring behind Orangeville race meets and was an organizer of the Orangeville Driving Club. In his 45 years as a harness-racing driver he covered an estimated 50,000 miles on the tracks of Canada and United States. He owned several famous horses and was a director of the Canadian Harness Racing Association and the Canadian Racing Association and great friends of the Honorable Earle Rowe.

His obituary reveals, "Dr. Riddell was generous with his means. He was open-handed and unostentatious in his giving. He was quick to support any deserving cause or charity and many were his donations to people who happened to need a helping hand."[10]

David L. Scott
Local residents were involved in Canadian history in many instances. A former mayor of Orangeville, David Scott moved to Orangeville from Hamilton in 1874. In 1884, he moved on to a new community in Saskatchewan called Regina, and was elected its first mayor. He organized a militia unit during the North West Rebellion[11] and earned the

The Tommy Marshall family were big—in their small way. Mr. Marshall was a well-known circus performer and worked across the North American continent. He was a regular at the CNE for many years and locals would take the train down to see the show. The town supplied Mr. Marshall with a fruit cart to assist with family income in the off-season.

208   ORANGEVILLE

rank of lieutenant colonel. He was the first chief justice of the Supreme Court of Alberta when the province was formed in 1905.

Mrs. J.H. Wylie

The women of Orangeville were not only resourceful, they were downright inventive: "Mrs. J.H. Wylie of Zina Street is at a Toronto exhibition demonstrating the new boiler lid of which she is the inventor and which has been named 'Pastugeta.' Last year Mrs. Wylie was awarded the bronze medal for having invented this useful boiler lid."[12]

Dr. James Simpson Island

Dr. James Simpson Island (1875–1933), a dentist and an inventor, was born and raised in Orangeville. Thanks to his genius, many of us who dread a trip to the dentist can expect a more pleasant visit. Not only was he the first dentist in Toronto to introduce sponge gold filling for teeth, but he also invented an electric engine for use on the dental drill. One can only imagine what it would have been like to receive dental work with the uneven and unpredictable use of a foot petal to run the drill.

Some of his other inventions can not claim to have changed the world, but are interesting none the less. He was responsible for a new process of ore refining and worked with the University of Toronto in the process of extracting nitric acid from the air by an electric process. He died in Toronto in 1933. The present Island Lake is named in honour of his family who lived in the red brick farmhouse on a point that used to be clearly visible across the reservoir. It was demolished in 2004.

Bob Cook

Bob Cook (1878–1949) was Orangeville's anti-hero of the early twentieth century. He was born in East Garafraxa and hung around Orangeville most of his life. Bob started to get into trouble very early in life and before long he had done it all—sheep stealing, bank robbery and liquor offences of all sorts from manufacturing to over consumption.

The Orangeville newspapers followed his exploits for decades, reporting every detail. He was a war hero who was wounded, and then discharged for striking his superior officer. He married a 14-year-old girl. Once when he broke out of the Grand Valley lock-up, he took the entire barred window door with him and then sent it back to them by railway express—collect! But Bob was a victim of his own reputation; he liked the attention and always tried to top his last caper.

Villains and Heroes

But in typical anti-hero style, he was loved and admired by everyone in town. He would always lend a hand to help anyone and more that one senior citizen in town remembers Bob crowding as many school kids in his car as possible and driving them to school. The Toronto *Globe and Mail* is quoted as saying, "Bob Cook, who was armed with two revolvers, ran amuck in Orangeville two years ago, defying the police and citizens who attempted to arrest him, is again in the toils. Cook, who was recently liberated from the penitentiary for wounding a policeman at Orangeville, is considered the most widely known jail-breaker in the United States and Canada. Cook's record of jail-breaking is unequalled. He has filed his way out of the lock-ups at Orangeville and the surrounding district on several occasions. Later he escaped from prison at St. Paul, Minnesota, and fled to western Canada, where he again duplicated the trick in a town near Calgary."[13]

Miss M.E. Barclay
In 1913, Miss M.E. Barclay was appointed superintendent of Lord Dufferin Hospital. She took on the role of running the hospital for the IODE, a group of women who built and operated the hospital. She had been trained by Dr. Abraham Groves[14] in Fergus and had begun her career by working as a private nurse.

Her appointment was a good choice. For a salary of $40 per month she was given two responsibilities: firstly, she was to organize the hospital and the staff, and, secondly, to run the nurses' training school at the hospital. She did both well. She lived at the hospital and was on call all day and all night. If someone called she would walk to their homes if necessary, to attend to them or send them on to the hospital. She was clever and pragmatic and knew how to work with little money. One story tells of her running out of bassinettes, so she converted bathtubs for use, lining them with pillows. Dozens of successful nurses trained under her. To say that the women of Orangeville were not strong and progressive would simply be wrong. Miss Barclay worked at the hospital until 1925.

Thomas C. West
Thomas West grew up in Orangeville. His father was a baker in town.

"Thomas C. West, a native of Orangeville, has been elected United States senator from California by a majority of 14,000. Tom studied law in this town many years ago, but has resided at San Francisco, Cal., for a long time, specializing in marriage law. He is a son of the late John West, who was one of the town's pioneer bakers. Mrs. W.J. Robinson of Toronto is a sister and the late R.F. West was a brother.

Tom's old boyhood friends who still live here, will be glad to learn of his latest success and we are sure he will fill the new position with distinction. He will assume office on the 8th of January next and the term is for four years."[15]

Mabel E. Watson

A number of Orangeville women have also made their mark on history, often for unusual reasons.

"Mabel Elizabeth Watson passed away May 1st, 1961, at the age of 81 years, at her residence on 32 Mill Street, Orangeville. She was born in Marsville, the daughter of Elizabeth Ann and Wilson Patterson and attended Ladies Teachers College in Toronto.

Mrs. Watson was the first lady to fly with the Canadian Air Mail, the first time it was inaugurated in 1929. She flew from Calgary to Winnipeg. She married William George Watson in Winnipeg in 1905, and then lived in Winnipeg, Calgary, Brampton and Orangeville."[16]

William Walsh

William Walsh's grandfather, Francis Leigh Walsh, was the registrar for Norfolk County for over 75 years. His father, Aquilla Walsh, was chairman of the commission formed to construct the Intercontinental Railway in 1868.

William Leigh Walsh (1857–1938) was the seventh mayor of the Town of Orangeville. He was a lawyer in town, having moved here in 1881 to join the firm of Maitland and D'Alton McCarthy. In all, he served as mayor three times.

In 1900, he went off to the Yukon and ran for the position of mayor of Dawson City, but was defeated. He moved to Calgary to open a law firm with Stewart McCarthy, who was Maitland McCarthy's son. In Alberta he soon became involved with provincial politics, and, in 1931, he was appointed Lieutenant-Governor of Alberta and was in that role until 1936. He died in Victoria, British Columbia.

Claire Wallace

Claire Wallace was one of the first women broadcasters in Canada. She was the daughter of William Wallace, who published *The Orangeville Advertiser* in the 1890s.

Villains and Heroes 211

Claire Wallace, whose vivacious talks on 'Tea Time Topics' over CFRB are followed with interest by many *Banner* readers, was the magnet, which attracted an overflowing audience to the schoolroom of St. Andrew's church Saturday night. Miss Wallace visited Orangeville under the auspices of [the] St. Andrew's Women's Association, which had set tables for tea for two hundred people, but found itself confronted with the task of entertaining close to three hundred persons. The gathering filled the main Sunday School room to capacity and overflowed into the two rooms at the side. A delectable menu was served by the ladies of the Society under the direction of Mrs. J.N. Brooks, President, and Mrs. Geo. B. Brown, Vice-President.

Introduced to the audience by Mr. A.D. McKitrick, Miss Wallace, who is debarred by contract from making public addresses, confined herself to answering questions. Despite this exacting restriction, she proved brightly entertaining and her remarks were keenly enjoyed. Most of the questions asked her related to radio and radio broadcasting. These she answered quite fully and conveyed a fund of interesting information in her replies. She also told something of her trip to England at the time of the Coronation and some of her experiences as a newspaper woman while in the old land. These and other incidents, related in a charmingly informal manner, served to while away an hour or longer in pleasant manner and won for the guest of the evening hearty rounds of applause when she resumed her seat.

Miss Wallace, who was born on First Avenue, Orangeville, was accompanied by her mother, Mrs. William Wallace, who was a school teacher here before her marriage to Mr. Wallace, at that time publisher of the *Orangeville Advertiser* and now Chairman of the Committee responsible for the Institutional Advertising sponsored by the Canadian Life Insurance Officers Association. Mrs. Wallace met a number of oldtime friends while here and enjoyed her visit to the old town very much...

Miss Wallace's Monday night broadcast was highly interesting to Orangeville listeners. She told of her visit to her hometown on Saturday, spoke of the tea and people she had met, described a visit to the Armstrong Foundry on Wellington St. and the work she saw being done there and gave a concise resume of the early history of the town."[17]

212   ORANGEVILLE

Judge Walter Tyrie Robb
Walter Robb was a native of Dunnville, Ontario. After graduating
from Osgoode Hall in 1914, he practised law in Cayuga and then in
Dunnville. He was appointed judge, County Court of Dufferin in
1931, and retained this position until his retirement on his 75th birthday in 1964.

"In 1944 the Ontario Government invited Judge Robb to become
the Chairman of the Liquor Licence Board of Ontario. He organized
this Board and has been and still is the Chairman [1963]."[18] He died
in Toronto at age 89.

M.H.J. McLary
Sometimes local heroes are known for what they did. For others, how-
ever, their work and reason for fame go unrecognized or forgotten.
Such is the story of M.H.J. McLary.

"Six years' labour by M.H.J. McLary, Orangeville toolmaker and
designer, on an invention that every farmer is waiting for, has resulted in complete blueprints and [the] acquisition of Canadian and
American patents for a weed destroying attachment for plows. A
model of Mr. McLary's creation will be constructed in the near
future, and when materials are available the inventor plans to build
his machine on a large scale in Orangeville.

The weed-destroying attachment relates to a method of and means
for cultivating the soil in the growing of crops, and comprises the pro-
vision of a burner apparatus for attachment to an agricultural imple-
ment such as a plow. From experiments, Mr. McLary has ascertained
that a very efficient method of destroying weeds and conditioning soil
is to subject the ground to the intense heat of a blow-torch while it is
being plowed. This completely destroys weeds as they are uprooted
and is particularly efficacious in killing twitch grass, which is most difficult to eradicate. Also, it is effective in killing insects and their lar-
vae, and results in a betterment of the soil with the assurance that it
is virtually free of weeds and their seeds.

He found that best results were obtained by using a burner at the
front of the plow and another at the rear, the front one being
arranged to throw a flame directly on the land in close proximity to
the point of the plowshare, and the other being arranged to throw
a flame on the turned soil of the furrow. The invention includes suitable blow-torch apparatus for treating the soil in this manner. This

comprises of suspended burners having downward directed nozzles to which hydrocarbon fuel is delivered under high pressure as from a tank in which air pressure is built up by a compressor. The burners have a preheating coil and protected against injury by encompassed guards. They are yieldably mounted by pivotal arms stressed by springs so as to swing backward to clear any obstruction such as a stone.

A distinctive feature of construction is that the burners are devised with a special flexible connection in the fuel line which accommodates the backward motion in riding over an obstruction. Mr. McLary's weed destroying attachment is attachable to gang plows, as well as plows having a single share."[19]

It is interesting to note that they now use steam machines to kill weeds in vineyards.

Maurice Cline
Mr. Cline was the high school principal at Orangeville High School for two generations of students. He was my principal when I started to high school in 1966. He left many legacies of his involvement with the community. First and foremost, he influenced thousands of young teenagers and was diligent at keeping them on the right track. He had a loud booming voice, but he always met everyone at their level. In spite of his position at the school he made the donuts in the cafeteria each lunch. Everyone wondered how he had lost a finger on his left hand, but no one dared to ask. When I asked John Handy, a former teacher under Mr. Cline to sum up his character, John replied "Maurice always gave a student a chance, always believed in him, but if a student did make him mad, that was the end." Mr. Cline was a true hero of Orangeville, always inspirational, and his home was always full of students.

A second legacy left to the community was Maurice Cline's collection of photographs taken in and around Orangeville. From the 1940s to the late 1970s, he took thousands of school, wedding, business and personal photos. The original negatives for these are held at the Dufferin County Museum and Archives.

Orangeville Lions Club
Growing up near Orangeville in the 1950s, I had my favourite haunts. One of them was the local Orangeville outdoor pool. It had been

The Orangeville Lions Club decided in 1948 that the town needed a swimming pool, so they literally built it themselves.

erected by the Orangeville Lions Club and for me these men were heroes. In Grand Valley all of us took swimming lessons in a deep hole behind the dam in the Grand River. So to come to town and smell the cleanness of the chlorinated water and to use a real diving board was amazing. The Orangeville's town council of the time felt that they could not afford to build and maintain a public pool, and some even felt that it was unnecessary as it would never be used. So the Lions Club took on the task.

In May 1954, with volunteer labour and money raised from the community, the project began. The plan included a cement block bathing house with a bright green roof and orange trim. When the pool opened that summer, the Orangeville Bottling Works supplied free cokes to everyone. To save money, the benches placed around the pool were recycled old pews from the refurbished Mono Mills United Church. We thought it was wondrerful!

However, once the Tony Rose Arena, with its plans for an indoor pool, opened in the late 1960s, the Lions pool was closed a few years later. A modern growing town tended to support the slicker indoor pool. This little Lions pool is long gone, but the memories of many a kid like me will make its builders heroes in Orangeville forever.

Max Braithwaite
John Victor Maxwell Braithwaite (1911–1995), born in Nokomis, Saskatchewan, was a well-known author before he arrived in Orangeville in the early 1950s. He quickly became involved with local groups and politics and was one of the first "outsiders" to tackle town council. He served as a councillor. Mr. Braithwaite brought attention to the town when he published, in 1973, a novel called *A Privilege and*

A Pleasure, which was based on incidents and characters in Orangeville (although he had changed the names to protect the guilty).That same year he won the Stephen Leacock medal of honour for his book *The Night We Stole the Mountie's Car.* He was a disciplined writer and was ably assisted by his wife Aileen.

The Braithwaites had five children. Their eldest daughter, Beryl, played a CBC character called Maggie Muggins. She was married to John Hart, who became known for replacing Clayton Moore as the Lone Ranger in 1952, but only for two seasons.

Max Braithewaite moved to Brighton, Ontario, and died at his home there in 1995 but was buried here in Orangeville at his request. He always felt that Orangeville was his true home.

Joanna Malouk

Joanna Malouk was the first woman councillor in Orangeville and one of the pioneers in education for the developmentally challenged children of Orangeville and Dufferin County area.

She was born in Lancashire, in the north of England in 1925. As a teenager and a free thinker, she was drawn to the Quaker Church and became a lifelong member of that religion after leaving the Roman Catholic faith. During the last year of the Second World War, she served in the British Navy as a "cipher," translating German transmissions using the newly developed "Enigma" deciphering machines. When the war ended, because of her active service during the war, the British government paid for her to get a university education. Joanna went to Oxford University.

After graduation, she spent a year learning how to teach "mental defectives" (teaching mentally handicapped children was a newly developing discipline at that time). For an adventure, she then went to Lebanon to teach English to adults at the American University in Beirut for a couple of years. While there she met her husband-to-be. They emigrated to Canada in the early 1950s and she took a job in Orangeville, Ontario, as the principal of a newly opened "Opportunity School" for mentally handicapped students. She served in this capacity for several years, and continued to instruct developmentally challenged young people in their homes once she left the school to raise a family.

In 1962, Joanne opened her own nursery school, Malouk Preparatory School, on the main level of her own home. She ran this school for ten years, as both a nursery school for children before they entered the school system and as a daycare centre from 1967 to 1972. She served on the Orangeville Town Council and on the Dufferin County School Board as a trustee. The Opportunity School was opened in Orangeville in 1955 by the Dufferin Association of Retarded Children. The purpose was to provide training programs for children with learning challenges to help them "grow intellectually, spiritually and physically, as well as emotionally, in order that adequate self-care, social adjustments, good planning of leisure time and satisfying usefulness may be realized."[20]

Veryl White
In the 1960s, the entire community followed the health of a local merchant. When he recovered, everyone was proud of the attention his surgery had brought to the town and of the hope he had given to many Canadians who suffered from heart disease.

A Canadian surgeon perfects a daring new operation that can mean a return to normal life for more than 5,000,000 heart-attack victims. Three months ago, a man was dying. He was 42. Veryle White was a grocery storekeeper in Orangeville, Ontario (population 5,200), married to a former nurse, Doreen, and the father of four fine sons.

The first sign of death came one evening four years earlier as he watched television at home. He recalls, "Suddenly, it was like a giant's hand squeezing my chest; I couldn't breathe." Weeks later, he had another attack in his store. Both were coronary occlusions, and White spent a month in the local hospital.

A year ago, a third seizure felled him. Months later, he still could not regain his strength. "I felt like an 80-year-old man," he says. "If I walked a block, I had pains." Doctors estimated the three attacks had robbed his heart of 70 per cent of its blood supply. Last July, White's doctor told him that only surgery might replace the lost blood. The physician sent him to Dr. Arthur Vineberg at Montreal's Royal Victoria Hospital. The decision was simple, White says, "I felt myself slipping; I knew it was operate or else." At the end of World War II, Dr. Arthur M. Vineberg set out to thwart the killing effects of coronary occlusion. In such an attack, a clot blocks the flow of blood through the arteries that surround and nourish the heart. The clot cannot pass because the artery's channel has been narrowed by an accumulation of hardened fat globules. With its blood source shut off, the heart dies. Dr. Vineberg's self-imposed task: restore the lost blood supply. After five years of research, Dr. Vineberg found a surgical answer. He freed one end of an artery that normally brings blood to the chest muscles and planted it in the heart. It rooted there and restored nearly 60 per cent of the heart's blood.

Patients fared well after surgery, but Dr. Vineberg was not satisfied with only 60 per cent. Patients deserved better than that; he wanted 100 per cent. He returned to the laboratory, resolved to find better ways. A year ago, he improved his original surgery with two new manoeuvres. The 100-per cent goal was now in sight.

When grocer White entered the Royal Victoria Hospital on August 26, he became the 74th patient to try the daring new surgery. Now it's over, and the operation has given him a second chance for a full life. Experts say that the Vineberg technique can do much for the more than five million persons in the United States and Canada whose hearts are dying from lack of blood.

A new X-ray technique helps decide whether Veryle White can benefit from the Vineberg operation. In this process, called cine arteriography, Dr. Skinner threads a hollow tube through an artery in White's armpit into the vessels feeding his heart. Next, Dr. Skinner injects radiopaque dye through the tube and, as the dye enters the blood circulating around the heart, a movie camera films a sequence of X-ray pictures. In the developed film, the dye pinpoints the location and extent of blockage caused by coronary occlusions. Viewed by a hospital team that includes Vineberg, Skinner, anesthesiologist Dr. John Wynands and cardiologist Dr. John Shanks, the White film showed three plugs, or obstructions. Now, ten days after surgery, Veryle White walks the hospital corridors with a firm step and colour in his cheeks. He is on a low fat, high protein diet and is taking an anticoagulant to lessen the chance of a coronary occlusion during convalescence. In another ten days, White will leave the Royal Victoria Hospital and go home. Within three to six months, he will enjoy the full effects of his three-wat surgery and can resume full activity. Even if more coronary clots occur, his heart will have the blood it needs. He's a happy man. So is Dr. Vineberg—with one regret. "So many others could enjoy the same gift of life," he days, "if only more doctors realized that surgery can correct coronary artery disease."[21]

And Many More…

There are dozens of other famous people who lived in the area. Many went to high school in town or were from the rural areas that made

Orangeville their centre. Such people would include Minervah (1872–1957) and Hannah Reid (1870–1955), born in Mono Township. Early Canadian female doctors they were founders of Women's College Hospital in Toronto. Minerva Reid was chief surgeon there from 1915 to 1925.

Also included would be Robert Gunn Bremner, born near Orangeville, who became the New Jersey state representative under his close friend, President Woodrow Wilson. Another example is W.J. Hughes who created and produced "Corn Flower," a pattern cut into glass that was sold and collected all across Canada during the '40s, '50s and '60s.

There were countless others. Many of them often referred to this area as their home and felt that Orangeville had helped in some way as they made their way to fame and fortune.

16

OFF TO WAR: CITIZENS WHO SERVED

THE MILITARY EXPERIENCE BROUGHT TO Orangeville by its
settlers was varied and vast.

Original land grants were often handed out anded out in lieu
of a pension for veteran soldiers from the Napoleonic Wars, and from
service in the War of 1812–14. Many local citizens served in the local
militia and were ready for the battle that never came during the Fenian scares of 1866. Orangeville has had citizens serve in every North
American conflict and two world wars. To tell all of their stories would
be impossible, these that follow are but a few.

Fought Under Duke Of Wellington
The Napoleonic Wars were a series of French army campaigns from
1800–15, led by Napoleon I against Russia and Great Britain and other
European nations. They ended in 1815 with the defeat of the French
by British general, the Duke of Wellington, at the Battle of Waterloo.

There resides now in the Town of Orangeville, an old veteran named
James Shaw, who served under Sir John Moore and the Duke of
Wellington in the Peninsular War, and who was present at twelve
general engagements, besides innumerable skirmishes, and who,
notwithstanding the severe hardships, which he must have endured,
and his advanced years, well retains all his faculties unimpaired,
stands as erect as a "soldier in the line" and walks with the elastic
step of a man of forty. We had a visit the other day from this Old
Veteran, and were entertained and edified by his vivid descriptions
of the terrible campaigns in which he participated, and the bloody
battles which he witnessed.

Mr. Shaw is a native of Ireland, having been born in the County of Monaghan in 1792, and is consequently in his eighty-third year. Enlisting into the 3rd Buffs he first served under Sir Hugh Dalrymple in Portugal, and was present at the surrender of the French at Lisbon, and the capture of the Russian fleet on the Tagus in August 1808. He fought under Sir John Moore, at the Battle of Corunna, in 1809, and was present at the Passage of the Duoro, the capture of Opporto, and the Battle of Basaco in 1810. He was at Albubern, under Gen. Beresford, in 1811, and took part in storming Almaras, under Gen. Hill in 1812. He fought under the Duke of Wellington in all the actions of the Pyrenees and the Battles of Nivelle and Nive in 1813. In 1814, he took part in the Battles of Ortis and Toulouse, and, crossing the Atlantic fought under Sir Geo. Provost at Lake Champlain and Plattsburg in the same year.

Though exposed in all these engagements to the fire of the enemy, he was singularly fortunate having been but once wounded. This was in one of the engagement on the Pyrenees, where he was struck by a ball which fractured his left jaw. He had, however, many hair-breadth escapes, especially in the Battle of Nive, when his knapsack was shot off his back.

This Old Veteran retired from the army, receiving a pension of one shilling sterling a day, which was last year increased to one shilling and sixpence. He has a retentive memory, and his description of the Generals under whom he served, and of the battles in which he fought, are vivid and highly interesting, and free from that view of egotism and bombast which too frequently permeate the "recollections" of old soldiers. He enjoys robust good health, goes regularly to Toronto to draw his pension, and has every appearance of being spared to enjoy it for many years yet to come. There are but few pensioners under Her Majesty living to-day, who have been in more engagements than Mr. Shaw.[1]

Crimean War

The Crimean War (1853–56) was a war between Russia and an alliance of Great Britain, France, Sardinia and Turkey. Most of the war was fought in the Crimea, a peninsula of the Ukraine lying between the Sea of Azoz and the Black Sea. The Crimean War is considered by historians to be the first modern conflict.

Basically, the war was fought for authority over the "Holy Land." It was here that Florence Nightingale (1820–1910) the English nurse and

Off to War: Citizens Who Served

medial reformer, became famous for her work in improving medical procedures, thus reducing mortality rates. Less famous and almost forgotten was a soldier, Hugh Lowrie, who lived a hero's life but died in the county jail located on Zina Street, Orangeville, a long way from the Black Sea.

There died in Orangeville, on Friday last, August 30, 1918 in the person of Hugh Lowrie, one of nature's gentlemen of the old school. He was born in Ayr, Scotland [on] May 2, 1832. And retained to the time of his death the accent and many characteristics of his native land. When scarcely more than a lad he went into the army, enlisting in the 2nd Dragoons, better known on many a hard fought field as the Scots Greys, and with that famous regiment served in the Crimean War, from the spring of 1854 to 1856. His most important engagements were the battle of Inkerman and the taking of Sebastopol, both of which he could tell many stirring incidents. For his services he received the Crimean and Turkish medals.

Hugh Lowrie, who was a local shoemaker, received the Turkish and Crimean Military Medals for his military service.

Taking his discharge after the war, he came to Canada and worked at his trade as a shoemaker. He had a shop of his own in Erin then moved to Grand Valley. He worked with Mr. Lawson until about nine years ago, when approaching old age rendered further labour impossible, and in default of [any] other home he came to the County Refuge at Orangeville where he died.

A small compassionate pension granted by the British Government in 1910 enabled him to add a few additional necessaries of life to those provided by the County and to end his days in comparative comfort, besides providing for his burial. He had been married in his earlier days, but from the time of settling in this part of the country was a widower without family or relatives, although he never lacked friends who esteemed him in the community in which he lived.[2]

American Civil War
Although the American Civil War (1861–65) was fought south of the border, far away from Orangeville, several local residents chose to join

the war. Most were not politically driven, but were lured by the pay that they could earn as a soldier. Some went for adventure. Few of them left any trace of their stories. This brief account in *The Sun*, gives a little insight and the name of one such individual:

> We understand that Mr. Richard Hewat has joined the Signal Corps of the United States Army. From a letter received by an acquaintance of his here, we learn that, though only a few weeks enlisted, he has already earned the confidence of his superior officers, and has been complimented for eminent services rendered the corps.[3]

Fenian Raids
A local militia was formed in 1865 in response to the potential threat of Fenian raids. These raids were attacks by members of the Irish Republican Brotherhood, a militant 19th Century nationalist organization founded in the United States, on British government forts and facilities in Canada. Their aim was to pressure Britain to withdraw from Ireland. The conflicts were close to the minds of many of the Irish Protestants living in Orangeville, who saw the ideas as Catholic-supported and a danger to their new country. Fears of the impending raids were fuelled locally by newspaper reports in the new Orangeville newspaper, *The Sun.*

By July 1866 the militia had received 5,000 rounds of ammunition and they were practising firing for the first time. New uniforms were shipped in from Toronto that same month and they put on their first dress parade. Over 3,000 people showed up for the event. Lunch was provided for the boys at the American Hotel. When the drill concluded in the afternoon, the Company marched to Thorpe's Hotel where a supper and several toasts followed. The local paper reported however that, "the cavalry horses, as was to be expected, did not understand the business well and the firing threw them into some confusion."[4] The militia uniforms of the time included shakos (a type of headgear featuring a tall cylindrical peaked cap) and redcoats. The shakos were ornamented at the front with a brilliant metal star enclosing a Canadian Beaver encircled by the words "Canada Militia" in raised letters, the whole thing surrounded by a representation of the Crown. The jackets had buttons with a matching insignia.

> A complementary supper will be given at Kelly's Hotel on Broadway to honour our gallant Volunteers, who went to the front in 1866 to repel Fenian Invasion. It is undeniable that the peace and security which we enjoy are mainly attributable to the patriotism of

Off to War: Citizens Who Served   223

our Volunteers and we therefore hope that our townsmen will show their high appreciation of such valuable services by patronizing by their presence the entertainment in honour of our citizen soldiers who so nobly risked their lives in defense of our country and our liberties. Tickets .50 each.[5]

When looking for material about Orangeville during the threat of the Fenian Raids, I found reference to an unknown resident of town who had written his memories of the period when he was a child. His story is about his father being drafted into the militia, his reminiscences of the Fenian Raids and of the local cadet company being formed.

In these piping times of peace it is almost impossible to realize that but for a few short years ago war's alarms were thundering at our very doors, and no doubt it was a surprise to some of our peace-loving citizens, who do not know a rifle from a canthook, to learn that our fathers were once "drafted" for active service with the colours. That they were not called upon to take the field does not alter the fact that their names were enrolled and that they were both ready and willing to risk life and limb in defence of Queen and country. Nor was the occasion merely a threatened invasion by an organized horde of irresponsible fanatics. It was much more serious than that.

So near the breaking point were relations between the British and American government in the early sixties that millions of pounds were expended by Great Britain in preparation of the struggle; British troops were rushed to Canada. British, French, Dutch and native-born Canadians were organized and armed for the fray. Needless to say the men of this country rose to the occasion, and although the first contingent was raised by "draft," i.e., by ballot, this was only done to avoid favouritism in the selection of the necessary number from among the thousands who volunteered. The men of Orangeville were at that time connected with the 2nd Battalion of Militia and those of Amaranth with the 1st Battalion. The following are the names of those who were drafted in Orangeville: 2nd Batt.—Thomas Fletcher, A. Best, John Hanna, Daniel Pisten, David Dunn, Robert Hewitt, James Corbett, Thomas Henry, Joseph Nelson, P. Mitchell, Samuel Allen, Charles Peran, Robert McKitrick, James Fead; Amaranth 1st Batt.—Phillip Watt, James Thompson, John Bell, Charles Wheaton, J. Mills, James Fennell, James Whitton, Hector Phillips, Joseph Pease, John Hughson, F. Durkin, William Tansley, R.J. Allen,

W. Cooney, T. McGarvey, H. Armstrong, R. Jefferson, William Irwin, William Curry, Patrick Curry.

Fortunately for all concerned and particularly for the government at Washington, diplomacy settled the differences and comparative quiet prevailed until the spring of '66, when the "army of Irish Liberators," assembled at different points along the United States' border and threatened to capture Canada and sweep the British Flag off the American continent. At this time the Canadian Volunteer Militia was pretty well organized, fairly well drilled and in fine fighting fettle, and when the news passed through the country that "The Fenians would cross at Fort Erie," thousands sprang to arms and a few took to the woods. In '66 odd as it may now seem, there was no telegraph line in all this upper district, and news could be sent no faster than a good horse could gallop. But bad news, then as now, could travel with lightning speed, and strange and fearsome indeed were the rumours that flew thick and fast up and down the concession lines.

One report would have it that the Fenians were massing east of Mono Mills; another, that they were descending upon the town from Adjala and with one canard and another, women were hysterical and men slept little night or day, and then always with one eye open. At

In 1866, the 36th Battalion mustered on Broadway prior to setting off for the American border to play their part in repelling the Fenian raiders. This photograph was later completed in oils by well-known artist Owen Staples and is now housed at the Dufferin County Museum & Archives.

Off to War: Citizens Who Served   225

last on Friday, June 1st, 1866, orders were received by the Orangeville company to turn out and report for duty at Toronto. Women wept and strong men trembled but the brave soldier boys, with two or three notable exceptions, rallied to the standard, piled into lumber wagons and hit the trail for Brampton where they entrained for the city. Many and fantastic are the tales that are told of the conduct of the men during the three weeks they were on "active marks."

The officers of the Orangeville company were: Captain Thomas Jull; Lieutenant Orange Lawrence; Ensign, William Parsons. When the bugle sounded the assembly on that historical June day the men as a rule responded with alacrity, willing and anxious to face the foe, but there were two or three whose hearts failed them, whose feet got cold, whose one idea seemed to be that the call meant certain death. To round up those [men] a squad was sent out under Corporal Andrew Jones. The corporal got his men, one in the bush, another in a cupboard and still another after a long chase, but as their trouble was merely stage fright and they afterwards proved to be gallant "sodgers" their names will not be given—though that could readily be done.

In Toronto the men were put through a gruelling course of instruction. When not on guard duty they were practising the goose step and bayonet exercise and were quite frequently turned out at midnight on false alarms. At first they were in momentary expectation of being ordered to the firing line, but as time passed they settled down to barrack duty and at the end of the third week returned home, sound to wind and limb and undismayed.

If on their departure there was consternation, on their return there was hilarity and tumultuous joy. Men, women and children from all the countryside trooped into headquarters and joined with the villagers in a rousing reception to the heroes just back from the wars. There was music, song and dancing bonfires and banquets, an days passed before business resumed the even tenor of its way.

In the absence of the fighting men, the homestayers were not idle. The families of the absentees were looked after to the Queen's taste. Farmers and their wives in the nearby townships brought in butter, eggs, potatoes and sides of pork, home-smoked hams and sacks of flour sufficient to keep the grass widows and the tow-headed kids for weeks and the women of the village knitted socks enough for a whole brigade of foot soldiers, and they were the socks that would wear—not the kind with clocks or yellow bumble bees. Possibly some of them are still in service.

226   ORANGEVILLE

At this period and for some time thereafter military excitement
was tense, and, in the spring of 1867, an uniformed cadet company
was organized in the village, a fact that will be news to some of the
boys of today. The uniforms consisted of a scarlet tunic, a forage cap
and belt, and miniature rifles were promised by the government. The
cadets were under the supervision of Captain Orange Lawrence and
the drill instructor was Sergeant Thomas Campbell...The cadets
were very popular; they were exceptionally well trained and were
always in evidence on ceremonial occasions. They took a prominent
part in a military review which was held here in celebrations of the
first Dominion Day, July 1, 1867. Under the guidance of Captain
Lawrence and Sergeant Campbell the cadets flourished...."[6]

But not everyone in town was on the same side during the Fenian
scare. "It is reported on reliable authority that J.H. Brown, late
Colonel in the Fenian army, who has recently been found guilty of a
breach of the United States neutrality laws, and sentenced to three
years imprisonment for his connection with the Fenian raid into Canada,
is the same J.H. Brown who carried on business in Cheltenham and
Orangeville some time ago and absconded, leaving several wholesale
merchants much the worse by their acquaintance with him."[7]

First World War
No family could represent Orangeville in the First World War better
than the Macpherson family. No less than four brothers signed up for
service. Sons of the local chief librarian, Dugald Macpherson and his
wife, Sarah (Wilson), each young man (John Ross, Donald Stuart,
Ewart Gladstone and Douglas William McPhee) brought fame to the
town in their own way.

An Arts undergraduate student at the University of Saskatchewan,
John Ross Macpherson signed up to the Princess Patricia's Canadian
Light Infantry (PPCLI) in 1914. On promotion to captain, Macpher-
son commanded "A" Company, and was awarded the Distinguished
Service Order (DSO) for his actions during the Battle of Passchendaele
in October 1917. He was promoted to the temporary rank of major in
August 1918. John Ross Macpherson was killed in action on August 26,
1918, at Jigsaw Wood, Monchy-Le-Preux, France, during the Battle of
Amiens. As few under the rank of major were awarded the DSO, the
designation signified extraordinary bravery.

Off to War: Citizens Who Served 227

His DSO citation reads:

> After a personal reconnaissance he led his company forward and surrounded and captured an enemy stronghold, together with its garrison, in spite of determined resistance and intense shellfire. His energy and initiative were entirely responsible for the success of the operation, which straightened out the line for a further successful operation on the following day.

Donald Macpherson enlisted in the Canadian Field Artillery on July 14, 1916. He was awarded the Military Medal (MM) in October 1917, for his role in the Battle of Passchendaele, the same action for which his brother, John Ross, was awarded the DSO. Donald Macpherson maintained detailed diaries during his wartime experience. His diary has been edited by his son, Ken and published (*A Soldier's Diary: The WWI Diaries of Donald Macpherson*) in 2001. Donald's son also served Canada in the Royal Canadian Navy. After the war, Donald Macpherson resumed his former career of teacher, and became an elementary school principal with the Toronto Board of Education.

The sons of Sarah and Dugald Macpherson served with distinction in the First World War; J. Ross Macpherson did not return. *Clockwise from top left*: Lieut. D.S. Macpherson, Capt. J. Ross Macpherson, Lieut. D.W. Macpherson and Lieut. Ewart G. Macpherson.

Ewart Gladstone Macpherson enlisted on December 8, 1915, in the 164th Battalion, CEF. Lieutenant Macpherson served in the Royal Flying Corps. During the war, Ewart delivered an "Air Mail" letter to his brother Donald, simply by flying over Donald's Officer Training Camp at Whitley, England. The method of delivery was tossing the letter over the side of the cockpit. The letter was delivered. (It survives today as part of the DCMA collections, having been donated to the museum by his family. It is marked "message delivered by aeroplane.") He rose to the rank of wing commander in the Royal Canadian Air Force in the Second World War.

Douglas Macpherson enlisted on September 10, 1916, in the 46th Battalion, CEF from Moose Jaw, Saskatchewan. He was awarded the Military Cross for his participation in the Battle of Amiens, August 1918. The citation for the granting of the Military Cross reads as follows:

During the attack he behaved with extraordinary courage and steadiness. He was incessantly backward and forward on the battlefield cheering on his men and getting them on in splendid order. On several occasions during the action he distinguished himself by his coolness and prompt action. He set the finest example to the troops he led.

The following is a letter written by Donald to his parents after hearing of his brother Ross's death:

London, Sept. 5th, 1918
Dear people o' mine—

My heart aches with the knowledge of the sorrow that has come upon us all, news of which reached Ewart and me here just today. My mind is numb as I write, and I do not know how to ease the suffering that I know is yours. If I could only be home to take you all in my arms and mingle my tears with yours until, perhaps, that Divine Peace of God might come upon us to rest our tortured minds and souls.

How are you bearing up under the weight of this blow, my folk? I pray that God, in his mercy, has comforted your sorrow, for no other power could guide you safely through these dark hours. Ewart and I here have fought it out together, and I think we are beginning to come again towards the light. But the shadow of this the darkest day of our lives will long remain; and I fear there are many hours yet before God's merciful Hand can heal the sorrow we have all suffered. It is only your sublime faith, mother, that can save us in this time of trouble. I know it has not failed you, and that knowledge is the refuge in which Ewart and I have at last found some measure of relief.

You have taught us boys, father & mother, that life is only worthwhile for the service we can render the world and our fellowmen. You looked on smiling bravely while all of us who could embarked on this great crusade for the freedom and liberty of all generations to come. You have passed in quiet courage and faith the weeks and months and years of anxious waiting, and inspired all your soldier sons to overcome the hardships and dangers and evil things that lay in the path of duty.

And now one of us has fallen, true and brave to the last, after a distinguished record of service that few can equal in this life for the cause of righteousness. Oh, people of mine, let's try to be proud and not sorrowful; for his life has been spent to the end in service for his fellow [men], and God has called him, in His wisdom to a place surely not so far away and where in a few short years we can hope to join him once again.

We have found out for certain that Douglas is still safe, and Ewart is now sending you a cable in which we have tried to bring you some degree of comfort, knowing that you like us are broken hearted with the loss of Ross and the loneliness that has come into our lives. We can obtain no information regarding the manner of his death, except that all the officers in his company were killed in the engagement. There is no doubt they all fought heroically to the end. I am writing the O.C. of the battalion for particulars.

I am sorry to know by your letter that you were still suffering anxiety on my account. You will know by now that I am getting well quickly. In a week or two I shall be walking quite freely, and shall make every effort to be promptly boarded and granted a furlough home. What chance there is of success I cannot say; so please do not build too confidently on it. But I shall not easily give up hope myself.

Does this letter bring comfort to you, people of mine? Oh I do hope it does a little. But my heart and head are like lead, and I cannot think of words that might help. Ewart is going to try to send a few lines too. He bore up bravely and had helped me wonderfully. I don't think I could have borne it if he had not been with me.

I shall try to write Marjorie tomorrow. Poor girl, she will suffer equally with us all and I do not know how to comfort her.

God bless you all, dear people. May He be very near to you these dreary days and nights. My deepest love flows out to you now as always.

Affectionately
Donald

Second World War
The Second World War reached Orangeville with the sad news of the death of Reginald Robb, son of Judge and Mrs. Walter T. Robb. A letter from him winged its way home and was received after his untimely death. The entire town mourned.

"This unfinished letter, its lines filled with the triumphant and unflinching spirit of its author under the shadow of death, has been bequeathed by a 25-year-old Canadian bomber pilot as his last message to a world in which he no longer lives. 'I am the lucky one as I have gone to the land where there is no time. It will be only a momentary lapse in the infinite before you are all with me, and so, courage!'

"So wrote Flight Sergeant Reg. Robb, before he was shot down while piloting a bomber against the enemy on February 26th. He left the unfinished letter in his Commanding Officer's possession with a message that it should be delivered to his father, Judge W.T. Robb, of Orangeville, when the simple arithmetic of death, which he knew so well, would call his number.

"It is published this Good Friday in the hope that its ringing message of faith and courage will bring some measure of hope, consolation and peace to other mothers and fathers:

Dear Dad, Mother and all the beloved Robb family:

I can give this letter no date, as it is possible that it may never be used, but in case anything goes wrong, this will be my last word to all of you.

Don't feel worry for me, as I've gone to something better and the day is not far removed when we shall be reunited. I have lived a happy life, and enjoyed it to the fullest—having made a host of friends and (I hope) very few enemies.

Always having been an idealist rather than a realist it was natural that I should answer the call of my conscience to join the service in a crusade against a barbarous enemy who threatens to annihilate mankind. I should never have been able to rest in peace for the rest of my days had I ignored the call. The greatest problem I had to solve was the one of the Robb family. I knew that, having been brought up a true Canadians that the whole family would plunge into the conflict body and soul, and that there would be hearts broken—those at home would could do nothing but patiently wait. Yes! They also serve! Whatever the end may be, you will all be able to proudly walk in any company and explain, "We did our bit." I am the lucky one, as I have gone to a land where there is no time. It will be only a momentary lapse in the infinite before you are all with me, and so courage!

Having considered our manner of living and making an odious comparison with the one which Hitler is trying to push on us, I could arrive at no other decision than to help preserve our civilization.

The country that had been so kind to our family was in danger.

Was the supreme sacrifice too much to give? No! A quarter of a century ago thousands of our young men were forced to make the same decision. They held up their part bravely, and died in the realization of having accomplished their goal. But the goal was not reached—it was only a lull in the storm. To us they threw the torch, and my only hope is that I have the fortitude and ability to be able to handle it in the same proud and unconquerable manner.

One of these nights I will climb into my plane and take off into the black. I shall ascend above the clouds to the peaceful atmosphere only realized by those chosen few who have been given the opportunity of meeting it. How strange it is—so serene, calm and clean. It is like being taken out of a world gone mad for blood, into a land of make-believe. White billowy clouds below, and the moon and stars brightly beaming above. I will sit back and thank God that he has showed me this divine pleasure in His sad world. I will take a deep breath of that sweet fresh air—for miles it will be thus— thinking to myself "God's in His Heaven, all's right with the world."

Suddenly the realization will sweep over me that all's not right with the world. I will be rudely awakened from my reverie with that peculiar odour associated with an aircraft. Fumes of burnt petrol stinging my nostrils—the ominous hum of my motors—I have reached my destination. Alas! I must descend to the cruel world once more. Even my kite senses the change. From the calm rocking back and forth it will begin to shudder as I give it more power. We will be tossed about by the turbulent clouds—confusion will reign everywhere. Blue pencils of light will stab out, searching frantically for the horribly scarred English cities. Bomb doors open. There go the messengers of death. One from London—one from Coventry— one from Birmingham—and so on until the monster will be repaid a thousand fold for the destruction of our people.

Suddenly there will be a horrible crash—we've had it! A lucky hit—or perhaps I should say an unlucky hit. Surprisingly I am not afraid—a peace that I never before knew engulfs me and I wait impatiently to pass through the gates into the unknown.

To you who are left behind is a task—a huge task. A new world order must be created where men can live in peace and plenty without fear or prejudice. It is up to you to see our job finally completed. No more lives must be sacrificed to satisfy the hunger of Mars. Beat your swords into ploughshares. Preach the gospel of "Peace on earth, good-will towards men." Never again allow the rivers of our world to run red with the blood of our youth. I am depending on you to aid in this movement."

The ancient philosopher, Confucius, once wrote: "It is not the truth that makes man great, but man that makes truth great!" This is the sort of man that must be moulded in the future generations, for if there is great truth on earth then there will be great men, and great men are certainly not those who try to become great at the expense of other people.[8]

As the days of the Second World War lengthened into months and years, the list of those serving on land, sea and in the air also grew. Young men and women went forth to play Orangeville's part in the services. At the same time others turned their hands to the factories, promoted the sale of war bonds, and assisted with the war effort in many ways, even making bandages. When the war was over, the Town of Orangeville saw fit to present each veteran with a gold ring bearing the inscription "Orangeville."

During the war, a corvette of the Royal Canadian Navy was launched under the name HMCS *Orangeville*. The navy had named all of its corvettes after Canadian towns and residents felt very honoured to have the name of their town included in the selection. Constructed in the shipyards of Henry Robb of Leith, Scotland, the ship was intended for the Royal Navy. The ship served on escort convoys from Newfoundland to Ireland and for searching out U Boats. In 1946, after the war, she was sold off to Nationalist China.

For many years the beautiful brass ship's bell was built into a showcase outside the Orangeville Royal Canadian Legion Branch 233. One night in the late 1990s the bell was stolen, and, despite numerous ads and attempts to locate it, the bell was never recovered, a fact still lamented by the many townsfolk with interest in Canadian military history.

17

ORANGEVILLE MOMENTS: SIGNIFICANCE IN CANADA

IF EVERY TOWN HAS ITS own claim to fame, then Orangeville must have one too. I have travelled to many places in my life to witness where someone was born or where someone famous is claimed to have slept. I have read dozens of historical plaques about battles and the first of something or other. There is no such plaque in Orangeville or any big sign claiming it to be the birthplace of some well-known hockey star. What did Orangeville do to set us apart, make us special or to influence the life and history of Canadians? If I were erecting a historical plaque for Orangeville, I would be honouring our inventors and our influence in Canadian politics.

It is the inventors of Orangeville, and there have been many of them, who have brought convenience and change to many lives. but most of their names have been long forgotten. Even before the village was incorporated, local inventors were giving the community a reputation for being progressive, always eager to try new things.

An ad in the April 11, 1867, edition of *The Sun,* for W. Daniels of Canada West stated, "The proprietor begs to announce to the Farmers of Amaranth, Mono, Caledon and Garafraxa and the surrounding country that he has opened a large establishment on East Broadway, for the Manufacture and Sale of Fanning Mills, horse rakes, straw cutters and rocking churns with every article warrented [sic]." These time-saving inventions freed the farmers from time consumptive labour and allowed that time to be used for clearing additional land or for extending their holdings.

Fanning mills, built by William Daniels of Orangeville, removed the seeds of weeds from the grain seeds, eliminating the need for constant

Fanning mills were one of the first conveniences that pioneer farmers could afford. Rather than winnowing their flailed grain, they could pour it into the fanning mill where a series of fans and sieves separated the grain from weed seed and chaff. William Daniels had a shop on Broadway where fanning mills were built to meet the local need. *Courtesy of the DCMA Artifact Collection.*

weeding of the plants that choked out their much-needed feed grain. The invention and ones similar to it caught on and changed Canadian agriculture.

Another truly Canadian invention was designed specifically for this region of Canada. "Mr. George Bell of Orangeville has invented a combined wagon and sleigh, designed to supercede all other vehicles during the broken seasons in Canada, when good wagoning or sleighing is uncertain. By an ingenious contrivance and the use of a small lever, the runners or wheels may be raised or lowered to suit circumstances, and the vehicle transferred into a sleigh or wagon. Mr. Bell has obtained a patent for his invention and intends soon bringing it before the public."[1]

And yet another great Orangeville invention is still being used today on local lawns and lawns around the world. The owners of Armstrong Foundry and Machine Shop took out a patent at the turn of the century for a hollow steel cylinder, which could be filled and weighted by water. When loaded it made a fine roller, and when empty it could be handled for easy storage. The invention proved very popular and the lawnroller quickly replaced the heavy wooden rollers made from the trunks of heavy trees, but their popularity brought on many copies shortly after their invention.

A creative man, James Armstrong, also invented a saw called the Dufferin Champion, which he manufactured in the foundry as well. Of an ingenious construction, it primarily was used for cutting long poles. Its safety design was attractive as many a pioneer man had lost fingers and limbs to mechanical saws. The foundry was located at the corner of Wellington and Armstrong streets along the river, in the former building of the King Brothers Furniture Company. The Armstrongs had acquired the building from the Kings in 1894.

A number of inventions were the result of the inventive mind of the grandson of the man Orangeville is named after—Orange Lawrence. In fact, Orange Jull is said to have added substantially to the industrial achievement of Canada. He gained national and even international fame for his inventiveness and practicality. Apparently, Orange Jull was extremely interested in innovations that increased the capacity of the mill that he operated in Orangeville. Jull spent long hours as a youth watching the operation of the mill and conceiving ideas that would later bring him fame. It is obvious that the use of waterpower and the ability to extract useful energy from it was dominant in his later inventions. In 1862, he modified a turbine wheel and penstock (a water intake structure that controls the flow of water) that was patented in Illinois that year. In 1875, he patented this device in Canada, and, as previously mentioned, adapted his design for use in his father's mill in 1876.

In addition to the turbine, Jull devised a paddlewheel, which was used extensively on the Great Lakes, and for which he received substantial compensation. The invention, which is said to have brought Jull to international recognition, was the rotary snowplough. In fact, it's said to be Canada's most important contribution to world railroading. In 1869, a Toronto dentist, J.W. Elliott, invented and patented a machine he called the "compound revolving snow shovel." Unable to secure the financial backing necessary to produce the plough, the patent lapsed. The Elliott Plough was subsequently improved and patented by Orange Jull in 1886. In conjunction with John and Edward Leslie, who operated a machine shop in Orangeville, Jull altered the original design. Between Orange Jull and the Leslie brothers, work on the development of the plough progressed. The rotary snowplough proved so successful that it was sold across the Americas, from Alaska to Argentina, as well as in Japan and France. Many of these plows were sold to the Canadian National and Canadian Pacific Railways for use in clearing the tracks in the Rocky Mountains.[2]

It is interesting to note that "The Elliott-Jull snowplough became standard equipment on North American railway lines against drifts, avalanches, and other obstructions. The basic plough now in use is derived from the Elliott-Jull design, which was standardized in 1911."[3] A book on trains says that Orange Jull was a "different sort than many inventors."[4] A good mechanic, he had sufficient means to follow his ideas through, and his ideas were in terms of a full-scale operating machine, not a model. He later had a falling out with the Leslies over profits and decided to go into the machine snowplough business for himself.

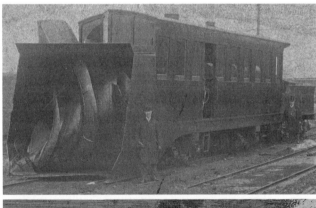

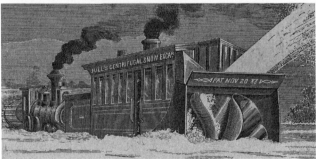

Top, Orange Jull applied the turbine principles learned at his father's Orangeville Flour Mill and adapted them to snow removal. The result was the rotary snowplough or snow blower, shown circa late 1870s; *bottom*, although somewhat modified, Jull's rotary snowplough is still used by railways to keep their track open in winter.

Orangeville Moments: Significance in Canada 237

Jull then designed an entirely different snow-collecting device, a huge cutter shaped like the head of an auger. He set up the Jull Manufacturing Co., with his financial backer, George Hobart, as president. They set up offices in Brooklyn and placed an order with the Southwark Foundry and Machine Co. of Philadelphia to build what he called the Jull Centrifugal Snow Excavator. This snowplough opened the way for a much longer winter rail use, increasing profits for companies, which normally could not trust the winter weather as the rail lines were often filled with snow. Jull, it seemed, just never stopped. One of Canada's foremost inventors in the snowplough industry, Orange Jull is credited with many successes, including several types of snowploughs he developed as full-scale operating machines, not models, in his hometown of Orangeville.

Orangeville itself has never played an important national political role, but it has significantly influenced politicians and civil servants at both the federal and provincial levels. In a strange way, politics have brought the attention of Canada to our little town.

A lawyer, Elgin Myers, came into Orangeville in 1878 and was appointed crown attorney for Dufferin County in 1891. A year later he attained national notoriety by advocating annexation to the United States. He insisted on the right to free speech, refusing to resign his public office. He was dismissed after only 17 months in office. Despite his stance, he served on town council as well as the county council, and was president of the Orangeville Board of Trade in 1901.

Elgin Myers was one of the very few known Liberals in Dufferin County ever to get a provincial appointment. Sir Oliver Mowat appointed the young Toronto lawyer to be the crown attorney and clerk of the peace for Dufferin County in 1891. Unfortunately, very shortly afterwards, Mr. Mowat had to send his appointee a letter asking for his resignation because of Mr. Myer's outspoken stand on the issue of union with the United States. The notion of continental union had developed long before Confederation and had never really gone away. When the federal Liberals, with the full support of Mowat's provincial Liberals, began to champion reciprocity (free trade) with the U.S. in the 1880–90s, the idea of going all the way and joining the United States came roaring back and found a raft of enthusiastic supporters, among them Orangeville's Elgin Myers.

Newspapers report that Mr. Myers was an eloquent speaker and letter writer in support of the cause. A first letter had been sent in May 1892 reminding the 37-year-old that his advocacy of union was "inconsistent with the position of an offer who in his county [is] charged with the administration of justice"[5] and pointed out that taking on the "boss" so publicly was an impropriety.

Elgin Myers continued to support his stand in the local Orangeville papers, but in August he was quietly replaced by W.J.L. McKay. He returned to private law practice. He moved to Sault Ste. Marie a few years later and died there in 1903. His body was returned to Forest Lawn Cemetery in the town that he had grown to love and call home. Canada lost one of the best speakers and advocates for continental union and soon the cause was forgotten. Had one of Orangeville's citizens been deprived of the free speech and tolerance that Oliver Mowat so firmly believed in and that had helped him win his knighthood. Some would say yes.

Another interesting lawyer involved with our town also made quite a name for himself, D'Alton McCarthy. Originally from Barrie, he, his brother Maitland and James Fead, a local banker, developed much of the subdivision along Zina Street, beginning in 1864, and hastened development towards the present-day Orangeville District Secondary School. Two of the streets in the area bear their names—McCarthy Street and Fead Street. At the time, Orangeville was newly incorporated, the railway was coming and settlers moving north and west were using the town as a staging site. The future looked bright and the three partners were convinced that the community was going to grow with the commercial district spreading along Broadway and up First Street, and residential development heading north and west, right where their property lay.

It may be claimed that D'Alton McCarthy changed Canadian political history. He was a very strong Orangeman, much opposed to extending any toleration of Roman Catholic or French language schooling rights in Manitoba. He headed up the radical faction of Orangemen and Tories, called McCarthyites, that led the opposition in the Manitoba Schools Debate.[6] They split the Canadian Conservative party, thus ending their 18 years as federal government in 1896.

Another prominent individual, Oscar D. Skelton, was born in Orangeville in 1878, the son of Jeremiah Skelton (an Orangeville merchant and afterwards a school principal) and his wife, Eliza Jane (Hall), a school teacher. Oscar's school years, both elementary and secondary, were in Orangeville. He earned his M.A. at Queen's University in 1900 and his Ph.D. at the University of Chicago in 1908.

In 1925, he became the Under-Secretary of State for External Affairs and ultimately political adviser to prime ministers Mackenzie

King and R.B. Bennett. He is the author of: *Socialism, a Critical Analysis*, 1910; *Economic History of Canada Since Confederation*, 1913; *The Railroad Builders*, 1916; *The Days of Sir Wilfrid Laurier*, 1916; *Life and Times of Sir A.T. Galt*, 1920; *Our Northern Neighbour*, 1920, and *Life and Letters of Sir Wilfrid Laurier*, 1921. "Governments have come and governments have gone, while Dr. Skelton stayed on as Under-Secretary, serving loyally premiers of different political opinion. Reliance was placed upon his good judgment and extensive knowledge of foreign affairs and constitutional questions by Mr. Bennett as well as Mr. King. In the determination of Canada's attitude towards the United States and the world, Dr. Skelton has given service of the greatest value. His wide knowledge of international questions, his judicial temperament and his unassailable integrity provide him with some of the most essential qualifications."[7] Oscar D. Skelton is considered by many to be the father of civil service in Canada. A recent book entitled *Marriage of Minds* tells the wonderful story of the life of both himself and his wife, Isabel.

Built by Orangeville merchant John Green in 1880, the house later belonged to his son Marshall Green and his wife Martha Jane Bowles. It was a favorite holiday spot of her young nephew, Lester Bowles Pearson. *Courtesy of John Woolner, Orangeville.*

But our most famous politician of all was none other than Lester Bowles Pearson. Although Mr. Pearson was not born here, his political ambition was roused here. His grandfather, Thomas Bowles and grandmother, Jane Lester, lived on West Broadway. Thomas Bowles was the first sheriff for the newly created County of Dufferin in 1881. A staunch Liberal, Mr. Bowles was appointed to the position by Sir Oliver Mowat, Liberal Premier of the province. Mr. Bowles was perhaps one of Orangeville's most tireless workers for the Temperance Movement. Lester Pearson's parents, Edwin A. Pearson and Annie Bowles (who had come to the area as a child from Peel County) met in Orangeville, his father being a local minister at First Avenue Methodist Church.

Most importantly, it was at the home of his maternal uncle, local merchant Marshall Green, that Lester got his first taste of politics. In his memoirs Mr. Pearson writes, "In Orangeville I also got my first taste of the thrill and excitement of electoral success. An uncle owned a general store there and one year, Uncle Marshall was elected mayor. We were at his home with the town band, and many citizens came to serenade him after the results were announced. This was true glory and I concluded then and there to become a politician so I could be mayor and have a band play outside my house."[8] It would seem he did a bit better than that. The historic bit of humour that adds to this tale is that Mr. Pearson was a Liberal and Orangeville has *always* been a strong Tory town.

Each time a class of Orangeville school students comes for a program at the Dufferin County Museum where I work, I always look at them and wonder which one will it be that brings fame and attention to Orangeville to continue our historic tradition of making us all proud.

EPILOGUE

I LIVE IN THE TOWN of Orangeville. I have made my home here for many years and intend to spend many more here. The future of Orangeville is important to me, and is important to many other people who live here, have lived here or have had family that have lived here.

It must be wonderful for descendants of the original settlers to come and still see some of the places where their ancestors worked and lived. How great it is for residents to proudly walk their visitors through town along shady streets and through the downtown heritage district. How strong is the emotion for many who although they have moved away, but still consider Orangeville as home. How comforting it is for visitors to come to our town, where despite the modern changes and growth of the town they are still greeted warmly on the street or treated to a random act of kindness. Somehow Orangeville has managed to keep its small town friendliness, its sense of community and sense of humour intact.

Who can predict the future of Orangeville? Not I. But there are, perhaps, some things that are learned from examining our history, insights that can aid in endeavouring to encourage a positive future, whatever form that future might take.

It will be the innovators, those with the pioneers' sense of going beyond and the risk takers who will shape our future. It will be the Orange Lawrences and Seneca Ketchums who will convince us all to take a chance and try something new. It will be the ones who, like those before them, will be generous with their time and with their means to benefit the community.

It will be the politicians who will shape the daily living in the future Orangeville. It will be the F.C. Stewarts, the Maitland McCarthys, and

The cast iron fountain at the Town Hall served three users—man, horse and dog. This is part of a set that once graced the main street. The other was taken for much needed scrap metal during the Second World War. *Courtesy of the Town of Orangeville.*

the Arnold Pattersons of the future who will make the decisions that effect our homes, our streets, our recreation and our community. Elect your future mayors and councillors wisely, as it is they who ultimately will make the decisions which will affect our town the most. Encourage our local representatives to hire capable and caring staff. It will be the clerks and planners of the future who will interpret those rules to make sure Orangeville changes and develops equitably and in line with federal and provincial policy. As a person living in a residential historic district, I am aware that it is the wisdom of our civil servants that will guide our town's way of life.

It will be the citizens of town that will guide us into the future. It will be the Mrs. Lalors, the Tommy Marshalls or the Macpherson brothers of the future that will make people say, "Orangeville, it must be a great town! Look at so and so and look what they have done."

The future of Orangeville will be influenced mostly by our location. Those swamps and hills that kept the settlers out of the area for so long, will be what draws and improves the quality of life for our future residents. Orangeville is at the headwaters of Ontario. So far our water is clean and plentiful and our town must look to the outside limits to protect it. The stream that brought the pioneers here still flows right through the centre of town. We must fight to make sure it flows through as long as the town exists. Residents of Orangeville are within a few miles of four conservation areas, three provincial parks, the Bruce Trail and sit on the brim of the Niagara Escarpment. How fortunate we are!

Orangeville is a town that is proud of its heritage and is trying to encourage residents and visitors to enjoy its charm and beauty as well as its changes and its growth. The town supports Heritage Orangeville and its work to protect both our built and natural heritage. They support The Dufferin County Museum & Archives where artifacts and the archival and photographic history of Orangeville are preserved for use now and for the future.

Historic information plaques are in place on many of Orangeville's older buildings. This plaque recognizes the house built in 1894 by merchant/tailor Andrew Hill and his wife Elizabeth. Orangeville is believed to be the only town that includes the names of the wives on their signs. I am fortunate that the Hill house is now my residence. Orangeville is truly a great place to live. *Courtesy of John Woolner, Orangeville.*

It has been a pleasure to tell you the stories of my town, the businesses, the people, the buildings, the events. Orangeville has been home to many stories, some of which have been captured here. But there are many more to come from Orangeville, the town with a vibrant past and a healthy future.

APPENDIX A

KETCHUM FAMILY TREE

Samuel Ketchum of Norwalk, Connecticut, was a descendant of Edward Ketchum, who arrived in Ipswich, Massachusetts, in 1635 from Cambridge, England.

```
Samuel Ketchum  m  Sarah Holbert
        |
   Peter  Isaac  Stephen  Lydia  Samuel
   |
JESSE* (1)  m  Mary Robbins
(1740–1826)
   |
   ├ SENECA  m  SARAH ANN MERCER (no family)
   │ (1772–1850) (Mono/Orangeville)
   ├ Sarah
   ├ Elizabeth
   ├ Henry
   ├ Oliver
   ├ Zebulon
   ├ JESSE (2)  m  (1st) Ann Love
   │                (2nd) Mary Ann Rubergall (1782–1867)
   ├ Mary
   ├ Abigal (infant death)
   ├ Hannah
   └ Abigal
```

* All capitalized names indicate people mentioned in this book.

APPENDIX A

JESSE (2) Ketchum   *m*   (1st) Ann Love
(1782–1867)   (?–1833)

- Lily Love (1802–?)
- Mary (1804–?)
- John (1806–1809)
- Fidelia (1808–1874)
- William (1810–1849)
- Anna (1812–1833)
- JESSE (3) (1820–1874)

After the death of his first wife, JESSE (2) married Mary Ann Rubergall (1801–1869). They had three children—Emma (1835–1869). Annie (1837–1851) and Henry who died in infancy (1839). Jesse lived in Toronto.

JESSE (3) Ketchum   *m*   (1st) Elizabeth Wilson

- OLIVER (1849–1899) – Orangeville Pottery
- Robert (1850–?)
- Catharine (1851–1872)
- Mary Elizabeth (1852–1926)   *m*   Thomas Stevenson, an Orangeville druggist
- Jane (1854)

JESSE (3) Ketchum   *m*   (2nd) Mary Colvin

- Jesse (4) (1857–1916) – tanner in Dundalk
- Margaret Helen (1858–1936)   *m*   Rev. George Burland Bull
- Cythria (1860–?)
- Amelia (1861–?)
- SENECA G. (1863–1903) – newspaper
- ZEBULON (1865–1937) – Orangeville lacrosse
- Annie Emma (1867–1905)
- John (1869–1870)
- Lily Love (1871–?)
- HENRY GEORGE (1872–1947) – Ketchum Sporting Goods–Ottawa

APPENDIX B

LAWRENCE FAMILY TREE

WILLIAM SOLOMON LAWRENCE   *m*   ESTHER DUTTON
(1757–1797)   (1758–?) (suicide)
Born Canaan, Connecticut   Born Littleton, Massachusetts
Parents immigrated
from Holland

- Experience (1781–?)
- Jonas (1782–1785)
- Rebecca (1784–1829)
- Erastus (1786–1839)
- Cyrus (1788–?) (suicide)
- Charlotte (1792–?) (died in Orangeville)
- Betsey (1794–1846) (suicide)
- ORANGE (1796–1861) (suicide) – married SARAH HOUSE

ORANGE LAWRENCE   *m*   SARAH HOUSE

- MARY (1822–1904)   *m*   ORANGE JULL who moved to Orangeville c.1857
- Cyrus
- Esther (1826–1884)
- RHODA (1829–1908)   *m*   JOHN WALKER REID of Orangeville
- FERRIS (1831–1913) – teacher in Orangeville
- Frances (1833–1913)   *m*   Dr. William Armstrong of Orangeville
- Charlotte (1835–infant death)
- ORANGE JR. (1842–1908) – Captain of Orangeville Militia
- Sarah (1846–1890)

NOTES

INTRODUCTION

1   Sidney Dickens, "History of Orangeville," unpublished manuscript, 1965; held at Dufferin County Museum & Archives.

1 – IN THE BEGINNING

1   Anna Jameson, *Winter Studies and Summer Rambles in Canada* (New York: Wiley Putman, 1839).

2   Early travellers and pioneer accounts tell of "clouds" of passenger pigeons and millions of them flying overhead in a 24-hour period. Overhunting for their sweet breast meat and extensive land cleaning led to their quick demise. Ontario passed a law for their protection in 1887, but it was too late. The last passenger pigeon sited and recorded in Dufferin County was in 1872. The last sighting in Ontario was in 1902 at Penetanguishene, Simcoe County.

3   Walter Massey Tovell (1916–2005) was the grandson of Susan Denton and Walter Massey of Massey Farm Equipment and City Dairy. He was raised on the Massey property near Dentonia Park in East York (now part of Toronto). Among his many accomplishments, he was a professor of geology at the University of Toronto; Board member, Niagara Escarpment Commission; on the staff of the Royal Ontario Museum (ROM) for 35 years and Director of the ROM from 1973–75; author of *Guide to the Geology of the Niagara Escarpment*; recipient of various National Heritage Awards; founding member of the Kortright Centre for Conservation; founder and patron of the Dufferin County Museum & Archives; and a philanthropist.

4   Dr. Walter M. Tovell (Lorraine Brown, ed.) *Guide to the Geology of the Niagara Escarpment*, published by the Niagara Escarpment Commission, 1992, 1.

5   Ibid, 14.

6   The Oak Ridges Moraine is a 160-kilometre ridge of sandy hills that starts at the Trent River and end at the Niagara Escarpment near Orangeville. It provides a unique natural habitant for many rare and sensitive animal and plant species. The hills are rich in aggregates which threaten the area, along with the development of the GTA. The moraine serves as a recharge area for groundwater and contains

numerous headwater streams. Current Ontario legislation is attempting to protect the Oak Ridges Moraine and restrict development within the area.

7 Tovell, 1991, 146.

8 J. David Wood, *Making Ontario: Agricultural Colonization and Landscape Re-creation Before the Railway* (Montreal: McGill-Queen's University Press, 2000), 106.

9 Ibid, 109.

10 "Recalling the Past," Special Issue of *The Orangeville Banner*, August 1975.

11 K.A. Armson, *Ontario Forests: A Historical Perspective* (Toronto: Fitzhenry & Whiteside, for the Ontario Forestry Association, 2001) 101.

12 Brendon M. Larson, John L. Riley, Elizabeth A. Snell and Helen G. Godschalk, *The Woodland Heritage of Southern Ontario: A Study of Ecological Change, Distribution and Significance* (Don Mills, ON: Federation of Ontario Naturalists, 1999) 28.

13 Ibid.

14 Ibid.

2 – EARLY STORIES OF THE SOURCE OF THE CREDIT

1 From Alexander McLachlan, "The Emigrant" (1861) in *The Poetical Works of Alexander McLachlan* (Toronto: William Briggs, 1900) 209.

2 The Queen's Bush refers to that area of the then still unsettled land that incorporates today's Bruce, Grey and parts of Huron, Waterloo and Wellington counties. It was acquired by treaty from the Chipewyan First Nation in 1836, but not surveyed and opened up for settlement until the 1850s. Prior to the formal surveying, a number of early settlers from the U.K. and many fugitive and free Blacks made their way into the area and squatted on the land. Many Blacks fleeing slavery actually were the first pioneers in the area and opened up the land for farming. Their work in clearing the land made the lots, once they were surveyed, more expensive, but they could not afford to purchase the land. Despite petitions to government, they were pushed aside and gradually left the area. For more information, see Linda Brown-Kubisch, *The Queen's Bush Settlement: Black Pioneers, 1839–1865* (Toronto: Natural Heritage Books, 2004).

3 Seneca Ketchum had to get across the swampy area, the source of the Credit River in order to access his land. The "Causeway" consisted of a series of log bridges connected together, about a kilometre in total length.

4 George Walton, *City of Toronto and the Home District Commercial Directory and Register, with Almanac and Calendar* (Toronto: Printed by T. Dalton and W.J. Coates, 1838).

5 Adelaide Leitch, *Into the High County: The Story of Dufferin: The Last 12,000 Years to 1974* (published by the Corporation of the County of Dufferin, 1975) 39.

6 *The Orangeville Advertiser*, September 1895.

7 Obituary of Isaac Newton, *The Sun*, February 12, 1929.

8 Water rights were "assigned" and registered on the deed of a property when sold. It assured the "owner" of the rights to use the flow of the water for power on his property downstream. It kept landowners situated upstream from damming the rivers and thus reducing the flow. After water power was replaced by steam and later electricity, the practice no longer was necessary.

9 *The Sun*, October 9, 1862.

NOTES   249

10   After being incorporated, the town could have joined Wellington County, Peel
     County or Simcoe County. Wellington County was chosen as Guelph was consid-
     ered more "convenient" than either Barrie or Brampton for transacting munici-
     pal business and attending County Council meetings.
11   *The Orangeville Advertiser*, October 28, 1869.
12   *The Sun*, October 29, 1863.
13   Ibid, March 10, 1910.
14   Diary of Jesse Ketchum, August 24, 1859, housed at Dufferin County Museum
     & Archives.
15   Bess Marshall, *A House For His Kingdom: The History of Westminster United
     Church and the Tributaries of Christianity That Have Streamed Into Her House*
     (Orangeville, ON: Westminster United Church, 1978) 139.
16   Ibid, 140.
17   *The Sun*, November 18, 1869.
18   Ibid, April 11, 1870.
19   Ibid, December 3, 1863.
20   Ibid, September 9, 1869.
21   Ibid, July 22, 1875.

3 – THEM DAMN YANKEES

1   *The Sun*, February 19, 1914.
2   John Strachan was born in Aberdeen, Scotland, in 1778, and emigrated to Canada
     in 1799. He was ordained an Episcopalian minister in 1802 and appointed to the
     Parish of Cornwall where he established a school, soon to be known as one of the
     best educational institutions in Canada. He moved to York in 1812 and soon
     became a part of the Family Compact. He was instrumental in the establishment
     of Grammar Schools and involved in the issue of Clergy Reserves, their control
     and their disposition. Appointed Bishop of Toronto in 1839, he also founded
     Trinity University in opposition to the University of Toronto. Strachan died in
     1867.
         John Strachan became acquainted with Jesse Ketchum (who lived in Toronto),
     through Ketchum's opposition to the Family Compact and through school issues
     in York. Seneca Ketchum was Jesse's brother and an Anglican lay preacher.
3   *The Orangeville Banner*, October 4, 1934.
4   Ibid, October 14, 1988.
5   Jesse Ketchum Diary, December 31, 1859. The diary is housed at the Dufferin
     County Museum & Archives.
6   Ibid, December 2, 1860.
7   The Ketchum family is descended from Edward Ketchum, who emigrated to
     Massachusetts from Cambridge, England in 1635. For the family tree see Appen-
     dix A on page 244.
8   *The Sun*, May 8, 1890.
9   Jesse Ketchum Diary, January 15, 1859.
10   When James II ascended to the English throne in 1688, he tried to re-establish
     the Roman Catholic religion as supreme in both church and state. Prince William
     of Orange, in Holland, came to England to regain "Protestant" rights and was

250   NOTES

placed on the throne by the Act of Settlement of British Parliament. When James
tried to regain his throne, King William defeated him at the "Battle of the Boyne"
on July 12, 1690. Since then, societies, known as the "Loyal Orange Lodge,"
were established to support Protestant principles. Orange Lodges arrived in
Canada with Irish settlers, as the Orange Order had become strong in their
homeland. Members brought a "Certificate of Membership" with them and
established lodges in their area. Local lodges that were established are as follows:
Lodge #2, The Maples, 1830; Lodge #84, Purple Valley (Mono), 1832; Lodge
#427, Orangeville, 1847; and Lodge #635, Orangeville, 1868.

11   "Dufferin 125," *The Orangeville Banner,* May 2006.

12   The Lawrence family are descended from William Solomon Lawrence who was
     born in Canaan, Connecticut. His parents had emigrated from Holland. For the
     Lawrence family tree, see Appendix B on page 246.

13   Alan Rayburn, "Orangeville Parade," a series of articles written for *The
     Orangeville Banner* in the late 1980s.

14   *The Sun,* October 20, 1864.

15   Donald A. McKenzie, *More Notices from Ontario's Methodist Papers, 1855–1872*
     (self-published, 1993).

16   The Founders Fair is a municipal street festival held in July, sponsored by the
     Orangeville Business Improvement Association (BIA). It features a street sale,
     children's activities and music. Started in the 1980s, the event celebrates the
     founding of Orangeville. In the 1990s, descendents of Orange Lawrence officially
     "opened the event." The festival continues to be held annually.

4 – ROADS AND RAILWAYS: GETTING TO TOWN

1   A chartered British company set up to colonize Upper Canada, the Canada Com-
     pany acquired over two million acres of land, much of which was near Lake
     Huron. That section of land became known as the Huron Tract. The Company
     had the area surveyed, and advertised extensively in Great Britain, then assisted
     with emigration to Upper Canada. John Galt of Scotland was the first on-site
     commissioner for the Company. For more information, see Robert C. Lee, *The
     Canada Company and the Huron Tract, 1826–1853: Personalities, Profits and Pol-
     itics* (Toronto: Natural Heritage Books, 2004).

2   The acquisition of Crown Land grants meant that settlers had to meet certain
     conditions regarding clearing the land and building roads in front of their prop-
     erty. Concessions and sideroads were opened by settlement duty and statute
     labour, donated by the landowner. Any further improvements to roads were left
     up to the inhabitants who lived along the road.

3   Leitch, *Into the High County,* 118.

4   *The Sun,* February 8, 1912.

5   Until 1829, the only route from Lake Ontario to Lake Erie included a portage
     around Niagara Falls from Queenston to Chippewa Creek. The first canal was
     constructed from 1829 to 1844 by William H. Merritt, who founded the Welland
     Canal Company. The second canal was constructed between 1845 and 1886. This
     was completed by the Ontario government to accommodate steamers, which were
     larger than sailing vessels. Both projects required much labour on the locks and

NOTES   251

canal systems. Work could be daily or weekly. Two more improvements have been
made since to keep shipping open to modern larger "Great Lakes" freighters.

6   Jesse Ketchum Diary, September 5, 1859.

7   *The Sun*, April 22, 1875.

8   In 1848, Charles Rankin, P.L.S. (Public Land Surveyor) was hired by the govern-
    ment of Upper Canada to survey a road from Toronto to Sydenham (Owen
    Sound). This and two other roads could then be used to bring settlers into unde-
    veloped land. Crown Land agents would place settlers on 50 acres of free land
    with an option to purchase another 150 acres. In 1851, Rankin declared the road
    still unfit. The road was turned over to the counties in 1858. Today, most of this
    colonization road is today's Provincial Highway 10.

9   *The Sun*, March 28, 1862

10 Ibid, February 19, 1874.

11 Ibid, February 3, 1876

12 Ibid, February 4, 1869.

13 The Grand Trunk Railway of Canada was proposed as the main trunk line through
    the United Province of Canada in 1851, and was formerly incorporated the next
    year. By 1856 a rail line connecting Montreal and Toronto was open for traffic.
    During this period, other railway construction had been undertaken west of Toron-
    to, towards Guelph and Stratford. This line was extended to Sarnia in 1859.

        In 1864, the Grand Trunk Railway took over the Champlain & St. Lawrence
    Railroad, Canada's first railway. By 1880, the Grand Trunk Railway system
    stretched from Chicago, Illinois, to the St. Lawrence River at Montreal, and to
    the Atlantic Ocean at Portland, Maine. and by 1923, some 125 smaller railway
    companies had merged into the Grand Trunk Railway.

        After facing heavy financial losses, the Grand Trunk Railway filed for bank-
    ruptcy in 1919. The federal government took over the railway that year, and, in
    1923, placed it under the management of the Canadian National Railway.

14 The Toronto, Grey & Bruce Railway (TG&B Railway) was located in southern
    Ontario, extending north from Toronto through Bolton to Orangeville and from
    there one branch continued north to Owen Sound and the other northwest
    through Harriston as far as Teeswater.

        In order to permit exploitation of lumber and resources in lands to the north
    and west of Toronto, and to encourage settlement, the TG&B Railway was char-
    tered in March 1868 to construct a line northwest from Toronto through
    Orangeville to a port on the shores of Lake Huron (Southampton), with branches
    to Kincardine and Owen Sound. Construction began in the fall of 1869 with the
    work being assigned to Francis Shanley, a contractor who had completed work
    on several railway fronts in the province. The first component of the line was for-
    mally opened for traffic from Toronto (Weston) through Orangeville to Mount
    Forest in December 1871, a distance of 87 miles.

        With the opening of the first component of the railway, the company initiated
    construction on a branch (known as the Grey Extension) from Fraxa Junction
    (near Orangeville) north to Owen Sound, a distance of 69 miles.

        With the line in full operation, it became evident early on that the use of nar-
    row gauge tracks to save the initial construction costs was a mistake, given the
    volume of traffic the line was carrying and the resultant wear and tear. To alter

the situation, however, would involve significant changes, reconstructing grades and curves along with the replacement of bridges and rolling stock. Such works would require a substantial outlay of funds, something the railway could not afford at the time. Realizing the work would need to be completed, financial arrangements were made by the bond holders of the line with the Grand Trunk Railway (GTR). The agreement reached stipulated that the Grand Trunk Railway would operate the line and retain a share of the profits, but would also make the changes necessary to bring the line up to a standard gauge. Accordingly, work commenced in the fall of 1880 and was completed by December 1881.

15 Sidney Dickens, "Early Stories of the Country Town," unpublished manuscript, 1965; housed at the Dufferin County Museum & Archives.

16 *The Sun*, May 9, 1872.

17 Ibid, May 3, 1906.

18 Norman R. Hawirko, "A Summary History of Orangeville's 1906 CPR Railway Station," in "Report to Orangeville Heritage Committee," February 6, 1984.

19 Ralph Beaumont, *Steam Trains to the Bruce* (Cheltenham, ON: Boston Mills Press, 1979).

5 – EARLY INDUSTRY: ENTERPRISE AND ENTREPRENEURS

1 *The Sun*, March 21, 1861.

2 Ibid, October 18, 1870.

3 *The Orangeville Banner*, August 4, 1927.

4 *The Sun*, March 21, 1861.

5 Alan Rayburn, *The Orangeville Banner*, January 31, 1990.

6 Full bound original copies exist at the Dufferin County Museum & Archives. Indices and microfilm are available to family researchers as well as those interested in finding out more about their community or their properties.

7 Alan Rayburn, February 17, 1989.

8 Jesse Ketchum Diary, January 7, 1860.

9 *The Sun*, February 4, 1869.

10 Ibid, August 1, 1863.

11 Ibid, August 20, 1868.

12 In 1839, Louis Jacques Mandé Daguerre of France announced his photographic process—the daguerreotype. It produced a finely detailed picture. A few weeks later, William Henry Fox Talbot of England announced his photogenic drawing process, which produced a paper negative from which any number of prints could be made. Fox Talbot is universally recognized as the father of modern photography. His ancestral home, Lacock Abbey in Wiltshire houses the Fox Talbot Museum. From John Hannavy, *Fox Talbot: An Illustrated Life of William Henry Fox Talbot, "Father of Modern Photography," 1800–1877* (Princes Risborough, U.K., Shire Publications, 1976).

13 *The Sun*, March 26, 1868.

14 Ibid, April 11, 1867.

15 Ibid, July 22, 1869.

16 Ibid, February 27, 1862.

17 Ibid, October 30, 1862.

NOTES 253

18 "Orangeville, The Town of Beautiful Homes," *The Orangeville Banner*, Special Edition, December 11, 1913.

19 *The Sun*, November 9, 1871.

20 Ibid, October 23, 1873.

21 Ibid, November 18, 1875.

6 – SUDDEN GROWTH: SUDDEN DECLINE

1 The Township of Luther was partially surveyed by Lewis Burwell in 1837 and completed in 1855 by William Phillips (PLS) of Richmond Hill. As a Catholic, Burwell named the very difficult to traverse swampy township after Martin Luther, a Protestant reformer. The Luther Swamp feeds the source of the Grand River. A community slowly grew along the banks of the Grand River called Joyce's Corners after an early settler, Mrs. George Joyce who opened the first tavern there. In 1874, the village changed its name to Manasseh after Manasseh Leeson, an Orangeville area developer. Two years later "Luther" was chosen as the name when the town officially got its first post office. In 1885, the name was officially changed to Grand Valley after "Grand Valley Brand Flour," which was produced in the village.

2 The present Town of Shelburne was founded in 1864 by William Jelly, who opened a tavern on the Toronto Sydenham Colonization Road. The village was called Jelly's Corners until the post office was established in 1869 and the names was changed to honour the Earl of Shelburne. Mr. Jelly was appointed as the first postmaster since the post office was located in his tavern.

   The Town of Shelburne is known nationally as the site of the Canadian National Old Time Fiddle Championships. Being located on the Toronto, Grey and Bruce Railway, the town achieved growth and prosperity at the same time as Orangeville.

3 *Handbook of Useful Information*, published by The Toronto, Grey and Bruce Railway Company, 1873.

4 Interview with Steve J. Brown, Archivist, Dufferin County Museum & Archives, March 15, 2006.

5 Sidney J. Dickens, "Progress and Prophecy Edition," *The Orangeville Banner*, August 1969.

6 *Toronto Telegram*, date unknown. Reprinted in *The Sun*, July 14, 1910.

7 Reverend Patrick Bell of Scotland arrived in Fergus, Ontario, in 1833 to become a tutor to Adam Fergusson's sons. He had invented the horse-pushed reaping machine in Scotland in 1827. Unfortunately, he failed to patent it and some years later, Cyrus McCormack of Staunton, Virginia, would take full credit for the invention. For more information on Patrick Bell, see Pat Mattaini Mestern, *Fergus: A Scottish Town By Birthright* (Toronto: Natural Heritage Books, 1995)

8 The Massey farm equipment started as a modest family business in Newcastle in 1848. Under three generations of enterprising Masseys, the company prospered and was relocated to Toronto in 1879

9 The Scott Act (the Canada Temperance Act) of 1878 extended the local option concept to cities and counties across the country

10 *The Sun*, November 17, 1887.

254   NOTES

11   Pauline Roulston, "The Urbanization of Nineteenth Century Orangeville,"
     unpublished MA Thesis, University of Toronto, 1974.
12   Leitch, *Into the High County*.

7 – TOWN OF CHANGE, 1900 TO 1914

1   An Arc light produces light by using an electric spark to generate heat between
     two carbon electrodes causing them to vaporize and burn. Carbon arc lamps saw
     extensive use throughout the world from the late 1870s on. Due to their intense
     heat they are not practical for lighting small interior spaces but survived for
     decades being used as streetlights. For many people of the time, an arc lamp was
     the first electrical device they had ever seen. From http://webexhibits.org/caus-
     esofcolor/3.html, accessed on August 27, 2006.
2   In 1906, as a member of the Ontario Legislature Adam Beck (born and raised in
     Baden, Ontario), introduced a bill which established the Hydro-Electric Power
     Commission of Ontario. He served as chairman of that body until his death in 1925.
3   *The Sun*, March 16, 1922.
4   Ibid, September, 1908.
5   *The Orangeville Banner*, May 18, 1911.
6   *The Sun*, December 15, 1910.
7   Ibid, May 8, 1910.
8   Ibid, September 12, 1911.
9   Prohibition in Canada was an attempt to forbid, by law, the selling and drinking
     of intoxicating beverages. Canadian Temperance groups began to rally for prohi-
     bition as early as the 1840s. In 1898, the movement was strong enough to force
     a national plebiscite (vote) on the issue. Although the majority of Canadians
     voted to support the cause, Sir Wilfrid Laurier, the prime minister, felt the major-
     ity result was not sufficiently large, especially in Quebec where a large majority
     voted against the cause.
         Before the First World War, much of the country was "dry" under "local
     option." Prohibition on a Canada-wide basis existed from 1917 to 1919, the major
     catalyst being the need for grain for the armed forces. Drinking establishments were
     closed. Alcohol could be purchased for "medical" and industrial uses only. Distillers
     and brewers, if properly licensed, could sell outside of the province and country.
         Although enforcement was difficult, crimes associated with alcohol dropped
     significantly, but many stills sprang up and illegal sales continued. In the U.S.
     prohibition was much stronger and lasted from 1920 to 1933. Quebec repealed
     the law first in 1919 and Ontario followed suit in 1927. Prince Edward Island
     remained dry until 1948.
10   *The Sun*, January 6, 1910.
11   Ibid, April 21, 1910.
12   Ibid, October 27, 1910.
13   Ibid, November 24, 1910.
14   The Imperial Order of Daughters of the Empire was founded in 1900 by a Mon-
     treal native, Margaret Polson Murray. It is a Canadian women's charitable organ-
     ization dedicated to improving the quality of life of children, youth and those in
     need through education, social service and citizenship programs.

NOTES 255

In Orangeville, the IODE was established on October 18, 1907, in the home of Miss Dewar, with 35 ladies taking the oath of allegiance. Originally they organized to establish a hospital for the Town of Orangeville and surrounding area. The name, Lord Dufferin Hospital, was chosen to honour Lord Dufferin after whom the county was named.

15 *The Sun*, February 16, 1907.
16 Adelaide Hunter Hoodless (1858–1910) was an ardent proponent of improved domestic and educational standards for rural women. She organized the first Women's Institute in 1897. The constitution was signed at the home Erland Lee of Stoney Creek (according to the laws of the time, a man had to sign the papers). The Women's Institutes movements gained worldwide participation.

More information can be found at the Hoodless homestead, now the Adelaide Hunter Hoodless Homestead, a museum near St. George, Ontario, and at the Erland Lee Home Museum near Stoney Creek, Ontario.

The Orangeville branch was organized in the summer of 1905. The first meeting was held at the home of Mrs. Henry Endacott. For more information on Adelaide Hunter Hoodless, see Cheryl MacDonald, *Adelaide Hoodless: Domestic Crusader* (Toronto: Dundurn Press, 1986).

8 – ORANGEVILLE BETWEEN THE WORLD WARS

1 *The Orangeville Banner*, actual date not known, 1952.
2 Ibid, April 14, 1927.
3 *The Orangeville Banner*, November 3, 1920.
4 *The Sun*, April 22, 1920.
5 *The Orangeville Banner*, January 23, 1930
6 From 1929–39, North America was in the throes of a severe economic depression brought on by the Wall Street Crash. It was compounded in Canada by the 1928 wheat crop price crash. A relief program was set up for families and work camps for single men. Thirty per cent of the Canadian workforce was unemployed and one in five Canadians were on government assistance. The era became known as the Great Depression.
7 *The Sun*, March 20, 1930.

9 – LOOK AT US NOW

1 *The Orangeville Banner*, July 19, 1978.
2 "Community Profile," a booklet produced by the Town of Orangeville in 1996.
3 Credit Valley Conservation Report, Part IV, 1956.
4 Colin Vaughan, "Beauty by Grandeur," a clipping dated October 19, 1977, newspaper source not identified.
5 A Heritage Conservation District is an area recognized by a municipality as having heritage value for the community. Part V of the Ontario Heritage Act specifies that a municipality may, by bylaw, define an area within its boundaries as a Heritage Conservation District.
6 Facade improvements approved under this program are eligible for a grant of 50% of the total cost of the project, to a maximum of $10,000.

256   NOTES

7 Jim Betts, "A Proposal for the Orangeville Theatre Project," April 1, 1993, sub-
   mitted to the Orangeville Town Council.
8 Interview with Mayor Drew Brown, January 12, 2006.
9 Ibid.

10 – MUNICIPAL HISTORY: GETTING THINGS DONE

1 *The Sun*, June 12, 1862.
2 Ibid, April 12, 1863.
3 Ibid, July 23, 1863.
4 *The Sun*, September 18, 1864.
5 Orangeville Bylaw #3, the originals are housed at Dufferin County Museum &
   Archives.
6 *The Sun*, August 29, 1861.
7 Ibid, June 18, 1874.
8 Ibid, April 29, 1875.
9 Ibid, June 8, 1876.
10 Ibid, May 1, 1878.
11 Orangeville Bylaws, a series of records housed at the Dufferin County Museum
   & Archives.
12 Andrew Carnegie was born in Scotland in 1835, the son of a weaver. In 1848, his
   family emigrated to the United States where they hoped to be able to avoid the
   industrialization that had so dramatically changed the weaving industry in Scotland. By the time he was 15 years old, Andrew had left school and was working
   as a messenger boy in Allegheny, Pennsylvania. It was here in Pennsylvania that
   he eventually built an industrial empire based on the manufacture of steel.
      Carnegie believed that anyone who was smart and worked hard could suc-
   ceed. He also believed that those who had acquired wealth had a moral obliga-
   tion to distribute much of their wealth to benefit society. On the other hand, he
   did not approve of charity.
      Of the $333 million that Carnegie gave away, ninety percent was distributed
   during his lifetime, much of it going to build 2,509 public libraries throughout
   the English-speaking world of his day in the United States, the United Kingdom,
   Ireland, Canada, South Africa, Australia and New Zealand. As he was quoted in
   the *New York Times* of 1903, "In a public library, men could at least share cultural opportunities on a basis of equality."
      Many of the Carnegie libraries in Ontario still stand today, albeit with substan-
   tial renovations, and continue to serve their communities well. There is no question that Carnegie, often regarded as the patron saint of libraries, left a valuable
   legacy across the towns and cities of Ontario. Adapted from *A History of the
   Grand Valley Carnegie Library*, published by the Dufferin County Museum &
   Archives, 2005.
13 Sidney Dickens, "Early Stories of the Country Town," unpublished manuscript,
   1965, at the Dufferin County Museum & Archives.
14 Interview with Mayor Drew Brown, January 12, 2006.

NOTES   257

11 – BROADWAY: STREET OF DREAMS

1   *The Sun*, December 22, 1869
2   Ibid, February 11, 1864.
3   Ibid.
4   Ibid, August 5, 1869.
5   Ibid, June 18, 1874.
6   Ibid, May 1, 1884.
7   *The Orangeville Banner*, December 5, 1929.
8   Ibid, "Progress and Prophecy Edition," August 1969.
9   Alan Rayburn, "Orangeville Parade" in *The Orangeville Banner,* July 19 &
    November 29, 1989.

12 – LANDMARKS IN TOWN

1   *The Sun*, February 18, 186
2   As quoted in Sidney Dickens, unpublished manuscript, 1965.
3   Sidney Dickens, 1965.
4   *The Advertiser*, August 17, 1876.
5   *The Sun*, taken from newspaper articles from May 23, 1901 to August 6, 1903.
6   *The Orangeville Banner*, July 1, 1998
7   *The Sun*, June 26, 1913.

13 – JUST FOR FUN

1   *The Sun*, August 29, 1861.
2   Ibid, May 28, 1863.
3   Information on the circus of 1863 taken from *The Orangeville Banner* Reprint,
    August 1, 1863
4   *The Sun*, February 11, 1864.
5   Ibid, September 1, 1864.
6   Ibid, July 3, 1867.
7   Ibid, March 9, 1871.
8   Ibid, July 14, 1910.
9   Ibid, May 25, 1876.
10 Ibid, July 14, 1910. Reprinted from the *Toronto Telegram* [date not given].
11 Ibid, January 3, 1887.
12 From an article written by Sidney J. Dickens, published in *The Orangeville Banner*, "Progress and Prophecy Edition," 1968.
13 Sidney Dickens, "Early Stories of the Country Town," 1965.
14 Sidney J. Dickens, *The Orangeville Banner*, "Progress and Prophecy Edition,"
    1970.
15 *The Orangeville Banner*, June 4, 1953.
16 Sidney J. Dickens, "Progress and Prophecy Edition," 1968.
17 "Historical Review of Orangeville," *The Orangeville Banner*, 1963.

258

NOTES

14 – AND BAD TIMES TOO

1 *The Sun*, October 20, 1870
2 Ibid, August 20, 1874.
3 Marshall, *A House For His Kingdom*, 132
4 *The Sun*, January 21, 1869.
5 Ibid, October 30, 1873.
6 Ibid, July 21, 1870.
7 Ibid, July 1, 1871
8 Ibid, December 11, 1873
9 *The Orangeville Banner*, June 16, 1918.
10 Laura Lennox and Brad McKinney, *Tornado Town: Remembering the 1985 Grand Valley Tornado* (Grand Valley, ON: self-published, 2005).
11 Ibid, November 7, 1935.
12 *The Sun*, February 11, 1904.

15 – VILLAINS AND HEROES

1 *The Sun*, October 10, 1862.
2 Thomas D'Arcy McGee (1825–1868) was an Irish-born Canadian politician, poet, historian and journalist. His extensive political career culminated in his attending the Charlottetown and Quebec Confederation conferences and being elected to the House of Commons in 1867. He was assassinated by a Fenian in 1868.
3 From an article by Archivist Steve Brown, published in *The Orangeville Banner*, July 19, 1978.
4 *The Orangeville Banner*, December 11, 1913.
5 *The Sun*, August 17, 1922.
6 Steve Brown, "Amazing but True," *In the Hills Magazine*, Spring 2006.
7 *The Advertiser*, September 1894.
8 J. Ross Robertson was the long-time prominent publisher of the *Toronto Telegram*. He wrote *Landmarks of Toronto*, 1894.
9 From "Dufferin in Toronto," a souvenir booklet, published by a group of Dufferin-born professional men who had established themselves in Toronto, August 1900.
10 *The Orangeville Banner*, November 25, 1943.
11 A number of Métis settlers, displaced from the land they had settled in the Batoche area of Saskatchewan, protested being forced off the land they had opened up to farming. When Ottawa ignored their letters of protest, they captured the store at Duck Lake on March 26, 1885. The North West Mounted Police were sent to expel them. The scene was set for what became known as the North West Rebellion of 1885 and ultimately the execution of Louis Riel.
12 *The Sun*, August 29, 1907.
13 Originally printed in *The Globe and Mail* (not recorded) and reprinted in *The Orangeville Banner* on January 11, 1912.
14 "Dr. Abraham Groves is best known as the first doctor to perform an appendectomy in North America, the first doctor to boil operating gloves (his riding gloves) and the first North American doctor to give a blood transfusion. His treatments were considered to be so radical that his fellow doctors tried to have

NOTES   259

him drummed out of the medical profession, citing lunacy as one reason. But
Groves' patients lived and his fame spread." Taken from Pat Mattaini Mestern,
Fergus: A Scottish Town by Birthright (Toronto: Natural Heritage Books, 1995).

15 *The Sun*, November 30, 1922.
16 *The Orangeville Banner*, May 6, 1961.
17 Ibid, October 28, 1937.
18 "Historical Review of Orangeville" as printed in *The Orangeville Banner*, 1963.
19 *Tara Leader*, March 1, 1945.
20 Ernest H. Dodds, "The History of Education in Dufferin County" (Grand Valley, ON: self-published, 1983).
21 *Look Magazine*, December 28, 1965.

16 – OFF TO WAR: CITIZENS WHO SERVED

1 *The Sun*, October 21, 1875.
2 Ibid, September 5, 1918.
3 Ibid, May 12, 1864.
4 Ibid, October 1, 1863.
5 Ibid, December 17, 1868,
6 Ibid, March 14, 1912.
7 Ibid, September 8, 1870.
8 *The Globe and Mail*, April 3, 1942.

17 – ORANGEVILLE MOMENTS: SIGNIFICANCE IN CANADA

1 *The Sun*, September 15, 1876.
2 *Trains: The Magazine of Railroading*, January 1987, 34.
3 Ibid, 30.
4 Ibid, 31.
5 Ken Weber, "Did Ontario Premier, Sir Oliver Mowat, Stomp on Free Speech in Dufferin County," in *In the Hills*, Autumn 2005.
6 The Manitoba Schools Question was a hot topic in the 19th century Canadian politics. It was a French-English issue, a Catholic-Protestant controversy, a conflict over the roles of the federal and provincial governments and a struggle about the proper relationship between church and state. It brought down the federal government, and Sir Wilfrid Laurier's short-lived resolution was a major defeat for language and educational rights outside the Province of Quebec. Information from Richard John Woolner, rjwoolner@sympatico.ca, accessed on September 5, 2006.
7 *Toronto Star*, date unknown.
8 For more information, see Terry Crowley, *Marriage of Minds: Isabel and Oscar Skelton Reinventing Canada* (Toronto: University of Toronto Press, 2003).
9 Lester B. Pearson, *Mike: The Memoirs of the Right Honourable Lester B. Pearson*, Vol. 1 (Toronto: University of Toronto Press, 1972) 11.

BIBLIOGRAPHY

A History of the Grand Valley Carnegie Library. Dufferin County Museum & Archives, 2005.

Armson, K.A., *Ontario Forests: A Historical Perspective*. Toronto: Fitzhenry & Whiteside, for the Ontario Forestry Association, 2001.

Beaumont, Ralph, *Steam Trains to the Bruce*. Cheltenham, ON: Boston Mills Press, 1979.

Brown, Steve, "Amazing But True," in *In the Hills Magazine*, Spring 2006.

Crowley, Terry, *Marriage of Minds: Isabel and Oscar Skelton Reinventing Canada*. Toronto: University of Toronto Press, 2003.

Dickens, Sidney, "Early Stories of the Country Town," Unpublished manuscript, 1965, at Dufferin County Museum & Archives.

Jameson, Anna, *Winter Studies and Summer Rambles in Canada*. New York: Wiley Putnam, 1839.

Larson, Brendan M., John L. Riley, Elizabeth A. Snell and Helen G. Godschalk, *The Woodland Heritage of Southern Ontario: A Study of Ecological Change, Distribution and Significance*. Don Mills, ON: Federation of Ontario Naturalists, 1999.

Leitch, Adelaide, *Into the High County: The Story of Dufferin: The Last 12,000 Years to 1974*. Corporation of the County of Dufferin, 1975.

Lennox, Laura and Brad McKinney, *Tornado Town: Remembering the 1985 Grand Valley Tornado*. Grand Valley, ON: self-published, 2005.

Marshall, Bess, *A House For His Kingdom: The History of Westminster United Church and the Tributaries of Christianity That Have Streamed Into Her House*. Orangeville, ON: Westminster United Church, 1978.

McLachlan, Alexander, "The Emigrant" (1861) in *The Poetical Works of Alexander McLachlan* (Toronto: William Briggs, 1900) 209.

Pearson, Lester B., *Mike: The Memoirs of the Right Honourable Lester B. Pearson*, Vol. 1. Toronto: University of Toronto Press, 1972.

Tovell, Walter, *Guide to the Geology of the Niagara Escarpment, With Field Trips*. Georgetown, ON: Niagara Escarpment Commission, 1992.

Walton, George, *City of Toronto and the Home District Commercial Directory and Register, with Almanac and Calendar*. Toronto: Printed by T. Dalton and W.J. Coates, 1838.

Weber, Ken, "Did Ontario Premier, Sir Oliver Mowat, Stomp on Free Speech in Dufferin County," in *In the Hills*, Autumn 2005.

Wood, J. David, *Making Ontario: Agricultural Colonization and Landscape Re-creation Before the Railway*. Montreal: McGill-Queen's University Press, 2000.

INDEX

Acrow Canada Limited, 107, 133
Adams, J.C., 107
Adams, Rob (Mayor), 135
Adjala, Township of, 58, 72, 135, 224
Agricultural Hall (Mono Mills), 191
Agricultural Labour Act, 104
Aiken, J.W. (Mr.), 193
Albion, Township of, 58, 139
Alexander, Ken, 152
Allen, Bob, 150
Allen, James, 125
Allen, Richard, 99, 100
Allen, R.J. (Mr.), 223
Allen, Samuel, 223
Alliston (ON), 147
Alton (ON), 45, 50, 84, 167, 190
Alton (Orange) Lodge, 175
Amaranth, Township of, 4, 5, 11, 15-17, 20, 28, 58, 72, 126, 175, 187, 201, 204, 223, 233
Amaranth Cricket Club, 179
Amaranth Mission (later Orangeville Mission), 17, 18, 45
Amaranth Settlement Road, 40
American Civil War, 221
American Hotel (Orangeville), 53, 222
American Trotting Association, 170
American War of Independence, 28
Anchor Flour Mills, 196
Ancient Order of United Workman, The, 146
Anderson, ___ (Mrs. Thomas), 77

Anderson, John, 123
Anderson, Thomas, 77
Anglican Church (Church of England), Anglican, 28, 55, 70, 160
Diocese of Toronto, 29
Arcadia Sweets (Orangeville), 98, 152
Argue, Thomas (Rev.), 70
Armagh, County of (Ireland), 19
Armitage & Company, 146
Armstrong, H. (Mr.), 224
Armstrong, James (Mr.), 140, 235
Armstrong & Robinson (foundry) (later Armstrong Foundry and Machine Shop), 163, 193, 211, 234
Arnott, James A., 151
Arnott, James D. (Mayor), 132
Art Walk of Tree Sculptures (Orangeville), 13
Arthur (ON), 51

Bacon, Miles, 18
Bailey, William T. (Mayor), 128, 150
Ballycroy (settlement) (Adjala), 65
Bank of Hamilton, 149
Bank of Commerce, 65, 129, 166
Bank of Toronto (Toronto Dominion Bank), 150, 152
Banting, Frank, 104
Baptists, 70
Barclay, M.E. (Miss), 90, 209
Barrie (ON), 120, 121, 238, 249
Bartlett, John (Rev.), 184

Beamsville (ON), 33
Beater, Mary, 53
Beatty & Co. (Fergus), 76
Bell, George, 53, 234
Bell, John, 223
Bell, Patrick (Rev.), 253
Bell's Hotel (Orangeville), 53, 173
    Bell's Hall, 123
Bell Telephone, 84
Belwood (ON), 22
Bennett, Polly (Miss), 17
Bennett, R.B. (Prime Minister), 239
Bennett, T.J., 81
Bennett, Winnifred (Miss), 182
Berlin (NJ), 105
Best, A., 223
Best Western Hotel, 52
Bethel Presbyterian Cemetery, 63
Bethel Presbyterian Church (Church of
    Scotland), 70, 126, 162
Betts, Jim, 111
Black, Howard, 105
Bloomer, Ed, 52
Bluebird Café, The, 153
Boer War, 79, 203
Bolton (ON), 45, 47, 65, 66, 139, 177
Bookless & Haley (Clothing Merchants),
    145
Bookless & Reid, General Merchants,
    145
Booth, James "Jim," 53
Bowles, Annie, see Annie Pearson
Bowles, Jane (Lester) (Mrs. Thomas),
    239
Bowles, Martha Jane, see Martha Jane
    Green
Bowles, Thomas (Sheriff), 149, 239
Bowles, W. (Mr.), 182
Bowles, W.H. (Dr.), 192
Bowling Green (hamlet) (Amaranth),
    180
Bowmanville (ON), 147
Bowsfield, Walter, 56
Bowsfield's Inn (Whittington), 45
Boy Scouts, 131, 132, 184
Boyer, Ed, 105
Boyne River, 4, 43

Braithwaite:
    Aileen, 215
    Beryl, see Beryl Hart
    John Victor Maxwell "Max," 133,
    214, 215
Brampton (ON), 39, 43, 45, 57, 64, 68,
    73, 97, 108, 112, 132, 134, 140, 175,
    177, 225, 249
Bredin, Gordon (Mayor), 105, 134
Bremner, Robert Gunn (Mr.), 218
Broadway, see Orangeville
Brooks, ___ (Mrs. J.N.), 211
Brooks, Herb, 151
Brooks, Mabel, 151
Brown, ___ (Mrs. Geo. B.), 211
Brown, L. (Mr.), 141
Brown, Drew (Mayor), 113, 114, 116,
    135, 136
Brown, Harry, 105
Brown, J.H., 226
Brown, Margaret (Mrs. Harry), 105
Brown, Steve, 72, 201
Bruce Trail, 3, 242
Bryan, Roy, 94
Bryan's Fuels (Orangeville), 195
Buckham, Thomas, 57, 58
Bulley, Fred, 184
Bun House, The (Orangeville), 60
Burlington (ON), 83
Buyers, ___ (Mr.), 140
Buyers & Meredith (Carriage Builders),
    47
Byam, J.W. (Rev.), 18
Bythia Street Public School, 121

CIBC (Canadian Imperial Bank of
    Commerce), 53, 154
C. Cullen Watchmaker, 62
Caledon (ON), 11, 45, 48, 183, 193
Caledon, Township of, 12, 37, 44, 58,
    66, 72, 74, 81, 119, 130, 139, 175,
    200, 206, 233
Caledon Lake, 96
Caledon Lake Company, 200
Caledon Mountain, 48, 194
Cameron, George, 105
Cameron, John H. (Hon.), 171

Campbell, ___ (Mr.), 44
Campbell, George Harold (Dr.)
 (Mayor), 130, 135, 150, 182, 199
Campbell, Thomas (Sergeant), 226
Campbell, William M., 56, 124
Campbell's Tannery (Orangeville), 10
Camilla (village), 41, 42, 191
Canada Company, 38, 250
Canada Presbyterian Zion Church, 70,
 71
Canada West (Ontario), 15
Canadian Bible Society, 29
Canadian Expeditionary Force, 158
Canadian Field Artillery (WWI), 227
Canadian Imperial Bank of Commerce,
 128
Canadian Harness Racing Association,
 170, 207
Canadian Lacrosse Association, 59, 75,
 176, 177
Canadian Life Insurance Officers Asso-
 ciation, 211
Canadian Military Institute, 158
Canadian National Exhibition (CNE),
 87, 207
Canadian National Railway, 236, 251
Canadian Order of Foresters, 146
Canadian Pacific Railway (CPR), 47-50,
 67, 79, 89, 106, 112, 195, 236
Canadian Racing Association, 207
Canadian Tire (Orangeville), 152
Canadian Volunteer Militia (Fenian
 Raids), 224
Canadian Westinghouse, 108
Cancilla, Jimmy, 152
Cando Contracting Ltd., 113
Carbert, ___ (Dr.), 140
Carload Food Market (formerly Superi-
 or Store), 153
Carlos Ventin Architects, 111, 159, 163
Carnegie, Andrew, 129, 166, 167, 256
Carnegie Foundation, 129
Carroll, ___ (Ms.), 65
Cartwright, Les, 109
Cataract (settlement) (Caledon), 18, 84,
 190
Cataract Electric Company, 130

Castle Leslie, 156, 157
Census, 1861
Centenary Church, 70
Centre Road, see Hurontario Street
Champlain, Samuel de, 7, 8
Chainway, The (Variety Store), 150
Chang, Harry (Prof.), 115
Chapman, T.W., 128, 148
Charity Society (Orangeville), 86
Charlestown (later Caledon), 29, 179
Cheltenham (hamlet) (Caledon), 226
Chisholm, Kenneth, 68, 70, 144, 148
Chisholm, Elliot & Green (Merchants),
 140, 149
Church of England, see Anglican
 Church
Church of Scotland, 55, 70
Claridge, Pam, 111
Clark, C., 60
Clark, Nellie (Miss), 182
Clarke, Phyllis, 133
Cline, Maurice, 213
Clippers, The (lacrosse team), 75
Clover Farm Grocery Store, 109, 185
Clorox Limited, 108
Clow & Foster (Builders), 126
Coffin House (Orangeville), 53
Coleridge (settlement) (Amaranth), 42,
 45
Collected Works, 201
Collingwood (ON), 42, 51, 84
Collister, W.A., 81
Colours in the Storm, 111
Colvin, Mary, see Mary Ketchum
Commercial House (Orangeville), 53, 89
Confederation (1867), 64, 237
Conservative Party (Tories), 73, 74,
 139, 171, 200, 238, 240
Consumer's Gas Company, 108
Cook, Bob, 208, 209
Cooney, W. (Mr.), 224
Corbet, John, 123, 124
Corbett, James, 223
Corbit, John, 68
Corn Flower, 218
Coronation Day (1953), 183, 211
Courtney, Gordon (Mayor), 135

Courtney, Jessie (Mrs.), 135
County of Dufferin Act, 72, 124
County Refuge (Orangeville), 221
Cowles, M.K.E. (Mr.), 64
Credit Flats, 3, 10, 11, 29, 30, 39, 114
Credit River, 3, 4, 6, 8-11, 20, 22, 48,
    52, 107, 113, 114, 130, 248
Credit Valley Conservation Report
    (1956), 107
Credit Valley Explorer, 113
Credit Valley Railway, 48, 50
Cressview Lake, 81
Cricket Club (Orangeville), 172
Crimean War, 68, 220, 221
Crozier and Fleming (Dry Goods), 145
Currie's Hotel (Camilla), 191
Curry, Harvey, 151
Curry, James, 53
Curry, Lloyd, 151
Curry, Patrick, 224
Curry, William, 224
Curry's Hardware, 151

Dahl, W.C., 145, 146
Dalton Patterson and Sons (Furniture),
    152
Daniels, Ernie, 149
Daniels, Minnie (Morrow) (Mrs.
    Ernie), 149
Daniels, William (Mr.), 233, 234
Davidson, Maurice, 152
Davison, Carm, 153
De Haas, Joseph, 106
Deagle, John M., 81, 84
Deagle System, 193
Debating and Mutual Improvement
    Society, 58
Dickens, Sidney, 132
Directory of the Home District (1837),
    11
Disney & Hertell (Hanover), 130
Distinguished Service Order (DSO),
    see First World War
D.J. Torrie Clothing Company, 110,
    150
Dobbie and Grierson (Builders), 161
Dodds, Fran (Miss), 183

Dodds, Robert, 11
Dods, J.M., 130, 167, 168
Dods Knitting Mill, 80, 81, 91, 103,
    107, 167
Dods Medicine Co., 181
Dominion Dental Council of Canada,
    199
Dominion Store (Orangeville), 151,
    152, 159
Donner, Sepha, 57, 60
Dryden, Al (Mr.), 40
Dufferin Area Hospital
Dufferin, County of, 13, 20, 50, 66, 71,
    92, 98, 101, 112-114, 133-135, 139,
    149, 153, 159-161, 166, 182, 193,
    199, 201, 202, 206, 215, 237, 239,
    247
Dufferin and Ava, Frederick Temple
    Blackwood, 1st Marquess of (Lord)
    (Gov. Gen.), 125, 179
Dufferin and Halton Rifles (164th), 82
Dufferin Agricultural Society, 200
Dufferin Area Hospital, 90
Dufferin Association for Retarded
    Children, 216
Dufferin Champion (a saw), 235
Dufferin Children's Aid Society, 200
Dufferin County Board of Education,
    135, 216
Dufferin County Courthouse, 71, 110,
    158, 161, 179, 183, 212
Dufferin County Jail, 76
Dufferin County Land Registry, 110
Dufferin County Museum & Archives
    (DMCA), 5, 135, 213, 224, 227, 240,
    242, 247, 252
Dufferin House (Orangeville), 53, 88,
    95
Dufferin Light and Power Company,
    130
Dufferin Old Boy's Association, 165,
    166, 181, 182
Dufferin Post, 59
Dufferins Lacrosse Clue, The (lacrosse
    team), 75, 176-178, 199
Dunbar, Francis Grant, 26, 123, 124,
    141, 158

Duncan, Jimmie, 93
Dundalk (ON), 146
Dundas Regiment (Riel Rebellion), 158
Dunn, Albert, 151
Dunn, David, 223
Dunnville (ON), 212
Durham (ON), 146
Durkin, F. (Mr.), 223
Dyer, Roy, 109

Earl's Hotel (Springbrook), 204
East, Richard, 190
East Garafraxa, Township of, 7, 27, 44, 59, 72, 105, 190, 208
East Luther, Township of, 72
East Indiaman, the, 60
East Luther, Township of, 4, 5
Ed Thompson and Company, 147
Edelbrock, Karl, 111, 166
Edmonton, see Snelgrove
Edward, Prince of Wales, 41, 42
Edward VII, King of England, 129
Edwards, Sandy, 167
Elgie's Hotel (Orangeville), 19
Elizabeth II, Queen, 184
Elliot, ___, (Mr.), 68
Elliott, J.W. (Dr.), 235
Elliott Plough, 235
Elliott-Jull snowplough, 235-236
Elora (ON), 40, 48
Emslie, ___ (Miss)
Endacott, ___ (Mrs. Henry), 255
Endacott, George, 148
Endacott, Henry (Mayor), 127, 128, 148, 149, 160
England, 16, 34, 46, 158, 211, 215, 227
Erin (ON), 40, 145, 201, 221
Erin, Township of (Wellington County), 58
Erskine, William, 148
Esquising, Township of (Halton County), 40
Eves, Ernie (Premier), 114
Ewing, Sam (Chief), 87, 99
Exchange Hotel (Orangeville), 187

Fair Day (Orangeville), 79, 95, 143, 189
Falconer, Fred, 151
Farmingham (settlement) (Amaranth), 45
Fead, James, 223, 238
Fead, James S., 139, 140
Fendley, Doug (Mayor), 132
Fenians, Fenian Raids, 58, 219, 222-226, 258
  36th Battalion, 224
  Amaranth 1st Battalion, 223
  Orangeville 2nd Battalion, 224
Fennell, James, 223
Fergus (ON), 40, 41, 76, 205, 209, 253
Fergus Road, 49
Ferguson, J.W. (Mr.), 176, 191
Ferguson's egg-grading station, 95
Ferns, Bob, 94
Filtro Electric, 108
First Avenue (United) Church, 70, 188
First Nations, Indigenous People, Native Peoples, Indians, 6-8, 12
First World War (WWI), 80-82, 88, 92, 168, 180, 226, 254
  Battle of Amiens, 226, 228
  Battle of Passchendaele, 226, 227
  Distinguished Service Order (DSO), 226, 227
  Military Cross (MC), 228
  Military Medal (MM), 227
Fish, Jasper Noble, 85
Fisher Price Toys, 108, 134
Flecker, Mike, 109
Fleming, George, 192
Flesherton (ON), 84
Fletcher, ___ (Mr.)
Fletcher, John, 124, 125
Fletcher, Thomas, 223
Foley, John (Mr.), 58, 120, 127
Foley, John Jr., 58, 59
Foley, Margaret, 58, 59
Forest Lawn Cemetery, 62, 63, 126, 147, 160, 169, 238
Forest Lawn Cemetery Company, 200
Forest Lawn Hotel (Orangeville), 53
Forks of the Credit Provincial Park, 113

INDEX 267

Foster, J. (Mr.), 173
Founders Fair (Orangeville), 36, 250
Fountain, Benjamin, 124
Frampton, Norman, 152
Franson, Eva (Miss), 183
Fraxa Station (settlement) (Amaranth), 89
Fruit Market and Confectionary Store (Orangeville), 84
Fuller, Allen & Holmes (General Merchants), 192

Gaines, "Joe," 94
Galbraith, ___ (Mrs.). 142
Galbraith, Robert, 145
Garafraxa, Township of, 11, 15, 16, 33, 34, 40, 58, 119, 121, 137, 157, 175, 233
Garafraxa Road, 40, 41
Gazette, The (Orangeville), 59
Gem Restaurant, 189
George V (King of England), 101
Georgetown (ON), 64
Georgetown Transportation Co., 134
Georgian Bay, 4, 8, 10, 38, 40
German, H.B., 64
Gibson, Don, 151
Gilchrist & Kent (Merchants), 147
Gillespie, Emerson, 147
Gillespie, John (Mr.), 204
Gillespie, W. (Mayor), 130
Gillespie's Hardware, 131
Glen Cross (settlement) (Mono), 18
Globe Hotel (Orangeville), 53
Goderich (ON), 38
Golden, Netta (Miss), 183
Gooding, Janice, 135
Gordon House (Orangeville), 53, 166
Gore of Garafraxa, The, 28, 33, 40, 44, 55
Governor's Road (Dundas Street), 38
Graham, ___ (Mr.), 175
Graham, James "Jimmie," 52, 96, 171
Graham's Hotel, 171
Grand Central Hotel (Orangeville), 88, 106, 154
Grand River, 4, 7, 22, 214, 253

Grand Trunk Hotel (Brampton), 64
Grand Trunk Railway, 45, 251, 252
Grand Valley (ON) (formerly Luther Village), 22, 66, 88, 92, 116, 145, 158, 159, 177, 193, 208, 221, 253
Grand Valley Agricultural Show, 88
Gray, Mathew Stickney (Rev.), 30
Gray, Ernie, 153
Gray, Mack, 206
Great Atlantic and Pacific Tea Company (A & P), 148, 150, 151
Great Depression, 84, 101, 102, 255
Green, ___ (Mr.), 44
Green, John, 68, 70, 124, 179, 239, 240
Green, Marshall (Mayor), 129, 147, 148, 239
Green, Martha Jane (Bowles), 239
Green & McBride Co. (General Merchants), 148
Greening Metal Products, 108, 133
Greenwood Cemetery, 27, 35, 60, 62, 63, 126, 128, 160, 204, 205
Grey, County of, 42, 55, 72, 248
Greystones Restaurant (Orangeville), 53, 54, 156
Griffin Bros., 39, 43
Grigg Co., The (Orangeville), 109
Griggs, A.J., 152
Griggs, George, 11, 33
Griggs, James, 11, 12, 27, 52
Grigg's Department Store, 152
Groves, Abraham (Dr.), 209, 258
Guelph (ON), 22, 24, 38, 41, 51, 71, 120, 121, 161

HMCS Orangeville, 232
Haddock, Marion, 105
Haley, Helen (Miss), 183
Haley, Hugh, 32, 44
Hall, Beverly (Miss), 183
Halton, County of, 33
Hamilton (ON), 56, 207
Hamilton, Andrew, 23, 24
Hamlyn, Jean, 133
Handy, John, 213
Hanna, John, 223

Hannahson:
   Alfred E. (Rev.), 33
   Arthur, 33
   Elizabeth, 32
   George, 32, 33
   John (Rev.), 32
   Mary (Mrs. George), 32, 33
Hanover (ON), 130
Harkess, A.M., 152
Harris Lodge, The (Masonic), 146
Harry Shiff's Fashion Wear, 151
Harshaw, ___ (Mr.), 205
Hart, Beryl (Braithwaite), 215
Hart, John, 215
Haywood, Herman, 105
Henderson, Alexander (Rev.), 70
Henderson, Joan (Miss), 183
Henderson, Thomas (Mayor), 130
Henry, James, 124, 127
Henry, Thomas (Dr.) (Mayor), 99
Henry, Thomas Jr. (Dr.), 179
Henry, Merve, 151
Henry, Thomas, 223
Heritage Orangeville, 242
Hewat, Richard, 222
Hewat, Robert, 124
Hewat, William (Dr.), 36, 142, 155,
   157, 158
Hewitt, Robert, 32, 223
Hewson, Thomas S. (Mayor), 98, 99,
   130
Hill, Alexander, 243
Hill, Elizabeth "Eliza," 243
Hill & Co. (Dry Goods), 192
Hoare, J.R. (Mayor), 132
Hobart, George, 237
Hockley Road, 43, 50, 51, 125, 186
Hockley Valley, 4, 125
Hockley Valley Resort, 145
Hodgson, Della, 96
Hodgson, Ruth, 96
Hogg, David "Dave" (Mr.), 170
Holmes, Alvin (Fire Chief), 184
Home District, 11
Hoodless, Adelaide Hunter, 90
Horning Mills (ON), 84, 130
Hotel Alexandra (Orangeville), 193

Hough, Rodney, 153
House, James Buffalo "J.B.," 34
House, J.B. (Mr.), 191
House, Sarah, see Sarah Lawrence
Hughes, Norris, 152
Hughes, William J., 218
Hughes & Norris Men's Wear, 152
Hughson, Abraham, 10, 17, 18
Hughson, John, 223
Hulse, J.H. (Mr.), 181, 192
Humber Institute of Technology and
   Advanced Technology, 115, 116
Humber River, 4, 9
Hunter, A.J. (Dr.), 150
Hunter, Keith, 152
Hunter, Thomas, 16
Hunter, William H., 67, 68
Hunter Rose Printers (Toronto), 201
Huron and Ontario Electric Railway, 84
Huron Colonization Road, 38
Huron First Nation, 7
Hurontario Street (Centre Road), 12,
   28, 39, 42, 43, 50
Husband & Galbraith (Dentists), 60
Huskinson, ___ (Mr.), 56
Huston, Margaret, 203
Huston, Robert, 154
Huston, Walter, 203
Huxtable, T.R., 84

IGA (Independent Grocers Alliance),
   152
IODE (Independent Order of Daugh-
   ters of the Empire), 89, 90, 184, 209,
   254
Inglewood (ON), 50
Ingram, ___ (Mr.), 57
Ireland, Irish, 19, 37, 38, 54, 58, 157,
   220, 222
Irish Republican Brotherhood, 222
Iroquois First Nation, 8
Irvine, ___ "Granny," 25
Irvine, ___ (Mrs. Robert), 183
Irvine, Bill, 151
Irwin, Francis, 173
Irwin, Sherri, 153
Irwin, William, 224

Island, Frank, 153
Island, James Simpson (Dr.), 208
Island, L.J. (Crown Attorney), 100
Island Lake (Orangeville), 10, 160, 208
Island Lake Conservation Area, 117

J.E. Smith & Co., 192
J. Kearns & Son (Dry Goods), 150
Jackson, Thomas, 123, 187
Jacques & Hayes (Cabinet Makers)
    (Toronto), 64
Jarvis, Beaumont, 166
Jarvis, J.W., 62
Jeaneration (Orangeville), 109
Jeffers and Sproule's Pharmacy, 109
Jeffers, Carson Valentine (Mayor), 130,
    150
Jeffers, Grant, 150
Jeffers Drug Store, 150
Jefferson, R. (Mr.), 224
Jelly, Lyn (Mr.), 117
Jelly, William, 117, 180, 253
Jelly's Corners, see Shelburne
Johnston, James, 18
Jolliffe, T.W. (Rev.), 70
Jones, Andrew (Corp.), 225
Joyce, ___ (Mrs. George), 253
Judge, George, 105
Jull:
    Mary (Lawrence) (Mrs. Thomas),
        34, 36, 156, 198, 246
    Orange, 6, 21, 36, 122, 198, 199,
        235-237
    Thomas (Capt.), 13, 20, 34, 36, 52,
        56, 121, 122, 124, 156, 198, 225
Jull Centrifugal Snow Excavator, 237
Jull Manufacturing Co., 237
Jull's Mill (Orangeville), 13, 20, 56,
    110, 149, 154, 190, 236

Kearns, Alberta (Miss), 183
Kearns, Graham, 150
Kearns, John, 150
Kearns, "Will," 150
Kelly, Jos. J., 193, 204
Kelly & Marshall (Hardware Store),
    204

Kelly's Hotel (Orangeville), 121
Ken Alexander's Haberdashery, 152
Kennedy, J.W. (Mr.), 65
Kenny, M. (Miss), 183
Kerr, ___ (Mr.), 172
Ketchum:
    Edward, 244, 249
    Hannah, 32
    Jesse Sr., 28, 29, 32, 244, 249
    Jesse (the Younger), 10, 13, 16, 17,
        28-32, 37, 65, 70, 119, 122, 137, 138,
        160, 174, 244
    Mary (Colvin) (Mrs. Jesse the
        Younger), 31, 65, 125, 160, 176, 245
    Mary Gladys (Miss Ainsworth), 32
    Oliver, 32, 174, 245
    Sarah Ann (Mercer) (Mrs. Seneca),
        28
    Seneca, 11, 13, 26, 28, 32, 114, 119,
        241, 244, 248, 249
    Seneca G., 59, 245
    Zebulon, 32
Ketchum family, 69
Ketchum Manufacturing Company, 32
Kilgour, ___ (Mr.), 84
Kincardine (ON), 100
King, Charles, 148, 163
King, Eleanor, 163
King, William Lyon Mackenzie (Prime
    Minister), 239
King, Thomas Theophilus, 163
King Bros. Furniture Company, 163,
    235
King Edward Hotel (Sudbury), 79
King House, 163
Kingston (ON), 28
Klappis:
    Blanche (O'Reilly), 98
    Jimmy, 98
    Harry, 98, 152
Klondike gold fields, 58, 202
Kurtz, Larry, 166
Kyle, Bob, 202

Lackey, Sam (Mayor), 133
Laidlaw, George, 50
Lake Erie, 4, 7

Lake Huron, 4, 7, 38, 42
Lake Ontario, 4, 7, 22, 38, 40
Lalor, Jane Huston (Mrs.), 203, 242
Lamplighter Drum and Bugle Corps
    (Berlin, NJ), 105
Large, John, 15
Large, Victor "Vic" (Mayor), 111, 135
Laurel (settlement) (Amaranth), 175
Lawrence:
    Esther (Dutton) (Mrs. W.S.), 33
    Ferris, 16, 34, 246
    Mary, see Mary Jull
    Orange (Capt.), 6, 11-14, 16, 18, 26,
    27, 30, 33-37, 40, 52, 58, 60, 116,
    117, 119, 137, 138, 155, 156, 157,
    174, 235, 241, 246, 250
    Orange Jr. (Capt.), 20, 34, 173, 225,
    226, 246
    Rhoda, see Rhoda Reid
    Sarah Ann (Mercer) (Mrs. Orange
    Sr.), 33, 156, 33
    William, 35
    William Solomon, 33
Lawrence, Jack, 60
Lawson, ___ (Mr.), 221
Lawson, F.J. (Mr.), 148
Leader, Herman, 185
Leeson, Mannaseh, 124, 253
Legate, Mary, see Mary Leslie
Leighton, Birdie (Miss), 183
Leighton's Shingle Mill, 190
Leith (Scotland), 232
Lemon, Bertha, 97
Lennox, A. (Mr.), 23, 24
Lent, L.B. (Mr.), 172
Leskey, Martin, 159
Leslie, Edward, 235
Leslie, Guy (Mr.) (J.P.), 24, 156, 157
Leslie, John, 235
Leslie, Mary Legate (Mrs. G.), 156, 157
Lester, Jane, see Jane Bowles
Lewis, Alexander (Rev.), 140
Lewis, Frederick (Dr.), 160
Lewis, George O. (Mayor), 130
Lewis, William, 43
Liberal Conservative Party, 74
Liberal Party, Liberals, 58, 237, 239, 240

Lilliston Canada, 108
Lindsay (ON), 146
Lindsay, Johnston (Mayor), 128
Liquor Licence Board of Ontario
    (LLBO), 212
Little, Sadie (Miss), 96, 97
Lloyd, ___ (Mrs.), 65
Lloyd, W.R. (Mr.), 187
Local Architectural Conservation and
    Advisory Committee (LACAC), 135
Longeway & Bros. (Dry Goods), 60, 187
Lord Dufferin Centre (Orangeville), 25
Lord Dufferin Hospital (Orangeville),
    89, 90, 99, 209, 255
Lowrie, Hugh, 221
Loyal Orange Lodge, 11, 33, 58, 169,
    171, 175, 250
Luther, Township of, 15, 16, 253
Luther Village, see Grand Valley
Lynn, Jas. "Jim" (Mr.), 205, 206

Macdonald, John A. (Sir) (Prime Minis-
    ter), 73, 74
MacGregor, Jim (Deputy Mayor), 116
Macpherson:
    Donald Stuart, 226-229, 242
    Douglas William McPhee, 226-229,
    242
    Dugald, 226, 227
    Ewart Gladstone, 226-228, 242
    John Ross, 226-228, 242
    Ken, 227
    Sarah (Wilson) (Mrs. Dugald), 226,
    227
Mackenzie, William Lyon, 12, 13
Macleod, ___ (Dr.), 99
Maher's Shoes, 153
Malouk, Johanna, 133, 215
Malouk Preparatory School
    (Orangeville), 215
Mammoth Store, The (Orangeville),
    187
Mann, Robert, 84
Manning Biscuit Company, 107
Manning Candy Co. Ltd., 133
Maple Leaf Store, The (Orangeville),
    146

Maples, The (settlement) (East Garafraxa), 18, 193
Mara, Thomas (Mr.), 177
Market Hill, see Mono Mills
Marksman's House (Hotel) (Orangeville), 23, 186
Marlane, Peter, 85
Marriage of the Minds, 239
Marshall, Allan, 150
Marshall, Frederick J. (Mayor), 129, 204
Marshall, Hazel (Miss), 129
Marshall, Jos. (Mr.), 204
Marshall, Netta (Miss), 182
Marshall, Tommy, 207
Marshall Green & Co., 147
Marshall's Harness Store, 95, 138
Marshall's Men's Wear, 109
Massey Harris Binder, 76
Massey Harris Company, 76
Matheson, Bruce, 59
Matheson, Helen B. (McKitrick), 59
Mathews, James A., 167
Matthews, H.S. (Rev.), 70
Maude, J.A. "Mac" (Mayor), 132
May, John (Mr.) (Saddle Maker), 121, 187
Maxi Taxi, 134
McAuley, F. (Mr.), 173
McBain, F.E., 17
McBride & Gillespie (Hardware), 148
McBride, D.H., 147, 148
McCarthy, Charleszina Hope Manners, 139
McCarthy, D'Alton, 139, 210, 238
McCarthy, Maitland (Mayor), 124, 139, 160, 173, 210, 238, 241
McCarthy, Stewart, 210
McCarthy & Fead (Lawyers), 149
McCarthyites (faction of Orangemen), 238
McCausland of Toronto, 141
McCleverty & Eastman (Dry Goods), 187
McCord Corporation, 133
McCulloch, Richard (Mayor), 132
McCutcheon, Laura, 95

McDonald, Donald, 78, 83
McDonald, J. (Mr.), 64
McDonald's, 169
McDonald's Planing Mill (Orangeville), 78, 83
McGarvey, Pat (Mr.), 205
McGarvey, T. (Mr.), 205, 224
McGee, Thomas D'Arcy (Hon.), 201, 258
McGowan, Alden, 151
McGowan, Alexander, 157, 158
McGowan, Elizabeth, 157, 158
McGuire, Blaney, 59
McGuire, Blaney Jr., 59
McIntyre, George, 192
McKay, W.E. (Rev.), 70, 179
McKay, W.J.L., 238
McKee, John, 181
McKeogh, Darcy (Hon.), 134
McKeown, Charles R. (Mayor), 130
McKinley Tariff (USA), 78
McKinney farm, 128
McKitrick, Alexander Dunlop "A.D.," 50, 59, 113, 130, 211
McKitrick, Helen B., see Helen Matheson
McKitrick, Robert, 56, 223
McKitrick, Samuel Henry "S.H." (J.P.), 23, 56, 124
McKitrick, Victor, 59
McKitrick Foundry, 56
McKitrick, Penfold, Huskinson & Co. Foundry, 56
McLachan:
   Alexander, "Bard of Amaranth," 9, 160, 200-202
   Clamina (Mrs. Alexander), 200
   Elizabeth M. (Miss), 95, 201, 202
   Mary, 201
   Audrey (Miss), 183
McLary, M.H.J. (Mr.), 212
McLaughlin's (later Mono Mills), 29
McLean, E. (Mr.), 59
McLean, George, 150
McLean, Morley, 151
McLeod, Pat, 135
McManus, George, 125

McMaster Binder, 76
McMaster Implements (Orangeville), 76
McMillan, W.C. (Mr.), 153, 194
McMillan's Village (now Erin), 201
McNab, Peter, 110, 123
McNeilly Bros. Foundry (NY), 164
McWilliams, N.T., 150
Meany, Patrick, 58, 66
Mechanics Club (lacrosse), 75, 177
Mechanics Institute, 126, 129, 166, 173, 201
Mechanics Institute Board, 173
Medical Hall (Orangeville), 58
Meek's Garage, 95
Meek, Jim, 150
Melancthon, Township of, 4, 16, 41, 42, 72, 130, 187
Melville (settlement) (Caledon), 10, 18, 45, 50, 190, 191
Menary, D. (Mr.), 187
Menary & Bros. (Blacksmith Shop), 187, 191
Mercer, Ann, see Ann Ketchum
Merchants Bank, 157
Merlina, Sam, 97, 152
Merryweather, ___ (Mrs.), 60
Methodist Church, Methodists, 17, 55, 70, 156, 160
Methodist Circuit, 17
Methodist Episcopal (M.E.) Church, 164, 174, 191
Military Cross (MC). see First World War
Military Medal (MM), see First World War
Mill Creek, 13, 14, 21, 23, 34, 37, 52, 119, 156, 186, 190
Miller, Chisholm, 34
Millroy, ___ (Mr.), 141
Mills, Ethel (Mrs.), 97
Mills, J. (Mr.), 223
Miss Sadie Little Millinery (Orangeville), 96
Mississauga First Nation, 6, 7
Mitchell, J. (Mr.), 179
Mitchell, P. (Mr.), 223

Mocha Berry (Coffee Shop), 153
Moffat, Bertha (Mrs.), 92
Mohawk First Nation, 8
Monaghan House, (Orangeville), 54
Monarch Master Manufacturing, 108
Mono, Township of, 11, 12, 15, 16, 28, 29, 39, 41-45, 58, 67, 72, 78, 99, 100, 105, 112, 119, 121, 125, 126, 137, 139, 160, 175, 187, 218
Mono Agricultural Society, 175, 176
Mono Mills (ON), 7, 9, 11, 28, 29, 41, 56, 65, 92, 144, 145, 173, 191, 224
Mono Mills Tannery, 56
Mono Mills United Church, 214
Mono Plaza (Orangeville), 193
Montgomery, Samuel, 124
Montreal Telegraph Company, 65
Moorehead, ___ (Mr.), 97
Moote, ___ (Mrs. James), 46, 47
Moote & Hodgson (Electrical Supplies), 150
Morrow, Bill, 152
Morrow, Minnie, see Minnie Daniels
Morrow, Myr, 152
Morrow, Russell, 152, 184
Mount Forest (ON), 72, 113, 146, 195
Mowat, Oliver (Sir) (Premier), 72, 74, 237-239
Mulberry Farm Antiques (Mono Mills), 145
Mulmur, Township of, 16, 42, 43, 72
Mungensen, Peter, 113
Mungovan, Dennis, 59
Municipal Institutional Act of Ontario, 124
Munro, Fisher, 58, 77
Myers, Elgin, 237, 238

Napoleonic Wars, 219
Nassau District, 11
Needles, Dan, 112
Nelson, G.S. (Mr.), 61
Nelson, Joseph, 223
Nestle's Infant Food Milk, 67
Neutral First Nation, 7
Newell, ___ (Mr.), 56
Newmarket (ON), 51

Newton:
  Isaac Sr. 12, 166
  Mary Ann "Granny," 13, 16, 25, 60
  William, 15
Niagara Escarpment, 3-6, 9, 113, 194,
  242, 247
Niagara Escarpment Plan, 112
Nichol, John James, 16
Nicholson, ___ (Mr.), 141
Nightingale, Florence, 220
Norfolk, County of, 210
Norris, ___ (Mrs.), 19
North Wellington Hotel (Orangeville),
  171
North West Rebellion, 207, 258
Nottawasaga Portage, 7
Nottawasaga River, 4, 8, 21, 22, 42, 44,
  125
Nottawasaga Valley, see Hockley Valley

199 Restaurant, 153
Oak Ridges Moraine, 4, 247, 248
Oakville (ON), 40
Old Kirk, see Church of Scotland
Ojibwa First Nation, 7
Olympians, The (lacrosse team), 177
Ontario and Quebec Railway Co., 50
Ontario Dental Association, 199
Ontario Good Roads Association, 100,
  200
Ontario Green Belt Plan, 112
Ontario Heritage Act, 71, 110, 156,
  159, 163, 255
Ontario Hydro-Electric Power Com-
  mission, 84, 130, 144, 254
Ontario Lacrosse Association, 59
Ontario Marble Works, 64
Ontario Municipal Board, 110
Opera House (Orangeville), 102, 110,
  111, 115, 150, 180, 203
Opportunity School (Orangeville), 215
Orange Lodge, see Loyal Orange
  Lodge
Orange Parade, 175
Orangeville (ON):
  Alexandra Park, 31, 157, 164-166,
  176, 184

Amanda Street, 21, 62
Armstrong Street, 48, 135, 163, 235
Banting Drive, 104, 105
Blind Line, 105
Bredin Parkway, 12, 18, 105
Brick Block, 65
Broadway (formerly Main Street),
  10, 13, 14, 16, 20, 23, 29-31, 34, 41,
  43, 41, 43, 46-48, 50, 52, 53, 59, 61,
  63-65, 69, 72, 73, 76, 83, 84, 91, 92,
  94. 96-99, 103, 105, 109, 116, 119,
  122, 124, 126, 128, 130, 131, 133,
  135, 137-153, 156, 164, 169, 173-
  176, 179, 180, 184, 186-194, 196,
  202, 224, 233, 234, 238, 239
Bythia Street, 16, 57, 105, 122, 179,
  193
Clara Street, 105
Chisholm Street, 68
Church Street, 18, 80, 130, 167, 174
Commercial Block, 140
Dawson Road, 106, 135, 140
Elgie Block, 65
Elizabeth Street, 93, 105, 201
Fairgrounds Shopping Mall, 61, 176
Faulkner Street, 104, 175, 188, 189
Fead Street, 136, 139, 188, 238
First Avenue, 17, 31, 70, 144, 155,
  157, 211, 238
First Street, 17, 18, 41, 53, 64, 70,
  72, 90, 98, 105, 124, 130, 140, 146-
  151, 174, 179, 191
Fourth Street, 50, 108
Goldgate subdivision, 12
Green Street, 46, 68
Henderson Block, 99
Historic District (Heritage Conser-
  vation District), 30, 110, 255
Idlewyld Park, 30, 109, 177
Jackson Block, 125, 131
James Street, 69, 149
Johanna Drive, 133
John Street, 16, 68, 81, 107, 108,
  124, 126, 131, 134, 135, 144, 155,
  156, 164, 179, 180, 190, 193
KayCee Gardens, 10, 57
Ketchum Block, 31, 110, 145, 151

Little York Street (later Sunnybrook Street), 36, 56, 94, 156
Main Street (later Broadway), 30, 137, 149
McCarthy Street, 238
Mill Street, 46, 54, 56, 61, 69, 72, 73, 84, 95-97, 116, 130, 131, 134, 135, 146, 149, 167, 174, 179, 187, 198, 210
Monora Park, 160, 179
North Ward, 29
Opera House, see Opera House (Orangeville)
Parsons Street, 62
Pattulo Block, 150
Prince of Wales Road (First Street), 21, 41-43
Sarah Street, 34
Second Avenue, 78, 83, 141
Second Street, 31, 70, 77, 78, 83, 95, 99, 130, 141, 144, 155, 157
Starrview Crescent, 105
Sherbourne Street, 30
Still Court, 136
Third Avenue, 141
Third Street, 107, 108, 15
Town Line, 13, 27, 34, 44, 46-48, 50, 68, 79, 134, 149
Union Block, 65
Veteran's Way, 116
Walsh Crescent, 136
Wellington Street, 18, 34, 52, 131, 147, 163, 211, 235
William Street, 68, 80
York Street, 16, 69, 117, 179
Zina Street, 13, 14, 17, 70, 76, 105, 139, 149, 161, 193, 221
Orangeville Advertiser, The, 12, 58, 204, 210
Orangeville Arena, 200
Orangeville Banner, The, 50, 59, 84, 85, 92, 113, 130, 134, 150, 185, 196, 211
Orangeville Board of Health, 36, 237
Orangeville Bottling Works, 214
Orangeville Board of Trade, 237
Orangeville Brampton Railway (OBRY), 112, 113

Orangeville Brampton Railway Access Group (OBRAG), 113
Orangeville Brass Band, 171
Orangeville Bus Service, 134
Orangeville Business Improvement Association (BIA), 250
Orangeville Casket Factory, 78
Orangeville Citizen, The, 53, 99, 111
Orangeville Citizen's Band, 73, 74, 96, 165, 184
Orangeville Curling Club, 200
Orangeville Dairy, 99
Orangeville Dairy Bar, 99
Orangeville (District) High School, 128, 188, 213, 238
Cadet Corps, 158
Orangeville Driving Club, 200, 207
Orangeville Drop-in Centre, 175
Orangeville Electric Light Co., 128, 202
Orangeville Fan Drill Company, 112
Orangeville Fairgrounds, 169, 179
Orangeville Fall Fair, 170, 175
Orangeville Figure Skating Club, 175
Orangeville Fire Hall, 126, 164
Orangeville Furniture Factory, 130
Orangeville Golf Club, 200, 203
Orangeville Health Committee, 126
Orangeville Horticultural Society, 69, 117, 180
Orangeville Historical Society, 6
Orangeville Hydro-Electric Commission, 199
Orangeville Infantry Company, 173
Orangeville Jazz and Blues Festival, 166
Orangeville Lawn Bowling Club, 179
Orangeville Lions Club, 109, 213, 214
Orangeville Monument Works, 64, 179
Orangeville Moraine, 4
Orangeville Novelty Works, 80
Orangeville Post Office, 13, 33, 41, 62, 63, 70, 106, 115, 116, 128, 149, 154, 192
Orangeville Pottery, 32
Orangeville Public Library, 53, 90, 110, 129, 134, 148, 166, 167
Orangeville Public Market, 159

INDEX 275

Orangeville Rotary Club, 174
Orangeville Snowshoe and Toboggan
    Club, 180
Orangeville Tannery, 56
Orangeville Tin Ware, 57
Orangeville Town Council, 53, 105,
    122, 124, 127, 132, 133, 134, 183,
    186, 214, 216, 237
Town Hall, 13, 16, 24, 26, 32, 46, 70,
    72, 79, 110, 115, 125, 126, 129, 135,
    158, 159, 165
Orangeville Turf Association, 170
O'Reilly, Blanche, see Blanche Klappis
Orr, E.N. (Mr.), 64
Orton, George Turner (Dr.), 74
Orton (Village), 95
Ottawa (ON), 75, 173
Owen Sound (ON), 40, 43, 47, 51, 69,
    84, 100, 251
Owen Sound Quarry, 50

Paisley, James (Mr.), 44, 47
Paisley House (Orangeville), 47, 53, 65,
    142
Papst, A. (Mr.), 65
Park Manor (Orangeville), 158
Parkinson, Boris, 134
Parkinson Centennial Public School, 134
Parkinson, Telford S. (Mayor), 130, 132
Parkinson, T.S. (Mrs.), 151
Parkinson Centennial Public School, 134
Parry Sound (ON), 79
Parsons, ___ (Mr.), 44
Parsons, John, 142
Parsons, William, 57, 173, 187, 225
Pascoe, Donna, 116
Patterson, Arnold (Mayor), 106, 133,
    134, 152, 193, 241
Patterson, Dalton, 152
Patterson, Don, 152
Patterson, Elizabeth Ann (Mrs. Wilson),
    210
Patterson, Hazel (Miss), 183
Patterson, Wilson, 210
Patterson's Furniture Store
    (Orangeville), 109, 152
Pattullo, Joseph, 123, 124

Pearson, Annie (Bowles), 239
Pearson, Edwin A., 239
Pearson, Lester Bowles, 239, 240
Pease, Joseph, 223
Peavoy, T.C., 99
Peel, County of, 37, 44, 72, 120, 171
Penfold, ___ (Mr.), 56
Pennsylvania Dutch, 12, 38
Pentecostal Tabernacle, 188
Pentland, Joe, 172
Peran, Charles, 223
Percival, ___ (Mrs.), 32
Perfect, "Ollie" (Mr.), 204
Perfect House (Orangeville), 53
Perth, County of, 201
Peter Hamilton Binder, 76
Petun First Nation, 7, 8
Phillips, Bill, 39
Phillips, Hector, 223
Pine River Power Company, 84
Pisten, Daniel, 223
Pocock, Archbishop, 134
Poems and Songs, 201
Polley, J. (Mr.), 125
Polyethylene Bag Canada, 108, 133
Port Credit (ON), 41, 51, 100
Portland Cement Company, 80
Presbyterian(s), 160, 166, 199, 200, 204
Preston, Charlotte (Mrs.), 158
Preston, J.A.V. (Colonel), 157, 159
Preston, John F., 158
Primrose (settlement) (Mono), 42, 43
Princess Patricia's Canadian Light
    Infantry (PPCLI), 226
Privilege and A Pleasure, A, 214, 215
Prohibition, 87, 88, 222, 254
Protestant(s), 19, 58, 70, 249, 250
Proton, Township of, 41
Purple Hill (settlement) (Mono), 6, 10,
    11, 26, 29, 39, 52, 53, 105, 141, 154,
    180
Purple Hill (Orange) Lodge, 175

Quaker Church, 215
Queen's Bush, 10, 41, 248
Queen's Hotel (Orangeville), 23, 53, 192
Queen's Track (Orangeville), 169

RCAF, see Royal Canadian Air Force
Railway House Hotel (Orangeville), 46,
    53, 54
Rankin, Charles, 41, 251
Rawn, Garnet, 106
Rayburn, Alan, 30, 34, 52, 150
Rayburn, Lorne, 105
Rayburn, Sophia (Mrs.), 134
Reading (settlement) (East Garafraxa),
    40, 157
Rebellion of 1837, 35
Red Onion (Orangeville), 53
Reid, Charlie, 153
Reid, Eugene, 104
Reid, Hannah (Dr.), 218
Reid, Harold, 151
Reid, J.C., 175
Reid, John Walker, 13, 34, 52, 156, 246
Reid, Mathew, 104
Reid, Minerva (Dr.), 218
Reid, Rhoda (Lawrence) (Mrs. J.W.),
    34, 156, 246
Reilly, E.A. (Miss), see E.A. Thompson
Rennicks, Fred, 105
Rich Hill (settlement) (Amaranth), 42
Richardson, ___ (Mrs. W.N.), 183
Richardson, W.N. (Mayor), 132, 183
Riddell, William Henry "W.H." (Dr.)
    (Mayor), 130, 170, 171, 179, 206
Riel Rebellion, 158
Ritchie, E.W. (Mr.), 146
Ritchie, F.W. (Mr.), 146
Ritchie, R.W. (Mr.), 146
Ritchie, Harry, 146, 182
Ritchie Brothers (Orangeville), 146
Robb:
    ___ (Mrs. W.T.), 229
    Reginald "Reg" (Flight Sergeant),
        229, 230
    Walter Tyrie (Judge), 59, 212, 229,
        230
Robb, Henry (Leith, Scotland), 232
Roberts, Shirley, 105
Robertson, J. Ross, 206
Robinson, ___ (Mr.), 141
Robinson, ___ (Mrs. W.J.), 210
Robinson, Charlie, 94

Robinson, John Ross, 206
Robinson, Murray, 105
Robinson, Nancy, 105
Robinson, T.J. (Mr.), 193
Robinson, Walter, 94
Robinson's Livery Stable (Orangeville),
    94, 193
Roman Catholic, 55, 58, 59, 160, 215,
    238, 249
Romano, Roxy, 79
Roney, Sam, 175
Rooney, R.W. (Dr.), 160, 193
Rose, Mary (Mayor), 135
Rowe, Earle (Hon.), 171, 207
Roy Bryan's Garage, 94
Royal Bank, 109
Royal Alexandra Theatre (Toronto),
    112
Royal Canadian Air Force (RCAF), 227
Royal Canadian Legion (Orangeville),
    105, 175, 179, 183, 184, 232
    Legion Hall, 179
Royal Canadian Navy, 227, 232
Royal College of Dental Surgeons, 199
Royal Flying Corps, 227
Royal Hotel (Orangeville), 53, 176
Royal Ontario Museum (ROM), 3
Royal Temperance Hotel (Orangeville),
    53
Royal Victoria Hospital (Montreal),
    216, 217
Rutledge, W. (Mr.), 14
Ryan, Joseph, 205
Ryan, William, 54

St. Andrew's Presbyterian Church (now
    Westminster), 33, 70, 162, 188, 211
St. Andrew's Women's Association,
    181, 211
St. John's Ambulance Brigade, 184
St. Mark's Anglican Church
    (Orangeville), 28, 141, 184, 191
St. Peter's Roman Catholic Church, 134
St. Peter's Roman Catholic School, 134
St. Thomas (ON), 50
St. Timothy's Roman Catholic Church,
    134

Safer, Alex, 81
Salvation Army, 101
Sanderson's Store, 138
Sarnia (ON), 33
Saugeen River, 4
Sault Ste. Marie (ON), 238
Scotland, 200, 201, 221, 232
Scott, C.I. (Dr.), 183
Scott, ___ (Mrs. C.I.), 183
Scott, David Lynch (Mayor), 207
Scott, Irwin, 109
Scott, Nan (Miss), 183
Scott Act, The (1885), 77, 253
Seaforth (ON), 75
Second World War (WWII), 103, 104,
    106, 130, 179, 216, 227, 229, 232,
    242
Shaw, Harry, 152
Shaw, James, 219, 220
Shelburne (ON) (formerly Jelly's Cor-
    ners), 42, 43, 66, 72, 84, 92, 117,
    177, 253
Sherburne, Elizabeth, 20
Shields & Gowanluck (Construction
    Company), 128
Shiff, Harry, 151
Simcoe, John Graves (Lieut.-Gov.), 39
Simcoe, County of, 44, 55, 69, 72, 120
Simpson, Isaac, 19
Skelton, Eliza Jane (Hall), 238
Skelton, Isabel (Mrs. Oscar), 239
Skelton, Jeremiah, 238
Skelton, Oscar D. (Dr.), 238
Smith, J.M., 155, 157
Smith, Walter, 153
Snelgrove (ON), 43
*Soldier's Diary, A: The WWI Diaries of
    Donald MacPherson*, 227
Sons of Scotland, 160
Soule, Cornelius J., 71, 161, 162, 163
South Arterial Road, 115
Spirit of Love and Other Poems, The,
    201
Springbrook (settlement) (East
    Garafraxa), 40, 53, 204
Springbrook Brickyards, 159
Springbrook Ghost, 203-206

Sproule, ___ (Tweedy) (Mrs.
    Nathaniel), 26
Sproule's Drug Store, 151
Stagg, Fred, 34
Stainforth, Elsie (Miss), 183
Stanley Park (Erin), 96
Staples, Owen, 224
Starr, Paul, 105
Steele, H.D. (Rev.), 70
Stephenson, John (Mr.), 57
Stevenson, Thomas (Mayor), 58, 128,
    141, 173, 179
Stewart, ___ (Mr.), 44
Stewart, Falkner Cornwall "F.C.," 20,
    74, 121, 122, 124, 125, 139, 173, 241
Stewart, Harry "Dime," 139
Stewart, Maitland "Silver," 139
Still, William (Mayor), 128
Stirton, Betty (Mrs.), 183
Stirton, Bill, 153, 183
Strachan, John (Bishop), 28, 29, 249
Streetsville (ON), 13, 48, 50
Stuart, Okill (Rev. Dr.), 28
Sudbury (ON), 79
Sun, The (Orangeville), 22, 23, 27, 35,
    56, 58-60, 64, 66, 86, 88-90, 100,
    102, 119, 127, 139, 142, 172, 180,
    222, 233
Superior Store (later Carload Food
    Market), 153
Supreme Court of Alberta, 208
Sutherland, Alexander, 200
Sutton, Eliza, 186
Sutton, William, 64, 186

Talbot, William Henry Fox, 252
Tansley, Ben Jr., 49
Tansley, William, 223
Teeswater (ON), 48
Temperance Movement, Temperance,
    71, 77, 87, 88, 239, 254
Theatre Orangeville, 110-112, 135, 159
Theatre Orangeville Youth Singers
    (TOYS), 112
Thompson, Albert, 153
Thompson, E.A. (Reilly) (Mrs. John),
    147

Thompson, Edward, 147
Thompson, James, 223
Thompson, John, 147
Thompson, John (Hon.), 74
Thompson, Ross, 105
Thompson, William S., 121
Thompson Brothers, 67, 146, 147
Thompson family of Mono, 67
Thomson, Tom, 111
Thorpe's Hotel (Orangeville), 222
Three Star Inn (Orangeville), 152
Tideman, Harry (Mayor), 106, 132,133
Tilt, J. (Mr.), 187
Tindley, ___ (Mr.), 61
Tom Lockyer Bridge, 114
Tony Rose Memorial Arena
    (Orangeville), 135, 214
Toronto (formerly York) (ON), 22, 30,
    32,41-43, 46, 50, 56, 62, 69, 79, 84-
    87, 95, 96, 107, 120, 121, 178, 201,
    204, 206, 208, 222, 225, 251
Toronto Board of Education, 227
Toronto Dominion Bank, 150
Toronto, Grey and Bruce Railway (TG
    & B), 45, 46, 48, 68, 251
Toronto Sydenham Colonization Road,
    41, 43, 251, 253
Torrie, Douglas J. "Doug," 150
Torrie's Clothing Store, see D.J. Torrie
    Clothing Company
Tovell, Walter Massey (Dr.), 3, 4, 247
Trafalgar (settlement), 11
Trafalgar, Township of, 11, 33, 34, 40
Trafalgar Road, 40
Train Station Restaurant (Orangeville),
    48
Tremaine Map of the County of Peel,
    37
Trimble, ___ (Mr.), 43
Trotter, Bert, 81
Trueman's Inn (Coleridge), 45
Tucker, Richard L. (Rev.), 70, 140
Tunstall's Cabinet Shop (Orangeville),
    64
Turnbull, Jean, 193
Turnbull, William, 76
Turnbull Binder, 76

Turner, H. (Mr.), 147
Turrell, Peter, 116
Tweedsmuir Memorial Presbyterian
    Church, 81, 179, 188, 200
Tweedy, John, 18
Tweedy, Samuel, 27
Tyrone, County of (Ireland), 19

UEL (United Empire Loyalists), 12, 28,
    38
Union Bus, 97
Union Carbide Limited, 108, 133
United Church of Canada, 162
United Extrusions Ltd., 134
United Farmers Organization, 102
United States, 32, 58, 98, 105, 170, 207,
    209, 217, 222, 224, 226, 237, 239
Upper Canada (later Canada West,
    then Ontario), 6, 8, 9, 38, 41
Upper Canada Religious Tract and
    Book Society, 28
Uptown Theatre (Orangeville), 98

Vandendam, John, 115
Ventin, Carlos, see Carlos Ventin
    Architects
Victoria, Queen, 42, 171, 172
Victoria Road, 42
Vineberg, Arthur (Dr.), 216, 217

W.C. Dahl & Co. (later Dahl Brothers),
    145, 146
Waite, William, 57
Waldemar (ON) (settlement) (Ama-
    ranth), 22
Wallace, ___ (Mr.) (Furniture Maker),
    190
Wallace, Claire (Miss), 210, 211
Wallace, Samuel (Magistrate), 35
Wallace, ___ (Mrs. William), 211
Wallace, William, 210, 211
Wallace's Inn (Farmingham), 45
Walkerton (ON), 51
Walsh, Aquilla, 210
Walsh, Francis Leigh, 210
Walsh, William Leigh "W.L." (Mayor),
    128, 210

INDEX 279

War of 1812-14, 219
Wardlaw, James, 159
Watson, C.W., 84
Watson, Mabel E. (Patterson) (Mrs. W.G.), 210
Watson, William George, 210
Watt, Henry, 101
Watt, Phillip, 223
Weaver's Drug Store, 151
Webb, Fred, 94, 99
Welland Canal, 40, 250
Wellborne, Bess (Miss), 183
Wellington, County of, 15, 44, 55, 69, 70, 72, 120, 123, 155-157, 248, 249
Wellington County Council, 119, 122
Wellington Hotel (Orangeville), 187
West, John, 210
West, R.F., 210
West, Thomas C., 209
West Simcoe Hotel (Orangeville), 53
Westinghouse, 134
Westminster United Church, 161, 162, 188
Weston (now part of Toronto), 45, 65
Whaley, Earl, 181
Whaley & Royce (Music Dealers) (Toronto), 181
Wheaton, Charles, 223
Wheelock, Charles J., 16, 30, 45, 100, 126, 160
White, Doreen (Mrs. Veryle), 216
White, J.J., 96
White, Veryle, 152, 216
White Elephants, The (lacrosse team), 75
Whittington (settlement) (Amaranth), 42
Whittler, ___ (Mrs.), 193
Whitton, James, 223
Widdis, ___ (Mrs.), 95
Wilcox, ___ (Mr.), 140
Wilcox, ___ (Mrs. A.), 174

Wilcox, Abiathar, 11, 12, 16-19, 105
Wilcox, George, 124
Wild, Ed, 150
Williams family, 161
Williamson, Gord, 105
Wilson, Fred, 99
Wilson, George, 99
Wilson, John (Justice), 123, 124
Wise, Alf, 150
Wise, Faith, 151
Wise, Jimmy, 150
Wise Bros. (Bakers), 85, 95, 150
Witter's Hotel (Orangeville), 43, 172
Women's College Hospital (Toronto), 218
Women's Institute, 90, 255
Woodbridge (ON), 84
Woodland, A.H., 152
Woolner family: 196, 197
    Connie, 196
    Gail (Mrs. Rick), 196
    Rick, 196, 197
World University Lacrosse Championship, 200
Wylie, Jane (Huston) (Mrs. J.H.), 208

Yonge Street, 38
York (later Toronto), 28, 29, 32, 33, 38
York Mills (village, now part of Toronto), 28, 29
Youmans, David, 173
Youmans' Store (Orangeville), 60
Young, Mae (Miss), 152
Young Men's Christian Association (YMCA), 179
Young Canadians, The (lacrosse team), 75
Yukon, Territory of, 79

Zion Presbyterian Church (later Westminster United Church), 161, 162

ABOUT THE AUTHOR

Wayne Townsend was born in East Luther, Dufferin County, and went to high school in Orangeville, moving there in 1972. He worked in the graphic art department of Drummond Business Forms in Orangeville for ten years as the supervisor. In 1988, Wayne was hired as the Curator of the Dufferin County Museum & Archives, opening their new facility at the corner of Highway 89 and Airport Road in 1994. Wayne has served on various local heritage committees and projects and is an active participant in numerous groups and activities. Since 1977 Wayne has been a resident in the historic district of Orangeville in a home built in 1894 by Alexander and Eliza Hill, Mr. Hill having been a local merchant tailor. Wayne, with his friend Kim Peters, operated a local hotel and restaurant in downtown Orangeville, in the Historic American Hotel (where he gathered many local stories), just up the street from the original site of Orange Lawrence's hotel.

Wayne continues in his role at the Dufferin County Museum establishing strong community relationships between the facility and the local residents. This is his second book on local Dufferin County history. His first, *Corn Flower: Creatively Canadian*, was published in 2001 by Natural Heritage Books.